The Bosun's Call

The Bosun's Call

Hugh Willis

The Pentland Press Limited
Edinburgh • Cambridge • Durham • USA

First published in 1999 by
The Pentland Press Ltd.
1 Hutton Close
South Church
Bishop Auckland
Durham

British Library Cataloguing in Publication Data.
A Catalogue record for this book is available
from the British Library.

ISBN 1 85821 615

Typeset by CBS, Felixstowe, Suffolk
Printed and bound in Great Britain by Bookcraft (Bath) Ltd.

To my Mother and in memory of my Father

CONTENTS

Sea Fever

I must down to the seas again, for the call of the running
   tide
Is a wild call and a clear call that may not be denied.

I must go down to the seas again, to the vagrant gypsy
   life,
To the gull's way and the whale's way where the wind's
   like a whetted knife;
And all I ask is a merry yarn from a laughing fellow-
   rover,
And quiet sleep and a sweet dream when the long trick's
   over.

John Masefield

Chapter 1

In The Beginning

He lashed her securely to the mast and quickly returned to the cockpit. It was dark except for the distant shore lights of Sheerness and the occasional flashes of red, white and green from the navigational buoys which marked the channel. She was tired, cold, miserable and not a little frightened. She held the hurricane lamp high above her head wondering when it would all end. Then with time, her arm began to flag and the lamp came lower.

'Higher, Peggy!' yelled my father from the comfort of the stern, 'we don't want another scare like that.' He sang out encouragingly as he peered into the darkness.

Five minutes beforehand they had sat without care in their unlit twenty-foot sloop, when, without warning, the black shape of an unlit barge came from under their lee and crossed their bows ten feet ahead.

Earlier, they had caught the last of the evening tide from Westcliff. They were heading for Queenborough and the Medway for the week-end. Mother had thought of reasons for not going but had finally given way to Father's insistent pleas.

There had been a warm south-westerly breeze as they had left the calm mooring and headed across the estuary toward the Kent coastline. Even so, sailing had never held any romance for Mother. It was dark and the moon hadn't yet risen, and she had

had to crawl around the decks with care. The blackness of the night had influenced Father's thinking – or lack of it.

He had decided – like the motorist without lights – that so long as *he* could see everything that moved for miles around, there was no problem. But it wasn't only that. He hadn't rigged the hurricane lamp on the mast because he hadn't fixed an eye-ring from which to hang it. That's where Mother's worth came in. He had hung it from her instead.

It wasn't until two hours later, when they had reached the safety of Queenborough jetty, that Father released Mother from the mast and led her aft to the comparative comfort of the cockpit. She always said that that was the night she had realised that sailing was a 'no-no'; it was her apocalypse. She never wanted to sail again with Father, or for that matter, with anyone. Ever again.

Father loved the sea. He didn't know it then, in 1933, that during the Second World War he would serve in the RNVR. However, that was in the future. Back in the present, it was just unfortunate, or as Father readily admitted, 'bad seamanship', that had allowed him to relax in conditions of good visibility without a light.

Meanwhile, sleeping peacefully down below and nine months old, I knew nothing of the events taking place up top, nor that the hand of fate was inexorably leading me toward a life at sea. Had I known, I might even have cried out from below.

During the next six years a lot of things happened in Europe which eventually brought about the Second World War. Things happened in our family too. Mother had been a nurse at Morefields Eye Hospital in London when they had first met. Father was employed by Cable and Wireless, and his mother had felt that he should have married someone from a better off home . . . 'You know, with money'. To make matters worse,

Father's three elder sisters didn't welcome Mother into the family, and Father's divided loyalty came to tear them apart. The final straw was his selfish devotion to his weekend sailing, when he would often race on both Saturday and Sunday and thus leave Mother lonely and furious.

They divorced, and I was farmed out to temporary minders and then boarding school, aged four. Father couldn't take care of me; he worked in London. Mother had to find work too; they couldn't afford two homes on Father's salary. It was miserable for us all and my memories of that time are a kaleidoscope of mixed emotions and fears.

The 'minder' pulled me to my feet from the bed, roughly took my hand, and steered me through the dark to the deserted dining room. It was spooky, cold and smelled of cedar polish and old chair coverings. The heavy curtains were closed; but from the single shaft of light cast by the mean shaded bulb in the gloomy hall, I saw among the shadows, Victorian hulks of furniture, sinister and glaring and leaning on the walls in silence.

'Till you learn to keep quiet, you'll sit here in the dark. Do you hear me?' she said, pulling out the great carver chair and thrusting me heavily on to its seat. With that, she swiftly left the room like a witch, viciously closing the door and leaving me to the terrors conjured up by the darkness of that lonely room. I sobbed quietly and wished that Mum would come soon.

Later, to glimpse another memory, I was sitting with Dad and Uncle Arthur by the window, with them singing: 'Run rabbit, run rabbit, run, run run.' The War was drawing closer and Hitler had already become the object of 'fun' in a worried land. They were doing their best to cheer me, just before the doctor called to lance my septic, swollen hand. I remember too, the soaked mask coming down on to my face and the dizzying, spinning sensation as the chloroform took me under.

Then a snapshot of excitement: going to Woolworths with my Mum on her day off, and in the place where she now worked. Seeing 'millions' of brightly wrapped sweets stacked higgledy-piggledy behind glass compartments. Toys galore: golden teddy bears, trains in bright red, dinky toy cars in their racing colours, submarines for the bath and gay spinners on the end of sticks which would whistle round and round in the wind. And on other counters, hammers, saws, nails and screws ready to be weighed and sold in brown paper bags; large ladies' drawers hanging limp, like windless ensigns, longing to be owned and hoisted.

Now I was a boarder at Lindisfarne school, with nurse and matron fussing over a motley bunch of disorientated little boys. The days were short but the nights seemed long as many of us drifted off to sleep dreaming of home and Mum and Dad. But suddenly everything changed again. Off to Granny's in the Austin 7, to stay a while in the Cotswolds, where she owned a village store. That was fun. Then Granny moved on to Northleach and bought a boarding house; so off once more, this time to Gloucester.

The month of August, 1939, was hot and the harvesting was well under way as the ominous clouds of war drew close. Northleach was a quiet rural village built of strong Cotswold stone, which breathed freely in the space of the surrounding countryside of farms and fields. The village life was remote from far-off Cheltenham and the villagers went about their country work, some running the local shops and others working the farms.

I would follow the reaper-binder, sometimes even ride like a king on the tractor; eyes peeled for rabbits, watching the golden corn being swept in by the twirling battens and the string-tight bunches of straw strewn astern. Later it was to be stooked by men in hats, their sleeves rolled high and their trousers tucked in their socks or tied with twine. Tea from old thermos flasks and lovely ham off the bone, jam sandwiches and apples. Then all too soon came the evening light, home to supper and later to a feather quilted bed which sucked me into its depths and security, to sleep.

'We're off to Cornwall – Father's there,' said Mother, as she collected me from Gran's and stowed my bits and pieces into the already crammed rear seat. The journey took for ever and I slept a lot as we swept through Southern England at 40 miles an hour, sometimes seeing khaki-coloured convoys as we headed west for Plymouth, the Torpoint ferry, and thence to Freathy Cliffs, where the little summer house stood on the cliffs and . . . Father waited.

The frightening thought of war and what might happen to us all had brought them back together and we were to be a family once again. They had quickly remarried at a registry office. Father, meanwhile, had joined the Royal Navy and done his basic training, and had been appointed to HMS *Raleigh*, near Torpoint, just across the River Tamar. The summer house would be temporary, until we had found a place nearer to the camp, and in between we would enjoy its gorgeous location overlooking the Cornish coastline and the sea. It had no power or light, it had no sewage system for lavatory or bath. In fact it didn't have a bath at all; instead it had a tub. I liked the thought of that.

They sent me to the local village school – about two miles away – and the first day I joined, the Mistress took us for dictation and punctuation. I had never heard of 'dictation' and 'punctuation' sounded nasty.

'Are you ready?' she said. 'Pick up your pencils. I will read it slowly so's you can get it down.' And then she commenced.

'The horse comma . . . walked . . . slowly . . . towards . . . Grandpa full stop . . . He looked . . . and said . . . comma . . .

there's . . . apostrophe . . . a good horse . . . comma . . . said
Grandpa . . . fullstop.'

I listened carefully, and wrote down everything she had said.
My spelling was atrocious but I had understood the interesting
story. I thought, however, that her choice of names for the horses
and Grandpa was weird. For I had understood her to say: 'The
horse, Comma, walked slowly towards Grandpa Fullstop.
"There's Apostrophe, a good horse, Comma," said Grandpa
Fullstop.'

Father loved living on the Cornish cliffs because whenever he
had any spare time he went down to the black jagged rocks to
fish for bass and pollock. Someone lent him a twenty-foot
bamboo rod and he would spend many hours close to the
foaming waves, standing solitary far below the cliffs on a ship-
like rock whose bow projected into the breaking waves; and
sometimes he would be lost from sight in the flying spray, only
to reappear a moment later. Mother, however, complained that
he was permanently hanging off the end of 'a bloody fishing
rod' instead of working in the garden. When he brought home a
great shining bass, she usually forgave him.

It was now late summer, the weather was still fine and I was
happy. On Saturdays the man came round with his horse and
cart to empty our Elsan and the chemical lavatories from the
summer homes. The chalets were scattered among the gorse-
and heather-laden cliffs in an abundance of wild flowers which
gave off their cocktail of perfumes.

He was a nice old man, who chatted in his broad Cornish
accent. He would let me pat his cart horse, Bess, who didn't
seem to mind the smelly cart. He let me open the iron lid on the
rusty tank and watch him deftly pour the brown liquid contents
into its bowels. I began to look forward to Saturdays.

Several weeks later, when Mother had gone shopping and left me to play in the garden, I saw my friend Bess clip clopping along the dusty cliff-top track with my other friend perched aloft on his reeking cart.

'Where's your Mum to, then?' he asked as we performed the usual ritual and I held the lid upright for him to pour the contents.

'She's gone shopping – may I come along with you and Bess?' I pleaded.

He gave me a long enquiring look from underneath his battered hat, which was weather-beaten and stained with time, just like his face.

'I's don't know about that, do us Bess?' he said, as he placed the empty Elsan on the grass. 'What'n your Mum say to that then, eh?' he added doubtfully.

Of course I told him that 'she would be ever so pleased . . . and anyway, Mum had thought it would be a very good idea.' So I glibly lied and climbed aboard his stinking chariot. He flipped the leather reins.

'Walk on, Bess . . . we 'opes you're right, young feller.'

That afternoon I got to meet all sorts of people, including some nice old ladies who knew Mother quite well. They asked me if she was aware where I was . . . and what I was doing, and I told them that 'Mum always lets me ride on the cart every week. She loves it very much.'

Two hours later, when our tank was near to overflowing, Mother overtook us in the Austin 7 wearing both a new hat and a look of disbelief. She swerved violently on to the verge and came to a slithering halt on the grass. Mother grabbed my hand and I flew off the cart like an athlete doing the flying angel over a gym box and landed on the grass. Bess whinnied in alarm, me old mucker flicked the reins hard and, contrary to her nature,

Bess broke into a fast trot down the road. The tank – never having been designed for speed – slopped its awful liquid contents liberally over the stern, laying its brown lavatorial trail in the dust as they trotted quickly into the distance. Meanwhile I was left to Mother's mercy.

Maybe it was just as well that Father had found us a house near HMS *Raleigh*. Within a week we had moved in. The place was enormous. It had an attic as a third floor, stables, outhouses and a half acre of garden with an orchard. It was, however, run down and neglected and needed a lot of work before it could be got back to its former days of glory. Father had got the place for a very low rent since no one else wanted to take on such burden, especially in war time.

With this in mind, Mother found Mrs Mullis and her boyfriend, Bill. They had nowhere to go and jumped at the chance of rent-free accommodation and board – on condition that they worked for their keep in and around the house. Both Mrs Mullis and Bill had their own bedrooms and shared a sitting room near the kitchen. They preferred the large farmhouse kitchen because when they were not working, they sat at the scrubbed kitchen table drinking tea and discussing the latest war news and how it was all so different from the old days.

Mrs Mullis was a graying, older woman, and I guessed her to be about the same age as my granny. She was a homely, buxom woman, who quickly settled into her new-found home. She enjoyed cooking, cleaning, pottering about the house and drinking her cups of tea. Bill was a big Irish navvy, a hulk of a man with a well used face, that readily broke into a broad grin at the slightest pretext. Like a true Irishman, he had a never-ending fund of stories, all of which had either happened to, or been witnessed by, himself. At week-ends or whenever he was between jobs, Father set him to work about the large garden, clearing the mass of undergrowth and brambles which had invaded the grounds over the years. Nevertheless, Bill was a happy man too. He had Mrs Mullis as his 'friend' and he had a new home which he liked. Moreover, what with the war, there was plenty of work around. Goering and his German airforce, however, had already made plans to upset the air of tranquillity which we had enjoyed during the period of the Phoney War.

Then Came the War

When the bombers came in earnest, our life style quickly changed. In the field alongside us they installed a barrage balloon and a machine gun post manned by ten airmen who kept watches day and night. Dozens of anti-aircraft batteries were sited around us. This was due to the large naval presence and the fuel-oil storage tanks, which lay half a mile up the road from Torpoint.

Initially, we didn't have an air-raid shelter, so the sergeant from the balloon site invited us to use theirs. By now the raids were mostly at night and we would fumble our way in the dark through a gap in the hedge, usually arriving as 'all hell broke loose' in the sky. It was comforting to be in a shelter, seated on large wooden boxes which filled most of the space. At times, as we looked out through the small entrance overlooking the valley, it was unreal. We would gaze out upon the magnificent 'fireworks' display and watch the guns spitting back into the black sky, the bombs exploding and the incendiaries providing the stage lighting. We felt so much safer in the shelter.

It was particularly exciting when the machine gun opened fire at the flares, which seemed to be suspended in the sky, occasionally firing at a deadly landmine as it floated down by parachute. It was only a little later that we became aware of the real purpose of the air raid shelter which had given us such comfort. A busy little airman kept coming into our unlit shelter.

''Scuse me, Mam, would you stand up a tick?' he'd say politely to my mother. Then he'd delve in the box she had been sitting on.

After a while Mother couldn't stand it any more.

'What the hell have you got in there, young man? Tea and biscuits for the lads?'

'Oh no, Mam, it's ammunition for the gun,' he said in an injured tone of voice.

'We keeps all the dangerous nasties, like grenades and such like, in 'ere,' he added as he departed with another box of ammunition.

Father decided that it was time that he built an Anderson air-raid shelter on the far side of our garden, just beyond the giant oak tree and thirty yards from the French windows of our sitting room. He fitted it out with a bunk and benches, a primus stove, jerry cans of water to provide hot drinks through the night, and plenty of blankets to keep us all warm.

After we had established our drill, we soon became adapted to the bombing. The moment the wailing of the siren began – that first note, an eerie rise and fall, always sent a momentary spasm of fear to the stomach – each of us quickly dressed in warm clothes, gathered up whatever items we had been tasked to carry, and then rushed to the shuttered French windows. When everyone was mustered and victuals and warm clothing had been checked, we would go to the shelter. It was not unusual, however, for the guns to be firing and the bombs and shrapnel falling before we were ready to head for the Anderson. Under these circumstances we would wait until we had heard the shrapnel crackle through the trees from the previous barrage. Then the moment it stopped, Mother would yell, 'Run!' and

Mrs Mullis and I would rush through the darkness and dive into the shelter as the next barrage began. This carried on until everyone was safely tucked inside.

Early one winter's evening there was no warning at all. Mother was on her knees laying the fire. I was standing nearby, idly watching as she laid the kindling on the tightly curled newspapers, whose headlines were, no doubt, filled with the usual gloom of war. Suddenly, we heard that fearful, high-pitched whistling note. Still kneeling, she turned towards me, arms outstretched, and our eyes locked in terror as the bomb exploded to our right. The house trembled as Mother hauled me to the floor beneath her. The second bomb – clearly from a stick of bombs – was deafening and much closer. It brought a cloud of soot cascading down the chimney which billowed across the room and made my nose and eyes sting. Unseen bits and pieces fell around and crashed to the floor. Meanwhile, trembling underneath my mother's body, I felt and heard the next shuddering explosion shatter the porch windows to our left. Our ears still rang in the moment's silence before the guns began to answer blindly into the – by now – empty sky.

For many little boys the fun came in the morning. Its reassuring light dispersed last night's fears, especially when we were busy searching for the shrapnel, which wasn't hard to find. Like collectors of marbles or cigarette cards, we knew the value of each piece in the 'market'. Bomb shrapnel rated higher than a fragment of AA shell; a fuse head from a shell, however, was highly prized, as were whole incendiary bomblets – that was, until Goering flooded the 'market' in later raids. Small parachutes from flares were a coveted collector's item and seldom found. For a time, with Hitler's help, you could say that we youngsters enjoyed a 'bull' market in the shrapnel trade.

Then came the time when they hit the fuel tanks. The sky was aflame and orange in colour for miles around. Black smoke billowed, accompanied by the stench of burning fuel oil, as streams of anxious men, frightened women and children, made their way out of the town towards the safety of the countryside. But they had nowhere particular in mind apart from somewhere to lay their heads without fear. We all knew that the bombers would return again and again to such a temptingly well-lit target.

That first evening Father shepherded a hundred or more women and children off the road into our house, while Mrs Mullis continuously brewed cups of tea. Mother bedded the children down wherever space could be found while Bill told them funny Irish stories. While the fuel tanks were burning out of control during the days and nights that followed, the people of Torpoint were convoyed out of town in trucks and cars, to sleep in barns or settle with country friends. Father drove us to an old barn some way out and I thought that life was one great adventure as I found myself tucked up in the old barn among the hay and straw, little understanding the grief and horror that were visited upon the many victims within the cities.

With very little warning I was packed off to boarding school. Mother had decided that it was too dangerous at home and that in any event the local school was decidedly limited. Seafield Park, a prep school, had been evacuated from the dangerous Portsmouth area to the Duke of Bedford's 'shooting box', Ensleigh, in Devon. The contrast was dramatic. It was another world; peaceful, rural countryside lay for miles around. We were cocooned and isolated within the magnificence of a beautiful estate, its large and elegant house perched snugly on the hillside overlooking the flowing River Tamar, which meandered its way through lush pastures and densely wooded banks below.

As the school holidays came and went and the years rolled

by, a whole range of factors came to influence my destiny. I concentrated my interests on the Royal Navy because 'My dad was part of it.' He had made model ships of *Ark Royal, King George V* and *Warspite*. Father was a Divisional Officer at HMS *Raleigh*, and I frequently visited the camp with him during the holidays. My school was steeped in naval connections and boys often left to join Dartmouth as thirteen-year-old cadets.

I read books about the sea and spent hours down by the water's edge. I looked across the harbour at the warships secured alongside their dockyard berths. They were being repaired and restored before heading out once again to join the battles of my vivid imagination. Among the Royal Naval warships, I remember the French battleship which always seemed to be there. She had a huge clock, like that of a church, high on her foremast.

And on a still day, the sounds and sights of frantic activity could be heard and seen from across the harbour: the echoes of the rivet-guns and the hammering of steel plates; the tall cranes swinging great loads and dumping them on to the decks and dockside; the constant flurry of movement among the tugs, busily scurrying about their tasks and importantly hooting their intentions for all to hear; the boats and launches ferrying gold-braided officers to their destinations through the chopped-up waters of a busy port.

But above all the noise and bustle, there were the frequent shrill pipes of the bosuns' calls, each one followed by a message over the ship's tannoy. They heralded orders and information to be conveyed to the disciplined men who manned the ships and they carried intimate messages pertaining to their daily lives. And all these intimate details echoed across the water to where I sat enthralled.

A shrill pipe: 'Spuds are now being issued from the spud locker', and then another, 'Cable party will be required to close up in 15 minutes time'. A pause, and then, from a further ship: 'Up Spirits. Rum is now being issued from the Spirit Room'. Or it might be a much less welcoming message: 'Night leave will be granted to "natives" only. The ship is under sailing orders'. The next day that ship had gone.

Those shrill pipes of the bosun's call made me tingle with excitement. They were my pipes of Pan, and they conjured, in my imagination, a life at sea in distant places. Every time I heard its note cry out, it seemed much closer than before.

School holidays were long but there was always so much to keep us youngsters interested and so many things to do. There was no television, and entertainment came from ninepence spent at the 'pictures', or maybe from the programmes on the radio: ITMA, with Tommy Handley, Worker's Playtime and Vera Lynn singing 'Blue Birds Over the White Cliffs of Dover.' This last didn't do much for boys, but did give hope to so many separated loved ones. Our fun came mostly from the depths of our imagination and ingenuity. We seemed to have so much freedom as children, taking off for the day with a bag of sandwiches and making our own fun; no 'nanny' state regulations, no drugs, no pornographic videos, no anxious mothers constantly fearing for our safety.

By now Mother was busy most days driving a mobile canteen, visiting outlying service camps and sites to bring them goodies: tea, cakes and buns, razor blades, Woodbine, Players, Gold Leaf and Capstan cigarettes, carbolic soap, Basildon Bond writing paper and many other luxuries designed to meet a host of wants. At first I went along with her but soon became bored of touring *army* camp sites. So to help pass the time while she was out on her rounds, Mother acquired a pony for me called Bobetta. It grazed in our orchard and ate all the apples it could reach. Mother knew nothing about horses whatsoever, but that hadn't stopped her from buying a pony trap, a gentle lame nag called Sally, and my pony, Bobetta.

I was fitted out with jodhpurs, and she with breeches, leather boots, riding crop, hat and jacket. Together, we made a fine pair of 'county' poseurs, scarcely knowing how to saddle and mount the beasts, let alone ride them. I don't think that Mother ever rode Sally; she just took her for a walk on the halter now and again. However, she quite fancied herself in her outfit, and her real 'horse' was the fifteen horsepower mobile canteen.

'After all,' she said in her 'county' voice, 'I drive mostly in the country, and one must look the part.' As for me, my jodhpurs were reserved for occasions when I could catch the elusive and frisky Bobetta.

During the term Bobetta ran wild around the garden, impudently whinnying at Mother whenever she called to her, 'Stop eating my lovely flowers and go back to the orchard.' On one occasion, as she caught hold of Bobetta's halter, she was dragged shrieking through the wickedly sharp pampas grass and came out the other side feeling she had been hauled through a shredder. When I came home for holidays, this well fed but under-exercised maniac of a pony had stored up the energy of ten race horses. One thing was very clear: Bobetta didn't want to be ridden.

But of course Mother would say sweetly, 'Darling, why don't you go and ride that lovely little pony? She's so looking forward to a nice walk.'

Harnessing and saddling were difficult, because neither Mother nor I knew where all the bits and pieces fitted – that is, until one day a kind farmer came along to teach us. Even he found Bobetta a handful.

'What you's bin feed'n 'er on, then . . . gunpowder?' Anyway, he told Mother that the horse had to be exercised, and soon.

When Mother came home from her round the following day, she told me that there was to be a gymkhana just outside Anthony – a village two miles away – and that it 'would be wonderful exercise for Bobetta, darling.'

'You must go. They run around and jump over things. It's awfully good fun – and they give prizes as well,' she added as bait. I had never jumped over anything and didn't fancy the thought, especially on Bobetta.

Mother left early and before I was up. She left wearing my jodhpurs since she didn't like wearing the painfully tight riding boots which went with her breeches. I struggled into her outfit, cursing because our feet were the same size and the boots were hell to get on. I had to take my socks off before they would fit.

At first all went well as we made our way towards Anthony. But after we had gone half a mile from home, Bobetta began stopping in her tracks every ten yards or so, turning her head and looking at me and back home whence she had come. We progressed in this manner for a further ten minutes until she finally stood her ground and wouldn't budge. There was only one thing for it. I got off and led her by the reins, pulling and tugging her while she stared at me, snorting, wide-eyed and rebellious.

By now my feet were killing me and I could feel the blisters forming on both heels. The sun beat down, the sweat poured from underneath Mother's riding hat and we still had a mile to go. I removed the riding boots and slinging them around my neck, carried on in bare feet. Every yard was a fight.

To this day I can still hardly believe that Mother could have got it so wrong. As we made our unsightly equestrian approach to the entrance, the wrought iron gates were locked shut and the park was deserted by man and beast alike. Not a sign of a horse or human presence was to be seen in any direction. I then spotted the notice on the gate:

'Gymkhana, 8th August – All Comers Welcome.' I had arrived one week early!

I mounted Bobetta in one angry, flying leap, the boots still round my neck, and giving her the hardest kick I could muster, flicked the reins and hollered, 'Get on, you bloody horse!' Without argument, she broke into a trot and then a canter and made off home and the orchard. And what a sight we must have made, me and the boots bouncing out of time to her every movement all the way home.

I never did do much riding after that, and shortly afterwards Mother sold both horses, the trap and its associated gear as a job lot for a 'song'. The only things that she kept were the breeches, the boots, the whip and my jodhpurs. 'They're right for the country,' she said, 'but the others must go.'

Mother had made many friends in the area – associated with her Church Army mobile canteen duties – and one such friendship was with Lady St Germans, who lived in Mount Edgecumbe, a magnificent estate not far away. Mother often popped in to visit her on the way back from her 'tea and bun' fight, driving her khaki monster, more like a tank than a van.

One day she arrived on the occasion of a garden fête held in aid of the war effort. She drove down the rhododendron-lined drive and arrived at the house to find those attending enjoying their expensive teas on the beautiful lawns which surrounded the elegant and historic house. A Royal Marine Band played patriotic military music, Vera Lynn hits and Cole Porter favourites; the guests nibbled genteelly at their thinly sliced cucumber sandwiches. Some tapped their feet in time to the beat while others just smiled and prayed to be seen. The setting was peaceful, the mood serene, redolent of pre-war ways and certainty; the sun forced shafts of light through the ancient oaks and elms as Lady St Germans floated mindfully among her flock.

In a moment the setting was transformed. Mother backed over the fire hydrant – rigged for emergencies – then, realising that something was underneath, she accelerated forwards and unstopped the pressurised main. A wide jet of water arched towards the lawn and descended on dozens of tea drinkers. The Royal Marines dispersed in confusion, trying vainly to keep their instruments dry. Women in Greer Garson hats screamed as their summer frocks clung to their thighs, and the ribbed outlines of heavy-stayed corsets became visible. Meanwhile men dressed in colonial, lightweight suits and Panama hats bought at Dunns all bravely took charge, recapturing their former military days by escorting the women and children clear as though beating a path to the *Titanic*'s lifeboats.

In spite of the war, life went on without too much trouble for the lucky ones. Mother and I sometimes went to the monthly concerts at the camp. Father also took me with him now and again, to trail behind him as he walked round the huts and talked to his Division. They were 'hostilities only' sailors, who, within a very short time, were to become the 'green' young matelots who fought (and some who died) off Norway, went down with *Hood*, battled their way to Russia with convoys, floated free of ships sunk at Crete, or perished with the *Prince of Wales* and *Repulse*.

Even in those dark war days some 'professionals' thought them gauche – novices to be tolerated. On one occasion Father was outraged when none of his sailors had received the fruit which had been delivered that day.

'Where have all the bananas gone, you bastard?' said Father to the Supply Officer in charge.

He soon found that there were 'wheels within wheels' and he'd upset an influential man who possessed power.

'The man's mad! Always chasing rations for his men. I can

only give them what I've got! Send him off to sea,' whined the senior Supply Officer in question.

It is sad to say that during those dark hours, the 'Black Market' thrived everywhere in the hands of racketeers. Men even went on strike for more wages while others fought and died.

And so he was sent off to sea. He was glad to go – but upset that justice hadn't been done. The senior officer, a pragmatic man, had hurried him on his way.

'Willis has always been trouble, he cares too much about little things. Doesn't know the realities of life.'

But Mother and I had seen what others had believed. We went to one last concert before he left. A thousand sailors sat waiting for the show to start, watching the officers take their seats. They knew and recognised the ones who cared, and meted out their scorn with groans and the slow stamping of feet to those who didn't. With unerring instinct, they singled out the 'fiddlers', the pompous, the ungenerous and the selfish 'yes' men. It didn't go unnoticed that Lieutenant Willis was greeted with deafening cheers. I felt proud of Father when they showed their affection for this stubborn, eccentric man who cared.

During his time at *Raleigh* he had brought so many volunteers back home; invited them to work with him on jobs about the house and in the garden. Then afterwards they would stay for supper, at ease amongst us all. They loved the fleeting freedom and the treasured sense of home. Father sat and fussed, and Mother smiled while heaping their plates with home-grown vegetables, though there was very little meat. For some it was their last taste of family life before meeting their fate at sea. Later I learned to understand; he had given them a taste of home.

They sent him to America to stand by a 'Woolworth' carrier.

Those generous 'Yanks' took the Royal Navy under their wing and to their hearts; Father, a careful man where outward demonstrations of sentiment are concerned, said: 'They're very much like us, you know. And they've all been so jolly kind.' In a while he sailed away in the new-found American-built 'Woolworth' aircraft carrier, HMS *Searcher*, which later joined the hunt for the *Tirpitz* lying in the fjords of Norway.

The tide turned and a sense of impending victory spread throughout the country. The might of America came to bear and Stalin sacrificed his millions on the Eastern front. From the beauty and safety of central Devon, even we schoolboys sensed the change as we watched the Lancasters and silver Flying Forts in their hundreds returning low, many of them with torn fuselage and badly damaged wings. They limped slowly, some barely airborne, engines shot away and propellers stopped. We watched them fly low overhead as they made their way home 'on a wing and a prayer'.

After the Normandy invasion, we marked our maps each day as the Allied forces advanced across Europe. By a hairbreadth the Doenitz submarines were beaten, hunted down by sea and air as each new technical advance gave us the edge in sonar, airborne high-definition radar, and the intelligence rewards gained from Enigma. The Yanks were hammering the Japs in historic battles at sea and clearing the bitterly defended Pacific islands in a surge of victories. And Father would soon be home.

After the Battle of the Bulge had been won, the war in Europe drew rapidly to a close. The V1s and their pop-popping engines were no longer to be heard; the V2s had ceased from delivering their first silent, but finally ear-splitting death. The merchantmen now arrived in their droves and thoughts of starvation were gone. Vera Lynn now sang with certain hope that: 'We'll Meet Again,

don't know where, don't know when,' and we all *knew* that it
would be *soon*.

Then The Peace

Suddenly it was over. The war had ended and Father came home.
When his leave was over, he returned to work at Cable and
Wireless. Once more, after nearly six years of war, he was wearing
a black coat, pin-striped trousers, starched white collar and tie
and a bowler hat. Daily he made his way to and from Southend-
on-Sea and the City of London. Gone was the war with its
paradoxical and often colourful life, which many of those who
had been lucky enough to survive unscathed had actually
enjoyed. Soon his mind turned blank with the boredom and
drudge of commuting and the mundane nature of his work.
Between times, at weekends, he sailed his boat like a wizard,
winning race after race with fanatical skill, and only then was he
truly happy. He was a man of strange contradictions. I remember
traipsing slowly astern of him, oars on shoulders, following him
along the crowded seafront to our boat. We weaved in and out
among clusters of bejewelled Jewish ladies – intimate groups
talking in Yiddish – as they lay back in straining deck chairs.

'Bloody Jews are everywhere. Look at 'em! Made their money
from the war.' When he said this sort of thing, I winced and fell
further astern, wondering why he had this irrational prejudice.

His close friend Marcus, who lived next door – and was known
by Father to be a Jew – would lend his new 'streamline' Vauxhall
to Father on special occasions, such as those on which my brother
was ferried back and forth to school each term. They were
comfortable with each other. Father was good with his hands
and often fixed things for Marcus that needed repairing.
Whenever confronted with the facts, my Father was dismissive:

'But that's beside the point! I like him, and don't care he's a Jew.'

'But Father,' I would say, 'what about Harry Denton? He's a Jew. I remember the day that he told that man who threatened you he would knock his block off if he didn't clear off,' I added. Harry Denton was six foot-three and large with it.

'But we're friends, my son,' he would reply in exasperation, though he would shuffle his feet and look uncomfortable. So in future I ignored his absurd ranting, just as Mother did, and got on with other things in life.

We were finding it hard to live on his salary, so I was sent to a polytechnic in Southend. Because of the cold weather – the winter of 1947 was wicked – I was made to wear the infamous jodhpurs to school. What with that and my 'toffy nosed' accent, especially among Essex-accented youth, I didn't get off to a very good start with my classmates. Our instructors were teaching us to lay bricks, boss lead sheeting, tongue-and-groove joints, and paint. It was hardly surprising that the incongruity of my attire got me into plenty of fights. I was constantly being asked where I had left my horse, and whether I happened to know Lord Fauntleroy. But Mother persisted.

'But darling, it's so much warmer in this frightful weather,' and so it bloody well was!

Meanwhile Mother had had some grandiose idea that the school might teach me to become an architect. Learning about bits of brick, things called King Closers and Queen Closers, bossing up lead boxes and chiselling wooden joints – it was hardly likely when all I was thinking about was the Navy.

Since money was short, I found myself a job as a paper boy. Mr Joiner ran the local news agent's. He had a big stomach, his hair was always cut 'short back and sides', he wore a Hitler moustache and smoked Woodbines. Cold winter mornings were hell. When I arrived at 6 a.m., he would be leaning over the counter with a Woodbine dangling from his mouth as he numbered each paper and stacked them into allocated delivery piles. Mr Joiner was one of those men who are always bustling to catch up – no matter how early I arrived, or how much ahead of time we were – as he pursued some illusory goal which was always just out of reach.

'About time too,' he would say as he looked up at the clock on the wall.

'Pass me that stack of *Chronicles*, lad!' he would bark. 'They forgot the bloody *Reynold's News* again,' he would say, pointing to the bundles of newspapers on the floor, all tightly held together with sisal string.

'Right, your first delivery's over 'ere. Off you go!' With that I would load up the heavy-framed delivery bike, built like a tank, and disappear into the foggy gloom.

My paper round was a large one, and twice more I would return to top up.

'Did you 'ave a *Dalton's Weekly* fer 32 Valkarie? He says he didn't get last week's – you didn't deliver it to 'er next door? The old cow'd keep it.' But Mr Joiner seldom waited for an answer.

'Come on, then, off you go! We 'aven't got all day. They got trains to catch.'

But I didn't mind because I was now rich. He paid me one pound sterling every week and I was the highest paid paper boy from our shop. Though I groaned, Mother made me save ten shillings every week; it was towards the sports bike that I so desperately wanted. One morning, however, I nearly lost my job.

It had snowed during the night – it was the bitter winter of 1947 – and at 6 o'clock that morning the icy north-east wind was blowing hard. As I came out of the shop door with my pile of papers, I slipped and fell backwards. Within seconds the wind attacked the scattered pile. I looked on in horror as the papers started to separate and blow away, some climbing like white kites into the dark as I frantically scrambled after the ones I could catch and scooped up the crumpled remnants into my arms.

Mr Joiner stood, hands on hips, framed in the light of the shop door as I returned in misery with a great armful of screwed-up newspapers – all that remained of the first delivery.

'That's one way to deliver 'em, lad,' he said sarcastically, 'Now you can come and 'elp me mark up another lot.'

He was very good about it, though. He docked my pay two shillings a week for five weeks.

'So's you'll learn to watch yer step in future' – and left it at that. But since it was nigh on Christmas, I more than made up for it in tips. I dressed up smartly, combed my hair, and during several evenings did the rounds of all my flats and houses.

'Good evening. Merry Christmas!' I would say cheerfully when a householder opened the door.

'I'm your paper boy who delivers no matter what the weather,' I would add piously. Then I would smile.

The reaction was generally favourable, though at times it could be a little begrudging. Some, however, were outright rude.

'Piss off, you little bastard! You either rip it in the letter box or leave it half out to get wet.'

My Jewish clientèle varied considerably. 'Don't worry yourself, Isaac,' one such lady might say, looking over her shoulder into the gloom of the hallway, 'It's our nice little boy that lights the cooker on the Sabbath.' Then maybe she'd give me half a crown with a smile. Some would be more direct.

'Jesus Christ, my boy! He's not one of *ours*!' and slam the door.

But I never called on the married man who waited for me to deliver the paper on Sunday mornings. Just as I was pushing the paper through the letter box, he would open the door and be standing there with his dressing gown wide open and a stupid grin on his face.

It was wonderful when the day came that I had saved fifteen pounds for my new bike. I had spotted just the one I wanted. Father came along to look at it. ' I wouldn't buy that one, Son,' he said seriously, 'It's not new and it's been made up from odds and ends. Why not save a little more and buy the new Raleigh?' But I didn't, and the one I had insisted on fell to pieces within a year. Father was very wise to let me buy it, because I would have been resentful. As it was, I learned the hard way, which is what most youngsters do.

I was now a regular crew member of the *Maybrook*, an 18-ft Thames Estuary One Design (TEOD) which Father raced every weekend of the season. Once again, this was much to Mother's annoyance. Father was still being sponsored to race *Maybrook* by George Baker. He had provided similar support for a number of years before the war with another TEOD, which I think was called *Vanity*. George was the proud owner, but rather like a race horse owner, he got Father to jockey his boats. He was proud of the many cups that Father won and kept them on display in his home. All the prize money went towards the annual upkeep of the boat and George derived his pleasure from the reflected glory which Father had won for him. Father didn't give a damn about the cups or the money; his pleasure was in racing the boat, which, without George, he wouldn't have been able to do.

There were three of us in the boat, two crew and Father at the helm. The other crew was most often a sixteen-stone butcher who, initially, knew absolutely nothing about sailing. He was brought along for his ballast value and muscles – the latter developed from carrying great sides of beef and the former, no doubt, from eating great quantities of it.

Captain Bligh's bad language had nothing on Father's. He could utter three expletives or insults between each word as he shouted instructions at both of us. This was usually when rounding a buoy, setting the spinnaker or jockeying for position. The butcher was a happy soul, whose large round face maintained an amiable, bovine expression through the worst of Father's ranting. He took not the slightest notice of the maniacal insults Father hurled at him, whereas I would sulk. The butcher knew that Father shouted to relieve his own bar-taught nerves, and that we, the crew, had nothing to do with it. At the time it confused me.

'Get your sixteen stone of offal off it's fat arse and hang out to windward!' he would bellow at the butcher.

'Don't be so hard on yourself, Alan, we're already half a mile ahead,' he would answer gently.

When the race was over and the finishing gun had gone, all the demons would instantly disappear. Whether we had won or not, he would sound our praises and thank us for having crewed so well. If we lost, he considered it to be entirely his own fault. More often we won or gained a place and went home to our mooring proud and happy. My Father was a brilliant tactician and feather-light helmsman. He knew the shore and tides, anticipated the shifts of wind, and covered his opponents like a cat with mice. Before the war, he had won thirty out of thirty-five races in *Vanity*.

In his day he was somewhat of a legend on the foreshore. I remember the occasion when we were leading in a race – in front of twenty boats – when we jibed on to a new course and the boom knocked his 'tatty' yachting cap into the water. He immediately jibed back and tacked towards his cap, while six boats immediately behind us overtook us as we were recovering it. I never thought he could do it, but one by one he fought his way past five of them and managed to pip the sixth over the line by a hair! He loved that bloody yachting cap.

Meanwhile, though he had taught me the skills of sailing and racing, I hadn't learned much at school, mostly due to my poor understanding of the basics. My plumbing and brickwork were a waste of space, because my mind was still set on the sea. Father tried to get me into a school called Sir John Cass, to train for the Merchant Navy, but I was a duffer at maths and the sciences. My grandfather had been a member of the Merchant Tailors but they wouldn't have me either. I was beginning to look like a lost cause, so they decided to send me to a sea training school – *any* sea training school that would have me.

Chapter 2

Fairthorne Manor

Fairthorne Manor is close to Botley village in Hampshire, and was then situated in unspoiled country surroundings looking down on the River Hamble. The school had just been opened. It was a small organisation which was run and financed through the YMCA. When my friend 'Flash' Acock and I joined, the staff comprised two training officers – one of whom was the Captain – and a chef. The Captain, John May, was an ex-Merchant Navy Master and his 'First Lieutenant' was a retired RNVR lieutenant-commander called Vince, otherwise known as 'Vincey'. And what a pair they were.

The Captain was an athletic man, who wore his forty years well and dressed the part with conviction. He was the manager and titular head of the organisation, dealing with all the administration and office work. He was also the front man when anyone of importance came to visit. He possessed a firm but easy-going manner and seldom shouted at us boys. Though he was the Captain, he appeared more like a headmaster than a salty seaman, although I have no doubt that he was a highly professional Merchant Seaman Captain.

Vincey, on the other hand, was always ready for action, clad in much used blue 'battle' dress, complete with gold buttons and shoulder straps and his old naval cap. He had an earthy smell, a mixture of dried cow pats, good Hampshire soil and salt brine. His eyes were blue under his battered cap, his features were aquiline, and his 'ampshire accent came through loud and clear like a farmer's. He was the practical man – the doer. Vincey could turn his hand to almost anything associated with the needs of living either on the land or on the tumbling sea. It was seldom that his eyes didn't twinkle, and if they didn't, those about him had better look out.

There were about a dozen of us boys to begin with, all around 15 years old, and we were the first to join this new school. When we arrived, there was no organisation to speak of, and they more or less made our programme up on a day-to-day basis. Vincey obviously believed in the old principle of an early morning run followed by a cold shower, as being good for the souls of all youngsters. We were told to run to the end of the drive and back, then to jump under the shower. After the first morning, many didn't run further than the nearest hiding-place, where they would get out of sight and hide for twenty minutes under the cover of the trees. This form of exercise was madness in winter but had some merit in summer. After the shower we would have breakfast, and then get ready for the day's instruction. The 'clean ship' routine, however, became an essential part of our training since there was no one else to do the work. We cleaned the manor house every day and gradually we began to notice the improvement. The floors were polished, the brightwork was polished, the lavatories were flushed with San Izal, the galley was scrubbed, and the mad chef – always dressed in white with a tall hat and armed with a long Sabatier knife – watched over us preparing the vegetables. After we had done that for several hours, we could start learning about the sea. Or so we thought.

Classroom instruction was almost non-existent. Vincey had already decided how best we should be employed after the housework was finished. He devoted three weeks to teaching us how to splice wire rigging. He weeded out those who showed no aptitude and put them to work with paint and brushes to brighten up the shabby manor house and outbuildings. The rest of us practised our splicing on spare bits of wire rope.

Thus we were split into two main work teams: the splicers and the painters. For about a month – during which time we became proficient splicers – I enjoyed the work and was proud of my new-found expertise. But then one day I accidentally found out why splicing was our only nautical subject. Vincey had jumped into his station wagon, loaded with all the work we had recently done.

'Get on with that next lot, lads. Gotta pop to Botley, won't be long.' When I saw the order bill left lying on the work bench, it all began to make sense. The order bill was from the local boat builder in Botley, listing another batch of rigging as per enclosed measurements. The boat builder provided the wire rope and whipping, and we did the work as part of our instruction, except that it constituted *all* of our instruction all of the time. That is, if you weren't one of the painters learning how to paint a ship's side. There is no doubt in my mind that the money we earned helped to keep the school afloat, as did the rabbits and pigeons brought back from the Captain's and Vincey's daily safaris in and around the grounds.

Anyway, several weeks after this discovery of the boat-builder's order bill, we must have completed all orders within the radius of his trade, since wire-splicing stopped abruptly – we started to learn a totally different trade.

'Right, my lads, get hold of them ladders and that there scaffolding. We're going to fix the roof,' said Vincey.

The roof in question was the old stables, about 80 foot long, and had probably last been tiled about a hundred years before.

30

All the unbroken slates had to be carefully removed and stacked for later use or sale. It took a week of intensive 'sea training' instruction before this task had been satisfactorily completed and we were ready for the next stage. Several more weeks were spent in ripping off the rotten battens, laying the bitumen sheeting, and nailing the replacement battens under the attentive supervision of Vincey. But when he saw that we were sufficiently competent to carry on alone, he would see us get started and then shout up to us on the roof.

'Won't be long, lads. Keep at it! Captain and me are off to get your dinners.'

Then he and the Captain, loaded with guns and ammunition, would take off to shoot pigeons, pheasant and rabbits in the extensive grounds.

Thousands of new tiles arrived by lorry early one morning and Vincey got us started straight away. But just as we had finished unloading, the Captain appeared and took Vincey to one side. He looked agitated, waving his arms around and repeatedly looking in our direction before hurrying off.

'Right, me lads, quick as you can! Get up to the house and change into your Sunday best. The Admiral's coming at 1000. And don't forget to wash your faces.'

This was the first that we had heard that there *was* an Admiral associated with the school. We had no idea what was going on as we doubled away to get changed. By 0930, we were sitting in the classroom, all spruced up and waiting for the mysterious Admiral to arrive. The Captain and Vincey were both in their best uniforms with medals and all, whereas normally they wore shooting jackets at about this time of the day.

'Now pay attention,' said the Captain. 'We are lucky enough to have two retired Admirals on the school board, and one of them – Admiral Elliot . . . unexpectedly . . . will be arriving shortly.' He didn't look particularly pleased with the thought, which showed in his taut smile. Nevertheless, he was concerned that we should be briefed as to our conduct in the presence of the Admiral.

'Should he address you, speak up because his hearing isn't very good,' he said, and then added, 'Remember this: each of you, just answer his questions. Otherwise, keep silent. Is that understood?' Vincey nodded vigorously in agreement.

Some of us understood all too well, and I silently toyed with the thought of asking the Admiral what he knew about tiling ships.

'Oh, by the way, he'll probably be giving you a short lecture on . . . gunnery,' concluded the Captain as he and Vincey went off for a quick planning meeting and a fag before the Admiral appeared.

I reflected that 'gunnery' was very much in keeping with the daily interests of our Captain and Vincey. However, it would be interesting to see how the Admiral would tackle the subject. And tackle it he did. In walked a distinguished, upright, white-haired gentleman with sea-blue eyes and a friendly smile. The Captain and Vincey stationed themselves like two close escorts, screening the capital ship from attack. Every word fired from the Admiral seemed to come 'words twice'. In his imagination he was on the rostrum addressing a thousand men on the quarterdeck of some great battleship. He asked a question, but being somewhat deaf, the answer fell short.

'What's your name? What's your name? Bedford, Bedford . . . No?' said the Admiral, smiling at the boy and cupping his ear, ready to collect the boy's returning vocal round of shot.

'*Oh . . . Redford, Redford.* Good . . . Good. Well done,' said the Admiral with a smile, then training right to straddle Vincey.

'Put it there . . . yes, yes . . . put it there,' as he pointed to the gramophone and several 78" records which Vincey had collected from the study.

'Now then . . . off you go . . . off you go!' said the Admiral to both the Captain and Vincey. They exchanged uneasy glances as they made their way to the door, leaving the Admiral to prepare his high-tech. equipment in readiness for naval instruction.

With boyish enthusiasm, he told us of his time spent at sea, for many years as a gunnery officer; how he had served in battleships, fought at Jutland, and about the *Royal Sovereign* – the 'Tidly Quid'. Today he would instruct us in both seamanship and gunnery, bringing live recordings to us, with the help of his gramophone; the sounds of the sea and sailors at work.

While he wound the 'His Master's Voice' gramophone, he told us that firstly we would learn to hoist the great steam picket boat – the biggest boat in the *Royal Sovereign*. With loving care, he placed his record on the gramophone turn-table and gently lowered the needle. A dreadful crackling sound came forth, followed by a muffled tinny voice, which the Admiral had to translate for us to understand.

'Take up the falls . . . marry the falls . . . hoist away!' cried the Admiral, while waving his hands in the air for emphasis.

This was followed by a crackled 'thump, thump, thump,' sound from the speaker horn. It lasted for a full minute and, as the Admiral explained, it was the sound of the sailors' feet on the wooden deck as they hauled on the boat's falls. His mind captured the scene vividly from the past, and his eyes sparkled as he nodded his head in time to the tramping feet.

'High enough . . . separate the falls . . . inboard fall hoist . . . high enough . . . marry the falls,' repeated the Admiral exultantly, as the record expired to its crackling conclusion.

'What do you say to that . . . eh? . . . What do you say to that, eh?' and to his pleasure, we broke into spontaneous applause.

Gunnery came next. 'You will now hear the guns of the *Royal Sovereign* firing at a battle practice target in the Channel,' he announced proudly, already preparing for the first broadside.

For the next two minutes the gramophone emitted periodic noises very similar to someone bringing up a troublesome quantity of phlegm. Meanwhile, in between the phlegm, the Admiral conducted his explanatory commentary.

'That was a full broadside. You probably noticed that the right gun of Y turret misfired,' he said gravely, pausing for a moment.

'I think that's the broadside, though, when we hit the target,' he concluded, his face brightening with satisfaction.

We enjoyed it and warmed to his enthusiasm. He came to share some of his moments from his bygone life at sea, and maybe whet our thoughts with his precious memories of ships and spray. The Captain and Vincey heard the final round of applause and poked their heads round the door; they were visibly relieved to see a smiling and satisfied Admiral. He waved us farewell and went off to talk more ships over pink gins and pheasant during lunch with the Captain and Vincey.

Some weeks later we met our other Admiral, Sir Geoffrey Layton, who had served in K Class submarines during the First World War. Apparently his submarine had been sunk in the Bosporus. He had subsequently been captured, then escaped and made his way back to England. In the Second World War he was in Singapore. He was present when the Service Chiefs were trying to come to terms with the Japanese invasion of Malaya. It was not a happy story, but he was a very jolly Admiral who had been in the wrong place at the wrong time.

John May and Vincey were a likeable pair. They had taken kindly to living in the Manor House, with its freedom, beauty and its game. They enjoyed the shooting and fishing, they worked hard to supplement the meagre funds available, and they were doing wonders with Fairthorne Manor – especially with a hell of a lot of help from us. We were treated fairly and fed well from their daily endeavours to rid the grounds of game. Fairthorne Manor must have sounded like a shooting range to the locals, and I often wondered whether – dressed in camouflage like jungle poachers – their search for food didn't bring them into conflict with adjacent owners and the local constabulary.

The only problem, as I saw it, was that we weren't learning a damn thing about maritime affairs – except painting, splicing and laying roofs. So I decided that something had to be done about it, and soon.

Several days later, high on the stable roof and laying tiles, I mutinied. I could hear Vincey and the Captain in the distance, engaged in game warfare as they banged away at anything which moved. I came down the ladder, jumped on to the chef's ancient sit up-and-beg bicycle, and pedalled down the half-mile drive to the open road. My destination was Curdridge, where the Admiral lived and where he dreamed of the sea.

I arrived at his house and saw a white mast which flew the Union Jack from the yard and several yacht club pennants hung from the halyards. Port and starboard lights adorned the wall on either side of the door. A ship's bell, boasting a magnificent bell rope, hung waiting to be rung by visitors or in case of fog. A freshly painted white lifebelt hung on a varnished stand ready for immediate use.

'Come in, dear boy, we'll talk and have some tea,' said the Admiral as he ushered me into his 'ship'. The hall was filled with nautical pictures, several barometers (both mercury and aneroid), a black silver-knobbed cane, two telescopes mounted on racks, a highly decorated Royal Marine drum and several ensigns. The sitting room was elegantly furnished: chairs and settees floated like ships on the sea of blue carpet, his Georgian side tables gleamed with polish, and a magnificent mahogany desk lay at rest by the window. As I gazed around the walls, it seemed that I was about to be run down by dozens of approaching ships, which bore down upon me with great bow waves from every picture.

He seated me at the desk, its deep patina reflecting my face, and handed me an old, finely bound book.

'Now you look through this, my boy, while I'm making tea. I won't be long,' he said, and then disappeared to the galley. It was a Midshipman's journal, dated somewhere around 1895, and covered the period when he had served in a gunboat up the Yangtze. The copperplate writing was faultless, the sketches, the diagrams, were superbly drawn, but the water colour paintings were individual works of art, their delicacy of colour and detail felt and captured the river settings and scenes of China. I became utterly absorbed and lost in wonder.

'You're lucky . . . they even delivered some buns to toast,' said the Admiral returning from the 'galley', carrying a silver tray laden with 'goodies' as he sailed in and hove to alongside me.

He answered my questions, and we talked and turned the pages of the journal and swallowed his toasted buns. Only after a while did he asks the question:

'And to what do I owe the honour of your visit then, my boy?' He said it casually as he looked at me with his penetrating blue eyes.

The purpose of my visit had been lost the moment I had opened his journal. I didn't know where or how to begin. In fact, I didn't really care about the matter any more, I was far too interested in everything else around me, not least the Admiral and his journal.

'Well, Sir . . . I was riding by and . . .' but I couldn't think how to continue.

'Yes, go on . . . go on. You were riding by . . . and you wanted to tell me something?' said the Admiral, and then continued.

'About *Warfleet*?' It seemed as though he were getting so close as to be reading my mind.

'Are you happy there, my boy?' He had now fixed me with a determined look of concentration, knowing he was close aboard.

'Yes, Sir, we're all happy there . . . except . . .'

He listened attentively and without interruption, as I told him of our concerns. I made it clear to him that everything was fine except for the matter of learning seamanship. 'If only we could be taught in class, go out in the boats on the river, and not spend our lives on the stable roof.' He gave a fleeting smile when I mentioned the stable roof.

As I left, he made it clear that, 'This is to be *our* secret. Don't say a word to anyone.' He made no comment or observation about anything or anyone.

'We'll put it right, my boy. Now off you go, back to your stable roof,' and smiled.

Two days later the Captain and Vincey mustered us in the classroom, and the former made an announcement. It seemed that he had been working on a new routine, which he thought might prove more beneficial . . . and as from today, we would be spending much more time under classroom instruction and . . . in the boats.

And so we did. Mind you, we ate far fewer rabbit and pigeon and instead thrived on bully beef, spam and powdered egg. Also Vincey did enjoy taking us on the river and down the Solent, choosing particularly vile weather and daring anyone to complain. He now made a point of following us, as best he could, on the chef's bike when we set off on our morning run, and the minimum time under the cold shower was two minutes. We continued doing necessary maintenance around the buildings, but never more than two hours a day. It was tougher, but much more fun.

I'm pretty sure that they knew who it was among us who was to blame for changing *their* routine, but they never let on by word or deed, and for that I admired them all the more. They could have made my life hell.

Came the day that Cunard shipping line rang the Captain saying that the *Queen Elizabeth*, all 84,000 tons of her, berthed in Southampton and due to sail in three hours, required a Bridge Boy. Could we provide one in time? It seemed that we were on their books – no doubt they had heard of our tiling capabilities – and having rung around several schools without success, had finally come to us in desperation.

Notwithstanding my mutinous record, I, being the senior boy, was offered first refusal by the Captain while Vincey stood by encouraging me to take the chance of a lifetime. The temptation to accept was so great that it hurt. To get my freedom by going to sea in the premier liner and experience a *Boy's Own* story come true, almost won. But then I thought of *Warspite, King George the Fifth*, the shrill notes of the bosun's call and . . . Dad. I couldn't let them down, nor forget my dreams.

The Captain saw my hesitation and gave me one minute in which to make up my mind. The second senior boy who stood beside me, Bray, was quivering with excitement as each moment passed. I felt his prayer as the silence drummed my ears and as thoughts of seeing the world in the *Queen Elizabeth* flashed through my mind. (Later, I learned that in fact she did the regular Southampton to New York run, and that I wouldn't have seen too much of the world).

'No, sir, it's the Royal Navy for me,' said I, as Bray let forth his 'yippee' loud and clear.

'Bray, pack your things . . . be ready within twenty minutes . . . Vincey, take him to the docks . . . and take Willis with you to let him see what he's missed,' said the Captain without malice, but with a tinge of hurt that I had not chosen his great service, the Merchant Navy.

We poured into the seasoned old station wagon and were on our way within thirty minutes, heading for the mighty *Queen Elizabeth*, which lay ready to depart and bound for New York. The car journey was like a nightmare, full of self-recrimination and doubt. Had I done the right thing? Was I missing the chance of a life time? Would I live to regret this day? What would my future be?

She looked magnificent: black hull with hundreds of portholes, white topsides and two huge red funnels, towering high into the sky above the dockside and dominating everything within sight. The ship looked majestic, a silent testimony to grandeur, wealth and the promise of romantic far-away lands across the seas. We were in awe and even Vincey, salt water flowing through his veins, commented:

'My, what a sight. I wish that I were starting new.' As I watched him speak so wistfully, his eyes were fired with excitement.

The last I ever saw of Bray was a small figure walking proudly up the gangway to his future. And as he reached the top, he turned and waved like a boy who had found his way to heaven . . . and was gone.

Vincey was, at heart, a gentle soul, and comforted me in my reflective depression on our empty journey back to *Warfleet*.

'Don't think about it, lad, you've made your bed. Now lie in it and make the bugger comfortable.'

In his prejudice, he silently agreed that I had made the proper choice to join the Royal Navy, but sensibly left me to carry the burden and make my decision come good. He understood that

I had probably made the first painful, and important, decision of my young life. He knew well that it was the first of so many more to come. But then, Vincey was a wise old salt, and maybe he already knew that ten days later I would have to meet another challenge: the lonely burden of command.

'Right, me lads, we'm off to sea,' said Vincey in his Hampshire voice, and then detailed us to load the 20 ft launch. We loaded water, provisions, fuel, towing hawsers, blocks and tackles, spare anchor, lead line, life jackets, charts and a host of other things which we thought we would never use on the trip.

Towing two sailing dinghies, we made our way gently down the river. It was another world in 1948. Lush woodland bordered the banks along the River Hamble, the wild birds thrived, the stillness could be heard between the mud-lined river banks as we wound our way through the upper reaches towards Bursledon Bridge and on past Moody's – several large tin shacks with slips where the boat builders worked their trade – and the 'Sailor's Return', a pub close to starboard, followed by a thin scattering of houses at the water's edge, and others nestled among the trees. Thence sharply round the bend to opening mud flats, and in the distance the wooden, black walls of *Mercury* – formerly a ship of the line, and HMS *Gannet* – riding high and filled with boys training for the sea. It was only two years since the remarkable Mrs Fry had died. She had otherwise been known as 'Beatie', and with her 'lover', founded this sea training school in 1885. Their affair had caused a great scandal at the time.

On we sailed, past small clumps of lonely yachts moored stem and stern between tall wooden posts and close to the channel. Then, over to port, in amongst the green and black of mud flats, lay the hulls of abandoned yachts up to their gunwales in ooze. I remember one such boat, a J Class yacht, later to be reborn – as were *Endeavour* and *Velsheda* – to grace the waters of the Solent with their beauty once again. Many years later, while sailing my own yacht in the Solent, I would see their lovely lines and remember that they represented the zenith of big yacht racing days, and recall that Father had crewed in several J class races off Southend when he was but seventeen.

It came on to rain, and as we passed Calshot, heading for Wooten Creek, the south-easterly wind began freshening. I remembered Father's little rhyme, 'First the rain and then the wind – Your topsails you must mind,' and the short steep waves caught us on the nose, buffeting our bows upward, and then falling quickly into space. The dinghies followed astern, labouring and jerking their way behind like two reluctant dogs fighting their leads.

Within the hour the sky had darkened and the wind had increased to 30 knots; the green, spiteful sea was whipped with white crests which broke over our bows, taking our way off with each shuddering jolt. Our cork lifejackets now comforted us as we looked inquiringly at Vincey, who grappled with the tiller, looking the fisherman in his dripping, sou' wester hat. Both dinghies now thrashed around like two snarling dogs and Vincey was grinning widely as he licked the salt water from his lips. We had become very quiet.

He gave us thirty minutes more of this before turning down sea and running before the wind, gently collecting our two strays to lurch and surf behind.

'Let's brew up, you lot. Get that kettle on,' said Vincey happily. 'You little buggers wanted to play in boats . . . didn't you? Well, now we're playing!' And having got his spear in, he made us take the helm in turns, cuffing us lightly when we got it wrong.

All along, Vincey had known our real destination. It was the head of Southampton Water, where we would berth alongside an MFV moored three hundred yards off shore, in which we would sleep for several nights.

Excitedly, we settled in and stowed our gear, pleased with the well-equipped galley and the small bridge, fitted with a compass, echo sounder and brass binnacle. Having made us polish all the brightwork on the bridge, Vincey spent the next hour or so instructing us on the mysteries of the magnetic compass. Flinders Bars and Kelvin Balls made us laugh, while variation and deviation made us think about CADET: 'Compass to True, Add East, Subtract West' was drummed into our heads till we got it right and Vincey was satisfied that we would not forget.

After a supper of beans, spam and canned tomatoes, with doorsteps of bread, Vincey called me to the tiny captain's cabin.

'I'm going ashore, lad. You're in command during my absence. No nonsense, mind.' With that, Vincey pulled his yachting cap firmly on his head, put a torch in his reefer jacket pocket and wrapped a woollen scarf around his neck. Apparently he had some important business to attend to on shore, and would be back at 2200. He would flash his torch three times, followed by a dash. This was Morse code for 'V', which meant that Vincey wanted the boat to fetch him.

I chose a crew of four to man the MFV's fourteen-foot dinghy, and we rowed him ashore in the dark. The wind was still blowing hard and the sea had a good chop on it, which sprayed over the bows and wet the crew.

'Keep a good lookout from 2150,' said Vincey as he climbed the steps and increased his pace toward the distant lights.

The lads dried off their wet garments over the oil stove and we settled down to read and chat, armed with tin mugs filled with tea and tangy canned milk. Came 2200 and no sign of a white light, flashing 'V' or anything else. The jetty lay barely visible in the darkness of the night and the wind blew hard as ever.

The loneliness of command descended heavily upon my shoulders. Was he standing on the jetty with a broken torch, willing me to come, even though no signal had been made? What time did the pub shut? There wasn't anywhere else to go in this desolate spot off Marchwood.

I called the crew and they grumbled all the way in to the jetty and all the way back, having seen no sign of Vincey. There were plaintive cries of,

'We told yer not to go, he would 'ave flashed his torch . . . Now we're wet again.' They settled down to moan and I was left with an unsolved problem. Where was he, and when would he bloody well show up? I stood with 'Flash' in the darkness of the bridge for an hour, peering into the blackness and listening to the rain and the wind howling.

The theory of the broken torch-light haunted me, so off we went once more to brave the miserable night. This time a new crew – chosen from the four remaining boys – bitched and moaned from start to finish during yet another abortive run. On returning aboard, they mixed in sullen groups, giving me the evil eye and muttering quiet threats under their breath. Flash and I retired to the bridge to continue our lookout vigil and wonder what the hell that Vincey was up to.

At midnight I called the first crew out again. All hell let loose as they told me to 'get stuffed' and made threatening gestures. This was bloody mutiny and I – like Captain Bligh – was in command. I retreated before the advancing mob, and as I was backing into the galley, Flash was suddenly at my side and we went in together. The mob, led by 'mouthy' Yates, stood two deep at the door and made to enter. Flash grabbed the heavy cast iron frying pan, while I grabbed an equally heavy pot. Our tactical advantage was considerable, since they could advance only on a narrow front, two abreast. We charged together, screaming like Dervishes, pot and pan on high, and saw them break left and right and run.

Ten minutes later, with Flash aboard, I led another sullen crew ashore.

Vincey's greeting came out of the dark, faintly resembling Stanley's opening remark to Livingstone.

'Ish . . . thaat you . . . me oold hearty . . . I hope it ish?' said Vincey, now visible, swaying gently behind the jetty rails and waving.

On the row back Vincey sang 'I wonder, oh I wonder, if the jaunty's made a blunder, when he said that he would marry me.' Then he gave us a garbled story which explained why he had been late. It seemed that his great aunt, who lived in Ringwood, had known the landlord's wife, whose sister was staying the night . . . and was very nice . . . so he couldn't say 'no' when they asked him to stay after closing time . . . they had wanted him to stay the night . . . and he had dropped his torch . . . so he couldn't signal his change of plans.

He was good as gold, however, once we had taken off his sea boots and got him into bed.

A month sped by and Christmas holidays were soon upon us. I had received my joining notice for the Royal Navy, which instructed me to present myself at HMS *Royal Arthur* on 17th February, 1949. It also informed me that since there were at present no seaman vacancies, I would join the Fleet Air Arm as a naval airman. It added, however, that my chances were high for subsequent transfer to the seaman branch. I made my farewells to Vincey and the Captain, promising to visit them when I got the chance, but a lot of water was to pass down the River Hamble before I saw them again in 1953.

Signing On

I joined HMS *Royal Arthur*, a new entry training establishment in Corsham Wiltshire, on 17 February 1949. I was one among five hundred new arrivals who poured through the main gates on that wet and windy day; most of the new entries were 17 or more years of age but I was 16 and a half.

For the next twelve weeks we were to undergo basic training far from the sea and in the heart of the unspoiled English countryside (then wearing its sombre winter coat of grey), while we froze each night in our wooden huts.

We were rushed hither and thither, hurried and bawled at, as we gathered up our uniforms, marked each item with our names, waited in never-ending queues for yet another medical, had our mouths roughly tugged and pulled by a mean-spirited and self-important dentist, were marched like amateurs to and from instruction, and learned to say 'Yes, sir' to everyone wearing a peaked cap.

They marched us up and down the parade ground, hour after hour in the biting cold, and taught us drill: to turn, to wheel, to right incline, to halt, to salute until we were dizzy with wonder and hungry as hell. Then came the rifle drill, which we performed – according to our instructor – 'like Portuguese militiamen after a night on the piss'.

As the weeks rolled by, I became more anxious about my transfer to the seaman branch, and constantly badgered my instructor for news.

'You're a bleedin' Naval Airman till the Navy says you're not . . . so shut your dripping, lad,' said my instructor every time I asked.

Twelve weeks later, having completed the basic training, my group of Naval Airmen were whisked off to Northern Ireland to

HMS *Gannet*, a naval air station near Londonderry, to start our specialist training. I don't really remember much about it, apart from a flight in a Barracuda, a dubious torpedo plane. At the time I was being used as a messenger for one of the squadrons, and I naively asked one of the officers if I could fly.

'I doubt it, lad, but I might be able to fix a flight for you . . . if you behave,' said the pilot with a grin.

He fixed it for the following day and just as I was about to get ready for this exciting trip, I was sent off to the other side of the airfield with a message and found on my return that the flight had gone. I was utterly miserable until we heard that the Barracuda in question had just ditched into Loch Foyle. The crew got out but later I learned that the plane had quickly sunk like a stone, and that the chances of an inexperienced passenger getting out would have been slim.

It was with considerable trepidation that I climbed into another Barracuda the next day. It was a monster of construction, with its dihedral wings poised high and looking like a disfigured eagle about to strike. Much to my disappointment, I wasn't given a parachute or, indeed, anything – not even a briefing. 'Jump in,' said the pilot. On either side of the fuselage were huge, plastic 'bubble' windows, and I was seated between them. It was a nerve-wracking experience, because as we gained height, I felt that I would fall off the narrow strip between my seat and feet, and drop earthwards through the windows to my death.

After an hour's flying, during which we skimmed over Loch Foyle at wave height – and I sought to catch a glimpse of yesterday's sunken Barracuda, I was exhilarated but a little relieved to touch down, clamber out and get my feet on the ground.

Apart from carrying messages and drinking tea in the squadron office, I don't think I learned anything during my eight weeks at *Gannet*. I do remember, however, that I did learn about one anatomical fact of life.

The cafeteria and galley staff were mainly made up of Wrens, and we green young sailors eyed the pretty ones as we queued for our meals, trays in hand, waiting for the dollops to descend upon the sectioned stainless steel plates. Their aim was often poor and one could enjoy the mix of steam duff pudding with soggy cabbage in its midst. Anyway, the banter between the braver sailors and the Wrens took many forms. One lad in front of me, who was always conscious of his hair style – all of us having been cropped nearly bald weeks beforehand – said proudly, as he stroked his new-grown mane.

'Me hair's nearly back to normal, now I'll trap the tarts.'

The pretty young Wren, ladle poised on high to drop a dollop of custard, looked him in the eye and delicately spoke.

'I got more hair on my fanny than you got on yer head,' and loaded his lamb chop with hot, runny Birds-eye.

Our 'acquaint' course was over and we set off from Londonderry by train, then across the Irish sea and southward towards Portsmouth, the billowing steam streaming horizontally from the surging locomotive, whose whistle shrieked adventure as we gathered speed and rattled over the rails towards the sea to join a ship.

HMS *Indefatigable* was a modern aircraft carrier, and we were joining her to continue our training at sea. We began to feel like real sailors and some more imaginative youngsters, hat flat aback, walked bow legged, in sorry imitation of a sailor's roll on heaving decks.

She was huge, and towered above us as we made our way up the forward gangway and into the maze of passageways, near-vertical ladders, hatches and watertight doors. Sailors in all manner of rigs were everywhere we turned; each one seemed bent on reaching some hidden destination that lay ahead, or up or down, through deck after deck in this warren of passageways and compartments.

We went to sea and watched the Seafires, Fireflies and Sea Furies launch and lift off the flight deck, each one at first climbing reluctantly into the air, then followed by another and another, until all were airborne and had become dots in the sky.

They would return later in small groups, and take up their pre-ordained recovery pattern. This brought them one by one into view of the batsman's signals, each plane wobbling in descent, answering the waved corrections in their final approach to the deck. Then at intervals they flashed over the round-down, their hook extended like an eagle's claw, catching one of the arrester wires laid out at intervals across the deck. They would pull up short under the restraining wire and come to a standstill just short of the rigid 'safety' barrier, which waits hungrily to mangle propellers, wings and sometimes the crews, should they miss the wires.

Several weeks go by and we return to Portsmouth harbour to paint the ship. Hundreds of sailors hang in nets, each with paint brush in hand and pot dangling nearby, high on the ship's side and superstructure with the water far below, clambering about like monkeys from 'fleet' to 'fleet', applying gallon after gallon of ubiquitous grey paint. Everything we paint is grey.

Then one day while hanging high above the water from a net, I hear a cry from above.

'Willis, yer transfer's come through. Yer Divisional Officer wants to see yer.'

The Shock

Long journeys by train were exciting events in the days of steam.

The smell of the station and the swirling steam conjured thoughts of holidays, change, strange places and new adventures. This was heightened all the more since I was to have my wish come true and become a *seaman*, just like my Dad. I was excited and happy.

By the time I reached Harwich, I was starving. I had eaten my bag meal even before I had reached Waterloo. My imagination had run riot as I had watched the green countryside roll by towards my destiny.

A dishevelled, peak-capped porter told me: 'There ain't no buffet 'ere, Jack,' and pointed me in the direction of the jetty, where I should catch the picket boat across the harbour to HMS *Ganges*.

The routine picket boat was approaching as I reached the jetty, and I looked across the harbour and caught my first glimpse of the *Ganges* Tower of Babel. The mast, sited on the hill, climbed high into the sky and almost seemed to disappear among the clouds; it was enormous; and I remembered the three-badge AB who had told me that I would have to climb it every day.

'Don't worry, mate, not many forl orf . . . and them as does drops on to the wire safety net. Mind you . . . they go through fast, like bleedin' chips!'

As we came alongside the jetty, the Coxswain of the picket boat leaned through his small bridge window and smiled.

'It's up the top of the hill . . . you can't miss it, just follow the trails of blood.'

I walked off down the jetty, hammock slung over my shoulder and towing my kit bag, feeling uneasy about the Coxswain's 'funny' remark, but comforting myself with the thought that he was only joking. I looked up and saw that a Lister baggage truck was parked on the road.

'Where's the others, then?' asked the sailor sitting on the

Lister's bench seat and smoking a cigarette.

I explained that I was alone and hadn't seen any others.

'You a bleedin' nozzer, then?' he said, looking at me with new-found contempt, adding.

'I'm 'ere for ship's company joiners, not bloody boy seamen.'

I judged that a proffered fag and a smile might get me a lift up the hill. He flicked his dog-end away and lit up.

'Orl rite, mate, 'op on.'

We chugged up the hill and into the approach road of *Ganges*. Two huge black wrought-iron gates lay at the far end; the gates had spikes painted in gold leaf and a decorated crest of HMS *Ganges* was mounted above the wrought-iron arch. He stopped in front of the closed gates and watched me with amusement as I off-loaded my kit.

'The Gestapo's in there, mate,' said my driver. 'Watch 'ow you go,' and he wheeled around smartly and was off back to the jetty.

The Regulating Office was a dismal room with a long counter which ran from end to end except for a counter flap halfway along. Three grim-faced petty officers sat on the other side of the counter on high stools doing paper work. The walls were filled with notices which ranged from: duty rosters, leave rosters, venereal disease prevention, duty free allowances, men under punishment routines and the Articles of War. It was, I thought, a heartening place at which to arrive. My reflections were quickly doused, as though by a bucket of cold water.

'And who may you be, standing there like a wet fart?' said one of the more aggressive looking Regulating Petty Officers.

'Er . . . Aircraftsman Willis, RPO, drafted for conversion to Boy Seaman from *Indefatigable*.'

'Sir! Not RPO. And stand to attention when you speak to me, you nasty little boy.' He climbed off his stool, lifted the counter flap and marched menacingly towards me. He halted within an inch of my face and glowered darkly down at me, both eyes bloodshot and looking most unfriendly.

'Sorry, R . . . sir, I was always told to . . .'

I thought his fat face would explode.

'Stand still. Speak when I tell you to speak . . . Understand?'

In fact I hadn't moved a muscle and was now speechless anyway.

The other petty officers looked up from their paperwork and fixed me with their hostile stares. My tormentor half-turned towards them and said, 'Ask the Master at Arms if he would be so good as to spare a moment of his valuable time.' He then returned his attention to me.

'Where did you get that fancy bleedin' dress from?' he snarled rhetorically, and then continued, 'this is not Haitch Hem Ess Pinafore, nor the stuffing girl guides,' he spluttered, so close to my face that I caught his spittle and felt the snort from his ugly nostrils.

My mind flashed through the past three months in the Navy. I had imagined myself by now to be a bit of a tiddly jack; for didn't I have a 'port and starboard' cap, and wasn't my tailor-made suit wide fronted and with bell bottom flares? You could cut your hand on the seven creases in my trousers and my badge was gold lace. And what about my Mediterranean blue collar and the tiddly bow in my cap? Surely I was dressed like a sailor.

Once again my thoughts were interrupted as the door at the far end opened, and in walked the King Crusher, the Master at Arms. He must have been all of six foot four inches from the soles of his shoes to the top of his cap. My immediate tormentor withdrew respectfully to one side in order that the Master at Arms could command a full frontal view of the offending object. He too halted within an inch of my head, which barely reached his collar. The petty officer leaned confidentially toward the great

51

man and spoke in a Fagin voice.

'He says 'e's joining *Ganges*, Master. An Airy Fairy from *Indefat.*' He then looked sideways, daring me to contradict.

The Master was standing rigidly to attention, his arms tightly held in to his sides. He took one military step backwards and leaned toward me at an angle of thirty degrees, thus making close contact with my face.

'So you're going to be one of us . . . but not looking like that, sonny.' He then turned toward the petty officers behind the counter, both of whom stood watching in approval.

'Have we a knife in here, RPO . . . so's I can rearrange this little jack-me-hearty?'

My blood ran cold. What the hell is he going to need a knife for? I asked myself.

A large 'pusser's' dirk was handed over the counter and the Master opened the blade lovingly. I thought of Sweeny Todd.

'Now, your collar looks proper washed out,' he said as he twirled me round, so that I had my back to him.

With two deft strokes of the knife, he cut the collar clean off my back, leaving the tattered remains hanging limp. Then he twirled me back again and removed my cap.

'That's not regulation issue,' he said, as he stabbed it repeatedly to death.

Then, with a gleam of satisfaction, he sliced down through the front of my jumper, thereby turning it into a jacket which opened, and then cut my bell bottom trousers to ribbons. Within three minutes I had been reduced to the status of a scarecrow.

The Master smiled as he handed back the knife.

'Now you look a proper sailor,' he said, turned about, and marched off back to his room.

I was humiliated and fought the tears back from my eyes as the petty officers viewed me with thinly disguised smiles of satisfaction on their mean little faces.

I was escorted to the Annexe where all newcomers – Nozzers by name – were indoctrinated prior to being released into the main camp. I was handed over to the Divisional Petty Officer, who looked at me in wonderment.

'What the bloody hell have you been up to, me old cocker? You look like you've been fighting the bleedin' Zulu's.'

I told him what had happened.

'Oh, my Gawd!' he laughed, but not unkindly. 'The bastards! Never mind, me old fruit, it can only get better.'

Chapter 3

HMS Ganges

Looking back on it after all these years, I still dislike most of the memories of my time in HMS *Ganges*. It was hell all the way. Of course, there were moments of happiness and fun when one was able to relax and lower one's guard, but not many. In between times there were long periods of monotony, stark living conditions and mind-boggling drudgery. But the most persistent theme, which occupied my thoughts through each long day and sometimes into the night, was survival.

And yet I can say truthfully that I have always been proud to have been a *Ganges* boy. I was to find out later when I joined the Fleet, that it was a mark of excellence and professionalism. We were trained exceedingly well and the method of teaching was based on the 'old fashioned' three Rs principle. Once the boys were taught how to splice a rope, blow a bosun's 'call', lash a hammock, secure and climb the life lines, it was never forgotten. We were taught a thousand and one seaman-like tasks, domestic necessities and time-honoured wrinkles, many of which still stand me in good stead to this very day.

Having recovered from the shock of my arrival at the gates of *Ganges*, I settled into the 'joining' routines that were the prime purpose of the Annexe. All new Boys were isolated in the Annexe for six weeks before being let loose across the road to *Ganges* proper. Firstly, they had to be taught the fundamentals of parade ground drill, how to wear their 'square rig' uniforms, address their superiors, absorb the basic Naval jargon and a host of other details that were part of their new way of life. They would probably never undergo such a shocking culture change as that experienced at *Ganges* for the rest of their lives.

I was issued with an entirely new kit and my *Royal Arthur* kit was burned in the boiler furnace. My new kit was more comprehensive and contained such esoteric items as a cylindrical, black enamelled hat box, 'night shoes' for evening wear, an attaché case for weekends, a new 'type' for marking my name on my clothes, and a remarkably well equipped sewing pack called a 'housewife'. This latter item was seldom out of my hands for the next two weeks and helped me occupy every spare moment of the day.

The officer in charge of the Annexe decided that since I had done a *'form'* of basic training as an 'Airy fairy' at HMS *Royal Arthur*, I was to confine my efforts to 'sewing in' my new kit and bedding. After that I would cross the road to join my appointed Division in the real world.

Thank God, my surname comprised six letters only, but I cursed my Mother and Father for giving me three Christian names. Every single item was to be stamped in paint – using my name type – then the name and initials were to be sewn into the garment in red silk. This included: handkerchiefs, socks, underwear, suits, shirts, trousers, blankets, sheets, hammocks – bedding was done in blue wool – and even gloves; and finally, the 'housewife' itself. As I sewed, hour after hour, I tried to imagine what it must be like for some poor devil called, say, ABC Williamson-Jones, sewing his name on every item and down to the last handkerchief. Having completed my kit, I was shown how to 'graft' my hammock lashings and make them into tiddly works of art. For years to come, these telltale signs on my kit and bedding announced from the hammock stowages that the owner was a professionally trained Boy Seaman.

With scarred fingers – caused by endless sewing – and once again looking like a forerunner of the Skinheads, owing to yet another balding haircut, and itching all over from the new blue serge suit, I doubled over the road to HMS *Ganges* and my destiny.

It was another world. The huge parade ground was dominated by the 140 ft mast, the massive drill shed and the unending squads of blue-suited Boys doubling to and from instruction. This was 'home' for more than two thousand Boys for the duration of their training, which would take a year to complete.

I had been assigned to Collingwood Division, which, like Hawke Division, was close to the parade ground. All the other messes were in either the long or short covered ways.

'Right, lad, get yer kit into 44 Mess and hurry up about it,' said my new class instructor, Kitchener, a tall large-nosed Chief Petty Officer.

My first impression on entering the mess was that the wooden parquet floor glistened like an ice rink. It gleamed and reflected every object within its orbit. The 'spit kids' looked like silver and you could see your face in them. The rows of beds – fallen in like a convoy about to move off – each had two blankets and were stacked uniformly and squared away with the accuracy of a nursing sister. Great reflector lamps hung down the length of the high-pitched dormitory roof, and the windows sparkled and drew reflections from the row upon row of polished aluminium lockers which disappeared into the distance through the main aisle. And it was empty; not a soul but me. All the others were at instruction.

When later we met, I was looked upon with hostile interest, as something of a freak for having joined late and entirely on my own. 'Who was I and where had I come from so suddenly to join them?' I was singled out as a newcomer. And to make matters worse, I didn't have the accent of a Geordie, a Londoner or come from Birmingham. 'He speaks proper posh . . . think yer better'n us then?' But I had been through it all before.

Next morning our Division was fallen in on the quarterdeck near the Commander's office and we waited for him to appear. My new boots were killing me and the lace of one had come undone. I bent down to retie it and was promptly booted up the backside. Furiously I turned round and looked at the Boy immediately behind me.

'Who did that?'

He laughed. 'Wanna make sommut of it?'

That was my first mistake. I did make something out of it. After we had got back to the mess, I fronted up to him. The only problem was that I had taken on one of the reigning *Ganges* boxing champions.

Luckily a Badge Boy stopped the fight before he killed me, but I was bleeding plentifully from my cut lip and nose before it had ended. While it was not a good start to my first day in the Division, it did tend to lend some mysterious easing of animosity toward me. I became less the leper and more the 'toffy' oddity.

As the weeks and months passed by, we learned so many different things; and what we learned was done the *Ganges* way. We mended our clothes, we darned our socks, we washed and ironed our clothes – done under the eagle eyes of instructors who were regularly among us till the moment we turned in at night. We marched, we climbed the mast, we went to school, we swam. Then another day would come. We 'pulled' the whalers and the cutters in the bitter winter weather, we sailed, did gun drill, played all manner of sports, tied knots till they were coming out of our ears, and always dreamed of food and home.

Everything we did was planned months ahead. The timing of each event was adhered to down to the minute. Laundry morning once a week, up at 0500, eat 'hard tack' biscuits fit to break your teeth while downing hot 'kye' – a chocolate drink with little milk or sugar – then off to the laundry. Each one armed with brush, scrubbing board, and a huge bar of 'pusser's' hard soap, we would scrub away under the eyes of the all-seeing Instructor. When satisfied that our clothes were clean, he would allow us to place them into the giant spinners, which to us looked like ship's turbine engines. Finally hundreds of garments, all names sewn in red silk, would be hung in the heated racks to dry.

Only then could we flee to breakfast and fight our utility sausage – bereft of meat – and savour the congealed, flattened egg which had suffered death an hour or so before its yellow, lifeless eye finally stared vacantly upward towards a gaping mouth.

Cooking food for two thousand Boys required some elements of care and planning: the ability to cook, careful choice of menus, culinary dedication, superb timing and imagination. The *Ganges* chefs failed handsomely on all counts. Their catch-all plan for cooking and timing was simple. They would boil and or fry everything to death starting four hours before the food would be eaten. The food would then suffer further agonies in great warming racks for an hour or more. Dedication and imagination were not on the menu. The only thing they didn't burn was salad; and that was limp, soggy and often sported slugs or caterpillars.

But, we ate everything. That included do-it-yourself pepper and mustard sandwiches – to take away the terrible taste of the wartime margarine. I'm convinced to this day that we were singled out to solve the margarine mountain in preparation for joining the EEC in later years. Once a week, however, we did manage to stave off hunger for an hour or two. That was on Pay Day.

Two thousand Boys would muster on the parade ground to be paid. We were fallen in by Divisions, and it seemed to take for ever before one arrived at the pay table. As one's name was called, one took one pace forward, off cap, 'Boy Second Class, Willis, Sir.' The Supply Officer would then place one shiny half crown on to the lid of one's hat – five shillings if one was a Boy first class. One then turned smartly left and ran off as fast as one's legs would move to join the queue for the canteen.

'One pint of "goffer" and four Banbury's please . . . oh, and a Mars bar,' was a typical order once one had commanded attention at the counter. Those over the age of sixteen were allowed to smoke. The smokers would usually buy a packet of five Woodbines, sold in a shiny green paper wrapper. But one could tell the 'Barons' – Boys First Class and Badge Boys – for they would order ten Capstan, Gold Flake or Players. One thing was certain though: everybody scoffed cakes and drank 'goffers'. The latter were sickly pink substitutes for cordial, and a pint of it made one feel a bit ill afterwards. Within an hour, it was all over until next pay day.

We had to go up the mast once a week and for most of us it was a bit scary the first time. Our class instructor, Chief Kitchener, didn't force us to go over the 'devil's elbow' on to the first platform until we were ready. Instead, we could go through the 'lubber's hole, which meant that we climbed vertically onto the platform, some eighty feet above the deck. But he was a good psychologist. Once one Boy had done it, the majority weren't going to be found wanting. In no time Boys were heading for the second platform, then up the Jacob's ladder – nearly one hundred and thirty feet high – and finally, shinning up the bare pole to the button. It was here that one hung on for grim death.

The 'devil's elbow' made the adrenaline run fast. At first, one didn't dare to look down. To reach the platform, one had to climb upwards and outwards at forty-five degrees. Thus one was hanging in mid-air with nothing between oneself and the deck . . . except the net. And we were frightened to death of the net. It was made of wire and held in position by twenty or so vertical steel supports. It was an often-repeated instructors' joke which I had already heard, 'If you miss the stanchions, lad, don't worry – you'll hit the net and go through like freshly sliced chips.' Hence the net was referred to as the 'chipper'. After a while, though, one didn't give it a thought. At weekends in fine weather Boys would play up the mast or take a book to read a hundred feet or so above the parade ground.

The 'button' boys were the heroes of the mast. They would stand to attention on the 'button' – the lightning conductor between their legs to steady them – and salute. This occurred on ceremonial occasions when the mast was manned, and the selected 'button' boy of the day would receive five shillings from the Captain. I made it to the button but I never dared stand up.

There were, of course, those who couldn't stand heights and who suffered misery every time they were made to go near the mast. It was obligatory to make the second platform and the Boys who hadn't done so suffered the humiliation of attending 'backward mast' class; just as the lads who couldn't swim went to early morning 'backward swimmers' class.

It still amuses me to think of the crazy penalties which were inflicted on us boys for all manner of misdemeanours. Boys who were punished for swearing would be made to fall in outside the Commander's office immediately after morning colours. They would stand in a forlorn row, each with a mug of soapy water in hand. At the order 'one', they would take a mouthful, at the order 'two', they would gargle for half a minute, at the order 'three', they would spit it out into a bucket. Whereupon, in chorus, they would sing out in unison.

'*Ahoy. Ahoy. This will make me a clean mouth Boy.*' This procedure was repeated three times, after which one was told to don one's gas mask for the rest of the day. It was to be worn at all times except when eating meals or at instruction.

Meanwhile, the backward swimmer had his problems too. He was made to wear a heavy cork life jacket all day long as a mark of his inability to keep his head above water. Equally funny – if you didn't get caught – were the Boys who were made to wear Second World War tin hats all day. This was because they had put 'bow waves' in their caps so as to look 'tiddly'. I remember seeing one Boy who had achieved a 'full house', and wore the lot. He looked much like a soldier from the Great War – gas mask, tin helmet and cork life-jacket – charging some unseen enemy as he doubled from one place of instruction to the next.

The whole establishment was a minefield of potential hazards. It was almost impossible to keep out of trouble. The do's and don't's of every-day life were, in their totality, beyond comprehension. One would have needed a 'double honours' in law to escape the system. Indeed, to be recognised as a smart-arsed sea lawyer was an offence in itself. One was then a 'lower-deck lawyer', subject to the Articles of War pertaining to mutiny and, '. . . shall suffer death or any such penalties herein to be proscribed . . .' Like all sailors, we were learning how to survive on the lower deck, which in short meant keeping your head down and keeping moving.

In spite of that, the system got me. Four weeks after joining my class, I was made the 'class leader'. Each one comprised thirty to forty Boys, and there were about ten classes in the Division – all at differing stages of progress. After each had been running for sixteen weeks with a succession of trial class leaders, one or more was rated-up to Badge Boy. Thereafter, the best of these could progress to Petty Officer Boy, and the élite might even become Instructor Boys. I had been given the temporary appointment of class leader – which carried little authority – and was responsible for taking charge of thirty-five Boys, doubling them to and from places of instruction and ensuring that they behaved themselves en route.

It was a hellish job. The class leader didn't wear the stripe of authority on his sleeve and the majority resented taking orders from one of their own kind. So there I was, lumbered on my own, with all the responsibility and none of the authority and privileges enjoyed by the Badge Boys. There was no doubt in my mind that it was made even more difficult because I had been dubbed 'the toffy-nosed bastard' due to my accent. I had only to order them to 'fall in', and someone would ask me 'who the bloody hell did I think I was, ordering them about?' They behaved like guardsmen when the instructors were present, and like revolutionaries from the Bastille when they weren't.

About a week after 'taking up office', I had had enough. They had plagued me all the way from the Division and were marching like a bunch of unruly farmers from Tolpuddle. Already I had been told to 'sod off' by half the class and they were laughing and joking as we approached the Main Gate. Instead of wheeling them left to our destination, I continued them on towards the 'Crusher's' hell hole, to cries of, 'were goin' in the wrong direction, you silly bastard!' and finally halted them directly outside the Master at Arm's office.

A hushed dawning of realisation descended upon them.

'What we doin' 'ere, Will?' said Benson uncomfortably – he

was one of the most objectionable among them – and now he was attempting a friendly tone of voice.

Two RPOs emerged from the office.

'What's this lot doin' here, then?' said one of them aggressively, as he fixed me with his SS stare.

'I want to run them in, sir,' I said, hardly believing my own words.

To an RPO the whiff of trouble was like the savoury smell of haute cuisine. He advanced upon me quickly, like a grizzly bear sniffing honey.

'Which one, lad. Just point 'im out.' And he fixed my worried, goggle-eyed class with a ferocious face as he marched up and down the files.

'All of them – the lot, sir,' I said with tremulous finality.

'Right . . . all of 'em . . . all of 'em?' said the RPO uncertainly, and sloped off to fetch the Master at Arms to deal with a serious outbreak of mutiny. He didn't fancy coping with what looked like another 'Invergordon' on his own.

It was a natural reflex. We all held our breath in the terrible presence of the 'King Crusher'. He was related to the Devil and did his dirty work. The mutiny was resolved with a simple observation and undisputed order.

'Class Leader, they've been naughty boys and I don't like naughty boys,' he said quietly, and in the manner a Mafia Godfather might use when passing sentence of death.

'Double them round the parade ground till dinner time, or until they drop.'

I was very lonely, standing in the middle of that great expanse, while my classmates endlessly doubled round the perimeter. They were models of behaviour and obeyed my every order. And when it was over, they gasped their way to dinner and plotted their revenge.

That evening after instruction I was sitting on my bed 'spit' and polishing my boots in an almost empty mess. I had been unofficially 'sent to Coventry' by my class and wasn't getting much change out of anyone else either. Meanwhile my classmates, led by Benson, were busily going round the other messses, drumming up support to have me taken outside and beaten up.

I heard the stamp and scuffle of feet as they gathered at the entrance to the mess. Cries of, 'Let's get the bastard' and 'We'll teach him who's in charge,' mingled with blood-curdling cheers. There was no doubt in my mind that they had come to get me.

Now I could see them at the bottom of the steps – many of them with webbing belts with heavy buckles in hand. 'Bloody hell!' I thought in fear. Their shouting, full of oaths, grew louder and a mass of them appeared at the door led by the evil-faced Benson. He needed his mob behind him, and spoke out only when he was sure of support. I stood up and waited for the inevitable, determined to get one blow on his ugly face before going down under the weight of numbers.

Quite suddenly they were no longer looking in my direction. They had turned to face a shouted order from behind.

'Stand aside! Leave the mess, all of you,' and in steamed ten Badge Boys, led by two Instructor Boys.

The mob sulkily dispersed and wandered off in groups towards the mast; there to vent their feelings in heated conversation rather than with buckled belts.

The senior Instructor Boy gave me good counsel, telling me to come to him in future if ever things got out of hand. They, the Badge Boys, would deal with it. My classmates sulked moodily for a week before we gradually returned to armed neutrality. Eventually it split us into two camps, with seventy percent for, and thirty against. Benson led the thirty per cent but they mostly confined themselves to whining discontent – 'dripping.' 'It ain't fair . . . why should we 'ave to do it?' But they did.

And so the months soldiered on, and we with them. Then came the time of the sixteenth week kit inspection, when we would be rated to Boy Seaman 1ˢᵗ Class. Lieutenant Alan-Williams was a correct, conscientious and efficient officer. He was responsible for the training, administration, and the welfare of the Division.

I was well aware that I would be rated up to Badge Boy once I had passed the formal kit inspection, and for several weeks we had been preparing for the day. Every article of kit that was suitably sized, was configured into the shape of a Swiss roll – the length of the Seamanship Manual – and secured by two pieces of white tape – at regulation spacing – at either end of each article. Every piece of kit one possessed had to be laid out on one's hammock in two long rows on the polished floor. It was designed to look like a piece of modern art, symbolically representational.

Two weeks before the day, we started to wear as little as we could get away with: our immaculate 'Swiss rolls' were being stored and preserved for inspection, wrapped in greaseproof paper. This process became more and more difficult since one had less and less to wear as the great moment drew nigh. Everything – but everything – had to be accountable and on display on the day. This was to be my undoing.

The day before the inspection, a few of us were at last issued with out tailor-made-to-measure 'sea suits'. The majority had already received them five days previously. This was to be our best No 1 uniform, which was to be worn only on special occasions. This presented me with a problem: how could I mark it in paint with my name type, have it dry, sew my name in red silk and then turn it into a 'Swiss roll' by tomorrow? I ducked the problem and stowed it in my locker.

'An absolutely first rate kit, Willis,' said Alan-Williams, with my Instructor smiling beside him. I was 'chuffed' to get such praise, especially after all the hard work. He made to move on to the next boy's inspection, then turned and said, 'Are you pleased with your 'sea suit?' He looked back to my kit and scanned its contents. 'Where is it?' he asked, in a sharper tone.

I explained the situation – as I had seen it – but somehow, he didn't see my point of view. I was given a 're-scrub' inspection in one week's time. The humiliation was total. I was grouped with the 'skates' and 'scabs' who had failed because of their ill-prepared, dirty and scruffy kits. I thought the world would end when pimply-faced Benson laughed and said, 'Now yer one of us, Will,' and carried on picking his nose.

But of course, the world didn't end and much to my surprise, I was told to continue as the class leader, although I 'wouldn't be rated to Badge Boy'. In its way, that was punishment enough. I licked my wounds and thought of other ways to earn some laurels.

Like a boy scout, I started collecting qualifications and badges. My first ambition was to become a 'Call' Boy. I wanted to possess a bosun's whistle in my own right. I wanted to be able to make those same shrill pipes that I had heard from across the water at Plymouth all those years ago. To blow the bosun's call with complete competence required skill and many hours of practice. My Chief Instructor loaned me a whistle and I blew it in all my spare moments. I blew it in the heads (lavatories), I blew it on the empty sports field and I blew it wherever I could find a place away from the frantic cries of 'I'll stuff that bloody thing up your arse if you don't stop.' I was permanently on the run to escape the anger of fellow messmates and instructors.

There were about twenty different calls to learn, and the most difficult was probably the 'dinner' call, which was originally meant to last for something like two minutes. Warbling and trilling had first to be mastered before any but the simplest pipes could be made. After several weeks of practice, I could: 'pipe down' (lights out) 'call the hands', 'hoist and lower boats', sound the 'still' and 'carry on', and in fact all manner of other arcane commands which had long since ceased to be used at sea. In practice, there were about five calls only which were still used regularly in the fleet. Within a month, nevertheless, I had mastered the lot and had undergone the exacting examination. I was now a qualified 'Call' Boy and was presented with my very own bosun's whistle.

Henceforth, I would no longer have to wear a white lanyard with my No 1 suit. Instead I proudly wore the silver bosun's chain and felt as grand as any Lord Mayor. I was now different from most others and could be distinguished from 'the rabble'.

In a short time I passed the examination for 'Coxswain', which allowed me to wear a badge, a ship's wheel on my sleeve – and qualified me to take out boats under sail and oars. To round it off, I then qualified as a marksman and wore a 'rifle' too. All this trophy-hunting went some way to saving face and restoring my pride for having not been made a Badge Boy.

Looking back over the years, I'm still surprised that I didn't suffer the indignities of 'Laundry Hill' and a 'beating'. Punishment was meted out in many forms. At the top of the list came a 'beating'; it was carried out with clinical ceremony in the gym and the offender was clad in a white duck suit. It was inflicted by a physical training instructor and witnessed by the Commander and his Regulating staff.

Each stroke of the cane was called and delivered slowly, to maximise the suspense and pain. The Royal Navy had enjoyed a long tradition of delivering corporal punishment to telling effect.

The punishment was never personal; the Captain sanctioned it, but he was merely carrying out the will and regulations embodied in the Articles of War and the Kings Regulations and Admiralty Instructions of My Lords Commissioners of the Admiralty. The ceremonial nature of the punishment ensured that it was seen to be an inevitable and impersonal retribution. While the cane hurt, the majesty of naval law was awful.

Doubling up and down 'Laundry Hill' – steep as Everest – however, was hardly easy going either. The Duty Petty Officer took charge of this event out of working hours. This ensured that his mind was focussed upon, and already prejudiced against, the unhappy offender. The practice ensured that if the Duty Instructor himself had to suffer, then most decidedly he would make the guilty pay. I seem to remember that Laundry Hill was also referred to as Faith, Hope and Charity, and the greatest of these, Charity, was marked by its absence.

Three times a year we went home for leave. During the term that was the 'star' in the sky that helped to hold us on course. It increased in brightness as the days passed and toward the end of term excitement blazed like the sun. During the final days it became infectious. Everyone was determined not to jeopardise his impending freedom. All was laughter and goodwill, and even the '*Gestapo*' were grudgingly tolerant.

We were up at 0400 on the day. Cleaning, squaring off the mess, getting dressed in our 'tiddly' suits and collecting our bag meals for the journey. Finally two thousand Boys would be mustered according to destination, to catch the fleet of buses to Ipswich Station, thence to disperse homewards to all parts of the British Isles . . . and freedom.

For the following three weeks, all over the country there would be cocky young sailors wearing HMS *Ganges* cap tallies, proudly wearing their uniforms for mums and dads, brothers and sisters, uncles and aunts and not least, for the local girls. In those days Britain was still openly proud of her Navy and the men who served. It was utterly unlike today, when sloppy fashions abound, gangs of lager louts roam the streets for victims, ill-informed 'peace-makers' scorn the uniform, terrorists kill soft targets, defence cuts and widespread cynicism are meted out to those who serve their country. No wonder the streets have been cleared of Jolly Jack and his fellow servicemen in uniform.

Too quickly it was all over. Returning to *Ganges* was likened to visiting a post-nuclear strike. The *Ganges* wasteland of bitter, cold-wintered East Anglia was 'ground zero'. Dark depressing skies cast their gloom upon the lifeless emptiness of the parade ground and the surrounding fields. The 'satanic' buildings stood like gutted shells and the mast, bleak in its nakedness, like a tree in winter. In solemn groups we would drift slowly to our messes and breathe in the all-too-familiar smells, stow our lockers, fix our beds and shed our No 1 suits for another day.

But as the mess begins to fill, the tempo gains pace. Snapshots of girls, books, presents, letters and the most unlikely possessions emerge from cases and lockers, proudly to be displayed, discussed and weighed according to their merit. Conversations quicken and soon the mess is alive.

'You wanna' know what I did?' and

'You won't believe this but . . .' and 'She's a gem; tits like ripe oranges.' We're back for yet another term.

Later comes 'lights out'. A deep hush descends upon us all. We lie there silently, alone, thinking of home.

'I wonder what Mum and Dad are doing now?'

And many a 'toughy' quietly wipes the tears on his sheet in the unnatural stillness of this first sad night away from home.

The resilience of youth is to be marvelled at. Within days it is as though we had never been on leave at all. It was all a beautiful dream to be treasured – and anyway, thank God, this is my last term at *Ganges* and then I'm off to sea.

But before that we had something else to look forward to. We were going to spend a day at sea in a Hunt-Class destroyer. It would come to Harwich and we were to embark by picket boat from the *Ganges* jetty. Some of our number made all manner of salty boasts about how 'My Dad took me out in his boat . . . well it wasn't exactly his boat, but we were at Clacton.' And another: 'Well, I used to go fishing with my uncle.'

The real experience in HMS *Bleasdale*, however, proved to be somewhat different.

It was a forbidding autumn morning. Or, as Chief Petty Officer Kitchener said in the vernacular,

'The equinoctial wind's blowing a bastard and the rain's pissin' down like pencils.' His large black oilskin was running wet as he marched the length of the mess.

'It's 0500. Now 'op out of your pits at the double.'

We picked up our bag meals, each in a stiff brown paper bag containing: two corned beef 'doorsteps', one apple, a packet of hard tack biscuits and a slice of rubbery Manchester tart, and made our way in the dark to the Shotley jetty. By the time we arrived, our paper bags were beginning to disintegrate and some were already chewing corn dog 'doorsteps' before they washed away.

Once aboard the *Bleasdale*, we found ourselves heading out into a north easterly gale in the blackness of the morning with the lights of Felixstowe and Harwich dropping astern. Not many of us really knew 'our arse from our elbow', as one of the ship's company observed, when *Bleasdale* was fifteen minutes out to sea and doing twenty knots. It wasn't spray that came over the bows, it was hundreds of tons of black, cold water, which slammed on to the fo'c'sle and rushed aft to the iron deck.

We were hurriedly taken below and allocated to various messdecks as the ship heaved, twisted and slammed into the sea. A great 'fanny' full of dark brown tea was poured into tin mugs and passed among us as we sat at the messdeck table. Its tannin content must have been capable of dissolving boots, and the thick 'Ideal' milk gave it the texture of oil. It tasted appalling, and we were used to tea with very few tea leaves *and* laced with bromide. It was the tea that helped to break the line. Two of our Boys turned white, then green, and rushed up the ladder to find the heads. Thereafter, it struck us in increasing numbers, quickly, like a cholera epidemic or the black death.

An hour later there were few Boys standing upright. We were scattered all over the ship, huddled in safe little hideaways and corners. About twenty Boys were 'dying' in the tiller flat among the spare oilskins, awnings and hawsers. Some were braving the upper deck, I among them, for we preferred to pass away in the fresh air than in the bowels of the ship. I had found a spot near the warmth of the funnel. At first I couldn't decide whether to succumb from exposure away from the funnel, or die from asphyxiation from the acrid funnel fumes which enveloped me. In the end, I compromised, standing clear of the smoke until I was numb with cold, and only returning to the fumes to thaw out.

The sailors – that is, the real ones – were magic. They did their best to look after us throughout the day, and it was a frequent sight to see them stuffing dry bread or ship's biscuits into green faces, rather like feeding sick parrots. One three-badge sailor made me laugh.

'Wanna' know the symptoms of sea-sickness, sonny?' he grinned, and then said, 'At first you think you're gonna' die. After a while, you're shit-scared you won't.'

Later, our spirits picked up when we heard the First Lieutenant make an announcement over the ship's tannoy.

'Do you hear there? We are now on our way back to Harwich and will be entering harbour in twenty minutes time.'

He had the grace not to 'hope that we had all enjoyed our day with them.'

What a sorry bunch we looked as we slowly made our way up the hill. We were a bedraggled lot, many still smelling of sick, with tell-tale stains and white faces that had aged. 'Sailors, home from the sea . . . were we,' and ever so grateful to be back on dry land.

Curious groups of Boys greeted us as we streamed back into the mess.

'How'd it go then?' they asked enthusiastically crowding round.

'Oh, not so bad . . . bit rough,' answered one pale lad laconically, but still looking decidedly bilious.

'Seen it worse,' said the Boy who had once fished with his uncle, and whose oilskin sleeves were still covered in sick.

But most of us quietly crept away to shower and to ponder on the wisdom of a life at sea. With the resilience of youth, however, and the human knack of forgetting what it was really like at the dentist, we soon managed to convince ourselves that, 'It wasn't quite so bad.' Anyway, the following day, Chief Kitchener soon took our minds off it with 4" gun drill.

'Gun's crew, number!' screamed the Chief. Every gunnery order was traditionally screamed two octaves higher than normal speech. This was followed by 'Gun's Crew, close up,' and those with numbers would rush to their allocated positions, standing or sitting rigidly to attention. The Captain of the gun, the Layer and Trainer were the positions we all liked most, but no sooner had you got one of those jobs than Kitchener would scream, 'Gun's crew, change round.' At first, it was all very baffling and we were particularly scared of the Loader's job.

The 4" shells were heavy and had to be thrust into the breech in one smooth action. As the tail end passed into the breech, it released the extractors and the heavy breech block shot upwards and swallowed the shell. The trouble was that it would swallow your fingers too if you didn't do it correctly.

'Clench yer right hand at the middle knuckles, and push through,' instructed the Chief. 'You'll know if you aint got it right, 'cos you won't be able to play the piano no more,' he added cheerfully.

We also learned to obey the important command, 'Still.' It was rather like playing 'statues' as a child. When the command was given, it signalled that something was wrong or about to go wrong; we were to freeze and not move a hair. This was particularly important with live firing when the gun suffered a mis-fire, because to open the breach would be fatal if the shell then decided to detonate. What with losing your fingers, getting your head knocked off by the recoil and the shell exploding in your midst, I then and there vowed that I would become a radar or sonar specialist. You could keep your guns!

The weeks passed quickly now, and the count-down to the end of our *Ganges* days was on. We sat or performed examinations every week, covering the many subjects of our schooling and seamanship knowledge and skills. Some of us would be sent from *Ganges* to join the Training Squadron – comprising three W-Class destroyers – to practice our skills at sea. Others would be drafted into vacant slots within the Fleet. The tension mounted as the Passing Out Parade approached. We scrubbed and polished for the big day.

And then it was upon us.

'Sound the Alert!' cried the Parade Commander.

'General Salute, present arms!' ordered the Guard

Commander; and at the same moment the Royal Marine Band burst into ten bars from *Iolanthe*. After that, the Guard was brought from the 'present' to the 'slope' and finally to the 'order', ready for the Captain's inspection.

I was proud to be a member of the guard that day. We wore white gaiters and webbing and our bayonets gleamed in the wintry sunshine as the Captain paused occasionally to speak to a member of the Guard. Our Divisional Officer closely escorted him, murmuring the name whenever he paused.

'Well, Willis, enjoyed yourself at *Ganges* . . . sorry to leave I suppose?' he said with a twinkle in his eyes. This was no time to rock the boat. I smiled and made some fatuous reply. He grinned and moved on.

It was a cold, wet and miserable day when we merrily got aboard the buses and headed for the station. As we passed through the Main gates of *Ganges* we were singing loud enough to bring several scowling RPOs scurrying from their 'gestapo headquarters'. But the bus flashed past and we watched through the rear window with glee, as taut with anger, they watched us escape into the distance.

At last we had found our freedom. Well – that's what we thought.

The Training Squadron

We joined the Training Squadron in Rosyth and our group was divided between four W-class destroyers. I was one of the boys allocated to the HMS *Wrangler*, and fifteen of us had our own mess. It was anarchy. The leading hand in charge didn't live in the mess, so that much of the time we were left to get on with mess life as best we could. Inevitably, the survival of the fittest brought the bullies and louts to the fore.

One of our number, a fellow called Willoughby, was as big as an ox and soon formed his personal clique of followers. They were all fawners and 'yes' men, who fed Willoughby's ego and laughed at every ridiculous remark he made. At meal times they gathered around him, ready to fetch and carry and listen in awe. Whatever he said was law, for we were all aware that if we argued with him, we would get thumped.

Willoughby always took charge of dishing out the meals. He would stand there, ladle in hand, smirking with power as he dolled out large portions to 'friends' and small ones to the rest of us. If anyone complained, he would take a ladleful off their plate.

'Wanna' make anythin' of it?' he would inquire and laugh when he was answered by silence. None of us did anything but scowl.

At tea time the mess was issued with half a pound of butter, bread, and a tin of jam. This was meant to be equally shared, but as usual Willoughby and his clique always took the lion's share. Each day there were boys who were left to go without.

On one occasion I came down from the bridge, having had the afternoon watch, and arrived in time to find that rations had all been dished out. Willoughby and his gang sat hogging the butter and jam at one end of the table. Without thinking, I took a spoon from the drawer and dived in among them, scooped up a dollop of butter and covered it in jam. Everyone froze and the mess went silent. Willoughby's fat face looked up at me in astonishment, which quickly changed to anger as he rose to his feet. Like the drowning man, I knew that I had to strike out first and fast. He advanced slowly toward me through the gap by the stanchion and then I struck. It was a haymaker of a blow. My fist missed his face and slammed into the stanchion, and I saw stars as he simultaneously knocked me flat on the deck.

Still dazed, I crawled to my feet in amongst the uproar. The whole mess was milling around shouting threats and preparing for battle. The worms had turned. My right hand felt as if it had been run over by a steam roller, and was already swelling fast. Then Willoughby was at my side,

'You all right, mate?' he said quietly, inspecting my hand. 'Let's get you to the sickbay – they'll fix it.'

We both returned smiling, with my arm in a sling. From then onwards Willoughby's reign of terror came to an end. Willoughby agreed that in future he and I should take it in turns to dish the food out. I always made sure that he, a big lad, got a goodly portion, while his former acolytes always got slightly under par. When he dished it out and came to his own turn, he would hesitate, ladle hovering over the pot unsure.

'Go on, mate, yer a big 'un,' we would say, and honour was satisfied all round.

The Training Squadron visited Dover, where we joined up with thirty destroyers or more. I can't recall the occasion for the gathering, but it was something to do with Royalty. Anyway, I'll never forget that magnificent sight. It was a warm sunny day, the sea was calm and the white cliffs of Dover reflected their ancient fortress might. The destroyers manoeuvred at speed into two long columns, their flashing bow waves each like a bone in the teeth. We took up station at 28 knots, separated by 400 yards from bridge to bridge. The ensigns, signal flags and pendants were taut in the wind as each ship raced to its appointed slot. The tingling whoop of sirens sounded – one for starboard and two for port – as ships indicated their direction of turn, streaming into their initial formation.

These were the elegant greyhounds of the sea, both young ships and old, driven with pride and élan, their names conjuring up the glory and triumph of the past. *Armada, Agincourt, Saintes* and *Trafalgar*, all modern Battle-Class destroyers. *Caprice, Cavalier, Chieftain* and *Cockade;* then more: *Wakeful, Whirlwind, Wrangler* and *Wizard* – *Grenville, Ulster* and *Undaunted.* On and on they came, demonstrating that Britain's Fleet was still very much alive.

We didn't know it then, but already the Fleet had started on its long, sad journey of decline. Only sixteen years from then, the Government would cancel the aircraft carrier programme, and thereby extract the Royal Navy's teeth.

Off we went to the Firth of Forth and Invergordon, much to the Scots' delight, and thence to Scapa Flow. All the while we were exercising seamanship and putting into practice the lessons learned at *Ganges:*

'Away seaboats crew', 'Man the falls', 'Man overboard!', 'Prepare to tow aft'.

These were among the many evolutions that filled our days. Soon we were shinning up lifelines, lowering and hoisting whalers almost like professionals. We gained confidence daily and for most of us, after several weeks, the seasickness of our earlier days had gone.

As we steamed up the Firth of Forth, we wondered at the sight that Admiral Beatty – in HMS *Queen Elizabeth* – must have seen as he led the Grand Fleet to rendezvous with the surrendering High Seas Fleet on 21 November, 1918. Later the German Fleet proceeded to Scapa Flow where they subsequently scuttled themselves. And of course we knew that Scapa Flow was the Royal Navy's big ship haven in both World Wars and was therefore steeped in recent naval history.

Quite suddenly the three months' training was over. We were sent on leave for two weeks, already knowing our next draft.

Boy Seaman 1st Class, H. Willis, was to report to HMS *Loch Scavaig* at Chatham Dockyard. The ship was programmed for a two-and-a-half year commission in the Mediterranean, and would depart to join the fleet at Malta in six weeks' time. I would now *belong to a real* ship's company.

Chapter 4

My First Ship

My first sight of *Loch Scavaig* was on a fine summer's day in Chatham Dockyard. She was being stored and provisioned for the start of her two-and-a-half year deployment to the Mediterranean. I was immediately disappointed because I had envisaged her as something like a dashing destroyer, and she didn't look the least bit like that. I suppose it was rather like expecting to see a Jaguar sports car and then finding out that it was really more like a sedate Ford Popular.

The Loch-Class frigates were built in the Second World War and proved themselves to be most efficient anti-submarine frigates. Their maximum speed was 19½ knots. Nevertheless, they possessed long range endurance and were comfortable ships; they accommodated one hundred and twenty-four officers and men. They were 307 feet in length, with a full load displacement of 2,260 tons and a beam of 38 ft. Additionally, they had the time-honoured reciprocating engines. Their main armament was vested in their sonar-detecting equipment and the Squid launcher, which was for throwing depth bombs. The forward gun – the 'popgun' – was a single 4" mounting, which was very basic in terms of gunnery control.

We continued storing and ammunitioning for a further two weeks before making our farewells to families and friends. The ship then headed down the Channel on its way to Malta. We were, however, going to visit Lisbon and Gibraltar en route.

When 'Woolly' West and I stepped ashore in Lisbon wearing our best white number six uniforms, we knew that we were *real* sailors at last. Two 'tiddly' jacks going ashore in a foreign port. Were we not to be envied? But still being Boy Seamen, our leave expired at 7 p.m., which meant that we had only some five hours within which to get drunk, and then sort out all the whoring that sailors apparently did. It didn't matter that we were both uncertain how to set about either.

When the young Sub-Lieutenant, the Officer of the Day, had finished inspecting us, he gave us a lecture on the pitfalls and dangers we would meet ashore. Most of the women in the red light area would probably have VD – he said this with a hint of embarrassment – and furthermore we were not to go to that part of the city. Neither Woolly nor I were sure of the exact implications of VD, other than that it could be quite nasty, and in any event, neither of us knew how to recognise this so-called red light area. We were further told not to drink the cheap brandy, which was readily available, lethal and very inexpensive.

'Drink good local port – it's much better for you and far safer,' concluded the Acting Sub-Lieutenant, probably recalling some bygone advice his father had given him when he first went to Dartmouth.

With these gems of wisdom, we hit the city. We seemed to walk for miles in the intense heat of the early afternoon before we saw anyone other than the occasional sleeping dockyard matey lying under a crane or a tree. The whole place was deserted except for a few people and the occasional vehicle which trundled past. How were we to know that we had ventured out in the middle of the city's siesta? Eventually we came to a deserted park and found an empty bench in the shade of a tree. Feeling hot and a trifle disillusioned, we sat down in order to reconsider our plan of action.

'I aint seen no bleedin' red lights . . . have you?' said Woolly, removing his cap and wiping his sweaty brow, adding that he was dying for a lemonade . . . or a cold beer if we could find somewhere open. Several moth-eaten mongrel dogs wagged their tails and sniffed at our bell bottomed trousers, until Woolly irritably told them to 'piss off.'

About an hour later we found a shop which was open and seemed to be a cross between a confectioner's and an off licence. Like two school boys, we gazed in the window at the goods on display and spotted a bottle clearly marked 'Aporto'.

'That'll be it,' said Woolly with all the conviction of an experienced drinker, 'we'll get a bottle of port and . . . drink it in the park until the red lights come on,' he ended lamely.

It tasted like hell and I kept telling Woolly that I was pretty sure that real port was much more red than this was.

'Rubbish,' said Woolly. 'There's losh of differen' shorts of port made all over, like,' he said authoritatively, as we took it in turns to slurp from the remains of the bottle, still seated on our park bench.

Luckily we later made our way back on board during supper time and there were only the Quartermaster and the Bosun's Mate on the gangway. Both of us were convinced that the other was 'stoned' and therefore each of us was doing his best to steady the other from falling over. Thus we must have looked like two wrestling monkeys as we made our unsteady progress towards the brow. I vaguely remember being told the following day that a chap called Pincher Martin had slung my hammock and tipped me into it just before I passed out. It seemed that Aporto was where they made the cheap and lethal brandy, and that port is either white or red in Portugal, and anyway port isn't spelt like that either.

Having spent two days only in Gibraltar – seeing the apes and sticking to beer – we arrived off the island of Malta G.C., ready to join the Mediterranean Fleet and really start seeing the world.

The 'Home' Port

Malta was very different in the early 1950s. No touristy high-rise hotels cluttering the skylines and there were very few visitors other than those associated with the Navy. It was delightfully sleepy and relaxed. The heat of the day, the salty sea air, the odour from Sliema Creek and the mixture of fish and baking cheesecakes combined to create that musty Mediterranean smell which is now familiar to so many tourists. No one on foot was in a hurry on shore; the only ones in a hurry were the maniacal Maltese drivers, and there weren't all that many vehicles on the roads in those days. They wanted to out-perform Stirling Moss. Maltese drivers have that warm-blooded Mediterranean temperament which admits of only thinly disguised tolerance towards all other road users. Tolerance ends the moment that the driver may have to avoid another object in his path, to wait in a queue or to slow down behind traffic. All these necessary practices were unpopular in an island where time was of no consequence. It was the principle that mattered. This was demonstrated by the frequent sick-cow lament from the blaring horns.

Dghaisamen, standing and facing forward as they rowed, would slowly wend their peaceful way when, without warning, they would yell suddenly and angrily in guttural Maltese at a boat passing nearby. When I asked what had been said, my dghaisaman replied easily.

'I say hello, how is dat sick mother you got doin'?' and after a few more strokes he would smile.

'He say she now good and go to pictures in Valletta.' He smiled approvingly. It had sounded, in guttural Maltese, as though they hated each other, but they were really good friends.

Malta was all fireworks and fiestas. Many of the streets were decorated with garishly coloured corner shrines, and baroque-style churches dominated many of them. Each bus had its shrine above the macho driver's head, and passengers would cross themselves frequently, especially when the bus lurched fast round a bend. I think they had a saint for every day of the year. Their parades were slow and glittering, with banners of silver, gold and rich colours. Large and heavy icons were carried aloft through the streets, which were full of spectators, including the ubiquitous priests and their followers. Their moods would be a mixture of wonder, gaiety, curiosity and devotion as they observed yet another holiday to give thanks to the saints.

But then Malta has a long Christian heritage. It dates back to A.D. 60 when St Paul was shipwrecked on the island, and his coming was commemorated with the naming of St Paul's Bay. Some of their churches and buildings were designed by great architects from the 16th and 17th centuries; for example the imposing fortifications and cathedrals in Valletta and at Medina and Gozo. Some have great domes which dominate the surrounding landscape of dusty brown earth and yellow stone. No expense was spared in the decoration of the interiors: gilded arcades and ceilings, beautifully ornate altars and canopies and walls covered in frescos and paintings. Many people are unaware that at the time when Nelson first brought British Seapower to bear in the Mediterranean, Malta was one of Europe's cultural centres. She then became one of Britain's most important maritime bases, on a par with Gibraltar. The Knights of St John were also pretty powerful marauders in their feuds with the Barbary pirates.

They also fought off 30,000 Turks during the bloody siege by Suleiman the Magnificent, the Sultan of Turkey. He had sent his general to 'annihilate the sons of dogs' of Maltese Christians. It was the French Knight, La Valletta, however, who inspired the people to withstand the onslaught and finally defeat the demoralised Turks some three months later. Their next great siege came more recently, during the Second World War, and called for great acts of courage in order to hold out while waiting for the relief convoys to fight their way through. This won the George Cross for the people of Malta.

In 1950 Malta was still 14 years away from independence, and much troubled political water was destined to flow before that date. It is particularly ironic that Mintoff, who became so controversial later, was a strong advocate of Malta's integration with Britain. He had found an ally in Mountbatten when he was C.-in-C. Mediterranean. The embryo plan foundered when Beaverbrook – that great 'finger in the pie' man – withdrew his support from motives of dislike for Mountbatten. The impending defence cuts in 1957 meant that the 13,000 dockyard workforce in Malta would be severely cut back. Britain ducked out of any commitment, even though a referendum in Malta showed that more than two-thirds of the population were in favour of integration. That was yet another of the 'might-have-beens' of the British Empire.

Nevertheless, in the early fifties Malta still reflected the same way of life that had existed in the late 1930s. During these latter years, Rear Admiral Cunningham had command of the destroyer flotillas and Mountbatten himself was in command of several destroyers. Mountbatten, though not always popular with his peers, inspired his ship's company to become Cock of the Fleet.

This was something that our own First Lieutenant, Lieutenant-Commander Joseph Bartosik, was determined to achieve in *Loch Scavaig*. He was a Polish naval officer who had fought in the Second World War and had subsequently transferred to the Royal Navy when the Russians had taken over his homeland.

The fleet in the early fifties no longer boasted the battleships or the same number of destroyers, but Malta was still run on a similar but smaller scale. The social life ashore and in the fleet hadn't changed that much. Polo was still played at the Marsa Club, cocktail parties were a way of life, horse racing continued and the traditional sports were well supported from the fleet and the shore. Only the better-off naval officers could occasionally afford to bring their families out during leave periods. The staff ashore, though – including dockyard civil servants – had 'married accompanied' appointments, and often brought their children with them. So Malta had a thriving community of servicemen, who brought millions of pounds into the economy. At that time the majority of Maltese people and British servicemen liked each other and accommodated their differences in harmony. Political stirrings were largely dormant, and would only show themselves when the livelihood of the workforce was later to be threatened.

The sailors had always enjoyed the social life in Malta. There was plenty of sport to meet all tastes; the island held numerous attractions for swimming, banyans, and there were dance clubs and bars galore all over the island. The notorious 'Gut' catered for those in need of female company.

Valletta's main street was thronged each evening by hundreds of young people, all out for a stroll and wanting to be seen in the cool of the night air, and to say 'Hello, how you doin'?' to their friends. English and American films were shown at the cinemas. The cafés were full of people watching the world pass by, as they sipped from their glasses of hot tea and lemon. The shops were plentiful and catered for most of the frugal wants of the Maltese and sailors alike.

For sailors the only thing that was in short supply were girls. Maltese girls wouldn't be seen alone with a sailor in uniform. The family and religious pressures forbade such a thing. They did, however, dance with them in public places when escorted by their girl friends. Thus the 'Gut' was able to thrive profitably; but then this was true throughout the Mediterranean. Thus any sailor who managed to find himself a British girl friend – the daughters of servicemen and civil servants stationed ashore – was greatly envied. It was for this reason that I and others were to join the Under Twenty Club in Valletta.

This, briefly, was the Malta which we sailors came to know and enjoy. It was to be our home port for the next two and a half years, and I still have very happy memories of it. Meanwhile, however, we had joined our Squadron and were now part of the Mediterranean Fleet. Already we had settled in to the daily ship's routine, but we still had so much to learn before we could confidently pull our weight and become *real* sailors.

But there was a nucleus of men among the ship's company who already possessed that experience and were ready to show us the way.

Pincher Martin

'Where do you think yer goin' with that bleedin' bucket, mate?' said Pincher, as he snatched it out of the young sailor's hand.

'I'm just gonna use it for . . .' but he got no further.

'I don't want no "just" men nickin' my buckets, son,' continued

Pincher, as he inspected it carefully for damage.

'You know the rules, me old cocker. No station card, no bleedin' bucket.'

The 'Lockerman', one for each part of ship – such as the fo'c'sle, the quarterdeck and the maintop – was responsible for all the cleaning gear; this included buckets, brooms, cloths and cotton waste, plus a host of other bits and pieces. He was a powerful man to be reckoned with. The keys to his locker and cupboards were permanently attached to his belt. They dangled there as a symbol of authority and power, and woe betide any man who entered his private domain without permission, whether in the presence of the 'Lockerman' or not.

In those days the Royal Navy still had plenty of able seamen, 'three-badgers', on the messdecks. They had already done 12 years man's service. Every four years from the age of 18, they had collected another good conduct badge and by the time they were thirty, assuming they didn't get into too much trouble, they became three-badge able seamen.

Many of these sailors were very happy to remain as able seamen and didn't want advancement. Most of them had a fund of knowledge and knew the ways of the Navy. In their own way, they became 'big fish' in a small pond by finding their niche; maybe as 'Lockerman', the Gunner's Yeoman, 'Tanky' the butcher, or 'Paints' the painter.

Such a man was Pincher Martin, who controlled the quarterdeck locker. When I first met him, he looked as old as Methuselah. He was thirty-one, stockily built, prematurely bald on top but with bushy black sideboards. His face was weather-beaten and looked brown even in winter. In the summer he became almost black and was frequently addressed by his peers as 'you silly old black bastard', which was a term of endearment.

He usually wore a broad grin, except when someone had either lost a broom or a bucket or had upset the smooth running of the quarterdeck locker. Pincher always knew who had lost what, because he only issued anything on receipt of the person's station card.

This card designated each man's watch and part of the watch. It was coloured either red or green for Port and Starboard Watch respectively. The logic was simple: no card meant no bucket, and no card at the gangway meant no run ashore. Anyway, if you didn't have a station card to hand over, you got nothing but a flea in your ear from Pincher. Therein lay the 'Lockerman's' power.

I first came into contact with Pincher when the Chief Boatswain's Mate, Petty Officer Spurway, otherwise known as the 'Buffer', detailed me to give Pincher a hand.

'What you want, lad?' said Pincher sharply, as I stood at the entrance to his Aladdin's Cave. Since I'd proffered no station card, he was suspicious.

'Buffer sent me to give you a hand,' I said defensively.

He looked at me with renewed interest.

'Oh, has he?' said Pincher, while continuing to open a sack of cotton waste.

'That's all right then. You's can 'elp me with gettin' the gear ready for washin' the ship's side, son.'

All the stages had to be positioned, buckets made ready, soft soap and cotton waste provided, ready in time for both watches of the hands. Apparently he was pleased with my efforts and I became his semi-unofficial helper when there was a big job on. He was very good at 'tiddly' rope work, every finger a marlin spike, and he took the time to teach me all sorts of wrinkles. Gradually, as the weeks went by, it became clear that he had taken me under his wing in a fatherly way. This became more apparent when the Buffer and other 'three-badgers' would poke their heads into the locker looking for Pincher.

'Where's yer seadad, son?' they would ask in a friendly manner. And that's how Pincher Martin became my 'seadad'.

This was a centuries-old naval tradition. Some of the 'older' hands would adopt a youngster unofficially and without the matter being discussed. It just happened by mutual and unspoken agreement. The naval expression for it was, 'to take someone under their wing' and that invariably made him a 'seadaddy'. Many of these characters, as I subsequently observed as I got older, were, for whatever reason, without close family ties. They were men who wanted a surrogate son. I can't ever remember meeting a bad one. I believe that was because any 'seadaddy' had to have the tacit agreement of all the other people in the system.

Pincher Martin was very correct and had an almost Victorian air of propriety about him. He observed my conduct and behaviour and would frequently correct me. I always knew that I would get hell from him if I didn't do a job properly or if I didn't clear up after a job was done. He checked my appearance in the mornings and gave me a 'bollocking' if my shirt was not clean and pressed. He used to swear with the best of them but if ever he heard me 'at it' he was as likely as not to say, 'Now that's a bleedin' 'nough of that, Will,' and he meant it. By then I had become known as 'Will' throughout the ship; it was short for 'Willis'. Sometimes they would use the diminutive of Hugh and call me Hughie, which made me crawl with embarrassment.

The messdeck space, one deck below the main deck and amidships, was shared between three different messes. I belonged to the Boys' Mess, which was starboard side aft. The sections were divided up by rows of messdeck lockers, stacked three high, and also divided by the hammock stowage. Nearly everyone slept in hammocks except the few who had somehow managed to get hold of a collapsible camp bed from naval stores. These camp beds were much prized, not because they were more comfortable, but because in off-duty hours the owner could take them on the upper deck and lie in the sun.

Each mess had a long pine table, firmly fixed to the deck, which was scrubbed white every day come hell or high water. The messdeck table was the centre of all activities. Three meals a day, numerous cups of 'char', the almost sacred and serious ceremony of the daily rum issue, when men under age were often told to clear the mess. And during the evenings, there would be cards, uckers (Ludo to naval rules), letter writing, model making, ironing clothes and reading. All these activities were conducted on and around the confines of the mess table. High politics, religion, the wardroom (the 'Pigs') and last night's run ashore were among the varied topics of conversation. Space and silence were at a premium, and it was the Leading Hand of the mess who would arbitrate when one or other was necessary.

It was not long after Pincher Martin became my 'seadaddy' that the following incident occurred. The Boy Seamen's mess catered for ten of us. A Leading Seaman called Pratt was in charge. As far as we Boys were concerned, it was Pratt by name and Pratt by nature. None of us could bear him since he resembled Shylock in both looks and mannerisms. How he came to be put in charge of the Boys' Mess was a mystery; they couldn't have found a less suitable Leading Hand throughout the Fleet. He was idle, sneaky, prone to pick favourites (none of whom liked him), his personal cleanliness was questionable and he appeared to have unnatural tendencies.

Pratt disliked me intensely. He frequently picked on me to do the dirty jobs, and one such job was to ditch the 'gash'. During the course of the day, all the slops were put into the 'gash' bucket and by the time supper was over, the bucket was brimful of food, gungy water and tea leaves. Prior to evening rounds, the bucket had to be taken down aft and ditched over the stern into the gash chute. Naturally, it was an unpopular task and particularly so in rough weather. In most messes the junior ratings used to take it in turns, but in the Boys' Mess it was the norm for Pratt to speak with a leer and a sneer.

'I think we'll let that luverly little bit of "skin", Will, do the honours tonight,' and then he would roll his eyes at me and spew out a cackling laugh.

Everyone knew that he was free with his hands when dealing with some of the smaller lads, but there was nothing much they could do about this. However, he had never touched me. He kept just within the limits so as not to be accused of outright indecency, and we all knew that *he* would be more likely to be believed if anyone complained. Pratt had been the Leading Hand of the Boys' Mess for about four months when eventually he got his comeuppance.

I and another lad, called Horace, had just cleared away the supper dishes; we were the 'cooks of the mess' that day. Pratt lay back, lounging on one of the locker seats, watching me with the usual sneer on his face as we squared away. It was an accepted rule that the 'cooks of the mess' were excused from ditching the gash. However, I knew what was coming.

'You've dun a good job there, "skin", now piss off down aft with the gash!' spat Pratt.

I bent over to pick up the bucket, hating him but resigned as ever. He leaned forward and put his hand between my legs from behind. I didn't give it a second thought; I swung round and fitted the entire bucket of tea-leaves, swill and food over his head.

There was an appalled silence for several seconds as he clawed the bucket off his head and threw it to the deck. The Boys in the mess were aghast. And so was I.

Pratt, looking like King Neptune rising from the sea, was dripping tea leaves and swill as he leapt to his feet in fury.

'I'm going to punch your rotten little head in, you snotty little bastard!' Pratt was considerably bigger than I was and there was every chance that he would. As he came towards me, hair matted and dripping swill, I commenced a slow rearguard retreat.

It was then that I heard the familiar voice of my 'seadad' say in a quiet and menacing tone of voice:

'I wouldn't be doin' that if I wus you, Pratt.'

A moment later the Boys' Mess was full to capacity as sailors from the other two messes poured in from different directions and fixed Pratt with unfriendly stares. Pratt, meanwhile, was busy brushing off tea leaves and bits of soggy paper, but by now he had got the message and prudently confined himself to one last outburst:

'You little bastard! I'll get you for this.'

He never did, because the next day he was relieved of his duties in the Boys' Mess. He was moved to the forward messdeck, under the eagle eye of a tough three-badge Leading Seaman, who stood no nonsense and knew the score. It subsequently transpired that the message that 'Pratt needs watching' had already been circulating in the ship through the 'grapevine'.

The only reprimand I got was from Pincher Martin.

'You shouldn't 'ave done that to a Leading Hand, son,' he said to me later. 'In future, leave that sort o' thing to me to sort out.'

Too Clever by Half

We had been berthed in Sliema Creek for about three weeks.

Malta was hot and sticky in the month of August. The whole Fleet had been told to economise on fuel consumption, and consequently our seatime had been curtailed.

Nobby and I were feeling pretty bored when we fell in for both Watches of the Hands that morning. We were both sent off to tidy the timber racks, situated under the bridge wings. We felt that this was a miserable, boring job and it only added to our sense of gloom – a feeling shared by many in the ship's company during the August heat.

After about thirty minutes of hauling out large pieces of jumbled shoring timber, one of our messmates, 'Knocker' White, happened to wander by with a bucket of soapy water in his hand. He loved to poke his nose in and revelled in gossip. He enjoyed feeling important whenever he came across a new story or rumour, which became the latest 'buzz'.

'What you two up to, then?' he asked in his nosy manner, as he lowered his bucket on to the deck.

'Doin' a job fer the First Lieutenant,' said Nobby with a grin, while throwing down another length of timber. 'It's very important, he wants it done quick.'

I looked at Nobby questioningly and he gave me a knowing wink.

'Remember the fo'c'sle deck above the paint shop got hammered in that gale off Sicily?' said Nobby. 'Well the First Lieutenant wants it shored up before we go to sea.'

Knocker's eyes widened with a keen hint of interest as he digested this valuable information. When Jimmy – otherwise known as the First Lieutenant or Joseph Bartosik – wanted something done quickly, he meant it. It was always best to keep on the right side of him.

'I'm just on my way there,' said Knocker importantly. 'Buffer's told me to give "Painty" a hand, cleanin' brushes. Anyfing I can

93

do?' he volunteered, now looking anxious to get in on the act.

'Too right, mate,' said Nobby as he lifted a length of timber and offered it to Knocker.

'You can leave yer bucket 'ere wiv us, and start ferrying this lot down to "Painty".

His eyes gleamed with satisfaction as he strutted off with the timber towards the forward hatch, the possessor of another 'buzz' to covet.

'Painty'll tell him to piss off,' I said, as we both laughed about it, expecting him to return any minute with a flea in his ear.

It was true, however, that we had taken great seas over the fo'c'sle during the gale, and both the First Lieutenant and the Engineer Officer had subsequently inspected the paintshop deckhead several weeks ago as a precautionary measure for signs of damage. But nothing more had come of it.

Knocker was gone for several minutes before he returned with a self-important smile on his face.

'Painty didn't know nuffin' about it 'avin' to be shored,' he said with satisfaction.

'They didn't tell 'im,' he added cheerfully, picking up another balk of shoring.

'He thought it were okay and were proper pissed off,' he added, as he headed forward once again.

'He's gonna give me a hand wiv it,' he said as he disappeared down the hatch.

'Hey, Nobby, we'll get done for this,' I said. 'What happens when Buffer finds out?'

'Don't worry, Will, he won't find out, 'cos after a couple more timbers, we'll let Knocker and Painty know it was all a joke,' said Nobby confidently.

'We'll stop it all . . . when he comes back, like,' he concluded, looking forward for Knocker.

Five minutes later he returned; he was now moving much faster and full of purpose.

'It's all in, 'and,' he cried triumphantly, 'Buffer's taken charge. He's down there wiv "Painty".'

'What do ya' mean, Buffer's taken charge?' said Nobby in shock. 'Who told 'im?'

'I did,' said Knocker smugly. 'He saw me wiv the timber and asked me what I was up to . . . and I told 'im, "The First Lieutenant wants the paint shop shored up, ready for when we go to sea, like".'

The trouble was that Buffer had known about the First Lieutenant's initial concern – everyone had. But the Buffer was like a madman and always jumped in with half the story about everything. He loved to show initiative, and in any event was probably hurt that the First Lieutenant hadn't kept him in the picture.

Nobby had turned pale and I wasn't feeling so good myself. Neither of us knew what to do. If we went down and told the Buffer that it was all a joke, he would 'kill' us. If we didn't stop him, he would *still* 'kill' us. While we deliberated on the best course of action, Knocker was working faster and faster as the Buffer yelled for more timber from below. Then suddenly matters got even worse. Two hands were detailed off by the Buffer to help Knocker ferry the timber to the paint shop. The situation had escalated out of control within minutes. By now we were sweating our guts out, unloading the bloody timber from the racks to keep pace with the demand. Even we were beginning to convince ourselves that the First Lieutenant really *did* want the paint shop shored up.

Then the Buffer's birdlike head emerged, head and shoulders above the forward hatch, sweat pouring down his face and his shirt stained with lots of dark patches under his arms and down

95

his back.

'Come on, lads, only four more timbers and we're done,' he said with evident satisfaction, and bobbed down the hatch.

'What do you think we'll get?' said Nobby miserably, as we passed the last piece of shoring to Knocker.

Nobby and I disappeared down to the messdeck and skulked over a fresh brew of tea. We sat and waited for the inevitable retribution which was certain to follow.

The rest was all hearsay and reportage, except that we both got fourteen days Number 11s and the Buffer made our lives hell for the following two months. The whole incident was made worse because the story went round the ship like a dose of salts, and everyone enjoyed it so much that the ship's morale went up ten points by dinner time.

Anyway, it appeared that the Buffer had proudly reported to the First Lieutenant's cabin, saluting like a guardsman.

'Ship's paint shop shored up, sir.'

'Mein Gott! Vot have you done?' said the First Lieutenant, almost reverting to his native Polish. It was shortly after that that the Buffer found us skulking in the mess.

The division between officers and the lower deck was very much greater than that of today. Orders from officers were not to be questioned and how was our impetuous Buffer to know that it was a joke? Joseph Bartosik was most imperious and had funny ways of doing things. He had not yet come to terms with English colloquialisms, let alone the psychology and attitudes of the British sailor. This was vividly exemplified several weeks later when the ship still lay sweating idly in the Creek.

Our whaler had been sanded down and its bottom gleamed with fresh layers of enamel paint; the First Lieutenant liked to keep it in racing condition and ready for any unexpected challenge. For several days the whaler had been lowered in the forenoon and then hoisted to the davit heads at dinner time and just when we were about to eat our meal. By and large, jolly jack is a good natured soul and made light of this task on both occasions, apart from making light-hearted comments about Jimmy's bleedin' whaler. On the third day, however, it had become a bit too much.

We cleared the mess and mustered at the whaler's falls. Having hoisted the whaler, we let out a derisive, good-humoured cheer which registered no more than irritation. Then we immediately dispersed below to get on with our, by now cold, dinners. As we sat at the table, our Leading Hand said that he would have a word with Buffer so's in future we could have our meal in peace. With that no more was said and the conversation drifted into tales of last night's run ashore and whatever else came to mind.

Shortly after we heard the pipe, not over the tannoy but moving through the ship from aft. It was the 'Still', used on ceremonial occasions such as Captain's rounds, giving advance warning of his approach. We all sat in wonder, speculating as it drew closer.

Suddenly the shrill pipe was at our door. There was the Coxswain dressed in Number Ones, pipe in hand and looking grim. Immediately behind him was the First Lieutenant, fully rigged in white uniform, sword and medals, and closely followed by the Officer of the Day similarly rigged.

'Attention in the mess!' cried the Coxswain, making way for Bartosik to come to the fore. He was calm and purposeful as he surveyed us gawping peasants.

'I vill now read the appropriate section from the Articles of War with regard to mutiny,' he announced. Taking the clipboard handed him by the Officer of the Day, he proceeded to do so. There were lots of 'Shall suffer death . . . or punishments in here-to-fore's . . .' in amongst the words as we sat stunned in silence, some still with their knives and forks half way to their mouths, wondering what the hell was going on. Having finished, he looked around the mess.

'Vill the men who have complaints vish to say so vile I am present?' he said with a wickedly aristocratic smile, his hand firmly clasping his as yet sheathed sword.

The Coxswain looked embarrassed and coughed. We waited in silence as he continued to stare expectantly at our uncomprehending faces.

'Very good, ve are happy that there vill be no mutiny today,' he said as he turned about and left the mess.

Nevertheless, thereafter he hoisted the whaler during working hours unless it was operationally necessary. He just hadn't understood that British sailors weren't like the Poles or the Russians, and that *Loch Scavaig* was not the good ship *Potemkin*.

The Ship's Painter

While we generally found that life was colourful and often full of fun, it seemed that this was largely due to the crazy scrapes that individuals managed to get themselves into. It almost looked as though we took it in turns to provide the humour for our messmates. Anyway, although he didn't know it, it was George's turn.

I first got to know him when I was given a 'job change', and became his Bosun's Mate. At long last I was free to blow my bosun's call officially, making the routine pipes and even piping the side on ceremonial occasions. George was one of four Quartermasters who kept watch on the gangway in harbour and ran the ship's routine. At sea we steered the ship and ran the routine from the wheelhouse. We were divided up into four watches and each Quartermaster had a young lad as his Bosun's

Mate. In harbour, the Bosun's Mate was the 'gofor', the 'kye' (hot chocolate) maker and the brasswork cleaner during the morning watch.

At sea, in the wheelhouse, George and I took 'tricks' on the wheel, which in fine weather might last for an hour at a time. The Officer of the Watch was one deck above us and passed his orders down through a voice pipe, which sounded as though he were talking to us from the end of a tunnel. Taking all things into account, it was a good job but it got a bit much when we were in harbour for long spells.

Anyway, George was a pretty easy-going sort of chap, so long as you did your job properly and didn't argue. He must have been about twenty-six years old because he had just picked up his second Good Conduct badge. George's face always looked solemn and he seldom smiled; it wasn't because he was miserable – he just always looked that way. His home town was Newcastle on Tyne and he spoke with a strong accent in a slow, deliberate delivery, giving emphasis to the particular point he was making.

During the 'quiet' hours of the night watches, George often spent his time telling me about some scheme or other that would 'mak' a few quid, mun,' and nothing would excite him more than to dream up a new way of making money. I remember that he even cut down on our night 'kye' issue, so's he could sell the chocolate slabs to other watchkeepers.

Each month, the Ship's Company was issued with soap and tobacco from the Naval Store. It was at a nominal cost and comprised two bars of 'pusser hard' – a bar of soap nine inches long, three inches wide and thick, which was used for washing our clothes – and either a half pound of tobacco 'tickler' (to roll your own) or a half pound of pipe tobacco. George had saved up a suitcase full of soap and tobacco, waiting for the day when he could make a big 'killing'. The only trouble was that he hadn't yet found a way to get this illegal contraband ashore. But he was still trying to think up the perfect money-making 'scam'. Little did I know then that George had already arranged the big 'scam'.

A month later, George's request for a 'job change' came through. The 'Buffer', after much pleading from George, gave him the duty of Ship's Painter. The paint shop was forward in the 'eyes' of the ship and 'Paints' was master of hundreds of gallons of black paint for the boot-topping, ship-side grey for almost everything, and white paint. In 1951 everything was still hard to come by. Paint was also a prized commodity in any walk of life, not to mention the white spirit and brushes. The Heads of Departments were always wanting to 'smarten' up their equipment and compartments for the next Captain's Rounds. George was now in a position of power.

He had been in the job for about three months and had settled in, and the 'Buffer' was pleased with the way that George exercised tight control over the Paint Shop stores. The Paint Shop was immaculate and all the tins and paint pots were neatly stowed and hung in rows; there was seldom a dirty paint brush to be found after 1730, when he got out his large bunch of keys and locked up for the night. He wore this new responsibility well, and with his new-found power came increased stature and presence. It was just when things were going so well that George met his downfall.

The ship was moored head and stern to buoys in Sliema Creek. We were undergoing two weeks' self-maintenance and were in the process of painting the ship from the topsides to the waterline. The ship's side had been painted – a major operation – and we were getting on with the superstructure. It was mid-day and 'Hands to Dinner' had just been piped; those who were old enough to draw their 'tots' of rum were huddled round the rum 'fanny' waiting for their tot to be poured by the 'rum-bosun'.

George was normally an early bird for rum issue, and the Leading Hand of the mess asked if anyone had seen him. I was sent up to the Paint Shop but it was locked.

His tot was put to one side and we got on with our dinners, thinking that he must have gone to another mess to visit a chum.

Just before 'Out Pipes', George appeared and came swooshing down the ladder-rails without touching the steps; he was as white as a ship's bollard.

'What's up, George?' asked the Leading Hand, as the rest of us stared.

'Nowt,' he said in his talkative Newcastle manner. He sat down despondently, head in his hands.

'George! What's up, Mate?' repeated the Leading Hand.

'The's nowt oop . . . Wes' me tot?' and having been handed the glass, he downed it in one.

It was then time to fall in on the upper deck, so we all 'trooped' off, wondering what the hell had upset George. We emerged through the hatch onto the upper deck and I heard someone ahead of us cry out.

'What the bloody hell's happened? The Creek's covered in it!' The rest of us spilled out into the bright sunshine to see 'what was up'.

The surface of Sliema Creek looked as if had been painted with ship's side grey. There was only a light breeze, and the water was as flat as a grey mill pond. Just off the starboard bow, no more than ten yards distant, lay a half-sinking dghaisa – a narrow and elegant Maltese rowing craft – with the Maltese dghaisaman clinging to the prow and yelling.

'Alla Madonna! That crazy bastard! He sink my bloody dghaisa . . . Isma Alura . . . I get him for this!'

The dghaisaman was grey, his boat was grey and even our

beautifully painted black 'boot topping', along the waterline of the ship, was neatly lined with grey. Both the First Lieutenant and the Buffer were staring down at this scene of destruction in disbelief. It was the Buffer who first 'twigged'.

'Where's that bleedin' *Painter*? bawled Spurway, 'Pipe for the bastard . . . Get 'im up 'ere right this minute!'

Later, when George was under arrest and in 'cells', the story began to emerge in detail. It appeared that George had made a deal with Vittorio, the dghaisaman, which included the sale of several five-gallon drums of grey paint, which were to be lowered over the ship's bow during the dinner hour. This was the time when everyone, including the ship's officers, were down below having their 'lunch' or 'dinner' and the whole Creek was quiet and deserted. Apparently everything was going well, that was until the barrel hitch holding the drum had slipped.

Down whistled the drum from twenty feet, straight through the bottom of the dghaisa, which was positioned nicely below. The drum split open on impact and the dghaisa was three parts submerged within minutes, leaving Vittorio to cling to the floating wreckage. George had given one look at the sinking dghaisa and fled.

During the time that it had taken George to escape to his messdeck, drink his tot and for us to appear on the upper deck, the grey paint had found its freedom and had spread rapidly over a large area of the Creek.

He went off to Detention Quarters for 28 days at Corradina, and the dghaisaman, Vittorio, chose the wise course of action and didn't sue for compensation. The First Lieutenant gave the 'Buffer' a bollocking for having chosen George to be Ship's Painter, and we cleaned the mess up, laughing ourselves silly all afternoon.

The soap and tobacco were still in George's suitcase when he rejoined us after his enforced 'holiday'; he held a messdeck sale shortly thereafter, selling his entire stock of soap and tobacco at greatly reduced prices. As a 'reward' for the paint fiasco, the Buffer gave him a 'job change'. He made him the 'Captain of the Heads', which entailed the daily cleaning of the ship's company lavatories from 0800 to 1630. I split my sides at the time but later George had the laugh on me.

For six months George was a broken man in the heads. He had nothing to barter, though I'm surprised that he didn't figure out a way to sell the 'bog' paper. However, one had to bear in mind that every sheet *was* marked 'Government Property'.

Chapter 5

Settling Down

Pincher Martin had been my unofficial 'seadad' for some time before he raised the subject of a 'run ashore'. Usually he would go ashore with his other 'three-badge' mates and I went ashore with 'Woolly' West and 'Nobby'; they were also seventeen and as 'green' as I was. The way Pincher put it to me was as if he was undertaking yet another aspect of his responsibilities as a 'seadad'.

'I bin thinkin' it's about time I took yer on a "run ashore", Will.' It was more a statement than a question.

'You can get into all sorts of trouble if yer don't know what yer up to,' he said, with a knowing look.

'Know what I mean?' he continued hopefully.

Pincher didn't like to go into unnecessary detail, especially if he thought it might become too delicate for my ears or even embarrass him. He preferred to make all-embracing generalisations, accompanied with a wink and a knowing look. Some things were better left unsaid.

'Well, Pincher, I won't drink too much if that's what you mean.'

I remembered months before that Pincher had slung my hammock when 'Woolly' West and I had returned on board. We were both 'tiddly', or , as Pincher put it, 'had smelt the barmaid's apron' and were behaving like two idiots.

'That's one of the things yer gotta learn, Will . . . how to drink proper that is . . . but there's a lot more ter learn . . . fer yer own protection like.'

Pincher winked and gave me one of his 'know what I mean' looks, paused, then said:

'Know what I mean?'We were off into Pincher's generalisations and I knew that he would be much happier if I just said 'Yes, Pincher.'

'Right then, be ready in yer "best bib and tucker" straight after supper.We'll catch the 1830 Liberty boat and get you back by 2300.'

Having just been rated Ordinary Seaman, my leave now expired at 2300. All night leave was given only to those who had reached the age of twenty.

From then onwards, Pincher would usually take me on a 'run ashore' about once a month. He undoubtedly looked upon this as a 'seadad's' duty. At all other times Pincher stayed ashore all night, catching the first boat back in the morning. He never discussed his 'runs ashore' with me, apart from saying, 'Stop burbling,Will, there's a good lad! . . . Me 'ead's not tuned in yet . . . Last night was a bit of a "goer" . . .'

The 'runs ashore' with Pincher were predictable. We would make our way to the red light district (Pincher always knew how to get there) against which the Officer of the Day had explicitly warned us. He would then find his favoured bar and we'd sit at a table from which he could assess the 'bar-girls'. They usually sat in pairs at separate tables, weighing up the potential trade and in readiness to take aboard willing customers. I was allowed to drink no more than three beers during the evening and frequently reminded to '. . . last 'em,Will, 'cos that's all yer 'avin.'

After a while (by this time Pincher would have downed at least four beers), he would broach the matter closest to his mind.

'Would yer like a bit o' company, Will?' he'd ask disinterestedly – almost as an afterthought and in a manner which suggested surprise, as though recognising that he had been remiss and should have asked before.

'I happens to know those two young ladies, over in the corner there,' he would say confidentially behind cupped hand.

'Now you's behave yerself. Mind yer language, Will.' And Pincher would then escort two giggling females back to our table. I dreaded his avuncular introductions.

'Right girls, this is young Will . . . me and 'im's havin' a few "bevies" before I takes him back to get some kip . . . He needs his shuteye.'

At this the girls would usually giggle and say 'Ah . . . poor thing,' and then I'd cringe and Pincher would give me a guilty look.

'What'll it be . . . two "sticky greens", girls?' Pincher would ask jovially, to avoid my injured gaze.

The expensive 'sticky greens' (two small liqueur glasses filled with green coloured water) would, on average, keep the two girls happy for about twenty minutes. As a general rule, if no further 'stickies' were forthcoming, they would be off back to their table in the corner. However, Pincher was obviously a good customer because two 'stickies' would usually last for an hour, assuming that the bar wasn't too busy. This was often the norm, since nothing much really happened in these bars until about midnight, by which time I would be tucked up in my hammock.

Thus my runs ashore with Pincher were more of an 'acquaint' course than an interactive run ashore. The 'cast' was present but the real show didn't actually commence until I was turned in. But I do remember one such occasion – I think it was in Syracuse – when the real 'show' may have started earlier. On that particular evening Pincher was blatantly going strong on one of the 'girls'. After about an hour, during which he was often huddled in confidential discussion with his 'chosen', he suddenly stood up.

'Right, then . . . won't be long, Will . . . gotta bitta business to discuss . . . now you sit 'ere and talk to her friend tills I gets back. Okay?'

He was gone for about thirty minutes and looked quite flushed and pleased with himself when he returned. By then it was 2230 and time for us to get back to catch the 2300 boat. Later I learned from one of his mates that Pincher had had to have a 'quickie' since he felt 'responsible like, to get me back on time.'

There came the time that we visited Cannes in the south of France. Pincher felt that another 'educational' run ashore was due. However, I had already been ashore on one occasion with 'Woolly' West. I had spotted a billboard advertising the appearance of 'Les Femmes de Chorus' at the Cannes Casino. Even my very limited French had allowed me to glean that this 'Chorus of beautiful girls would dance naked, covered in gold paint, in the Grand Salon Variety Show!

'Pincher,' I said, 'would you mind if I chose where we go tonight?' He looked at me questioningly.

'Don't yer like our runs ashore, Will?'

'Of course I do, Pincher, it's just that I've always had an ambition to see what it's like in a real Casino.' Pincher didn't look convinced, so I stumbled on.

'You know, Pincher, like Monte Carlo . . . surely you remember "The Man Who Broke the Bank at Monte Carlo"? Well Cannes has a big Casino too.' He looked at me as if I were stark 'bonkers' and out of my mind.

'We can't go in there, mate. That's fer toffs! . . . Anyways, you and me aint gamblin' and the like.'

I pleaded with him and promised not to gamble. All I wanted to do was to go and have a drink and see what it looked like. He shook his head in wonder and then reluctantly he agreed.

'Will, I don't think we'll get through the bleedin' door, let alone get a drink. And anyway, beer'll cost a fortune!'

It was a warm summer evening and we went ashore in our best white No 6 uniforms. I knew that the show was due to commence at 2000 and that we would have a couple of hours to 'kill' before 'Les Femmes' appeared in all their gold-painted naked glory. We would have to sip our drinks slowly, and that was a bit of a worry because Pincher never sipped anything slowly. But I was an optimist and very determined to see a whole bunch of women dancing naked.

We made our way to the imposing entrance of the Casino. Two magnificent doormen dressed in white uniforms, shoulders covered in gold braid and looking like Admirals of the Fleet, stood at the top of the steps in front of the entrance. They appeared quite regal as they ushered in their important evening customers. Pincher had by now dropped back several paces behind me, and was muttering something about being 'bloody mad to think we'll get away with it . . .' However, I had done my homework.

'Monsieur, mon ami et moi . . . nous desirons . . . dans le . . .'

The elegant doorman interrupted me in perfect English. 'But of course you may visit our wonderful Casino. It is a pleasure!' and he escorted me, and an astonished Pincher Martin, through the grand entrance into the magnificence of unashamed wealth.

The reception foyer was enormous. The domed ceiling seemed to rise up forever. Huge potted palms, marble floors, soaring pillars and dozens of white-jacketed waiters carrying sparkling drinks held on high. We both stood, caps in hand, wondering in which direction to proceed.

It was then that I spotted an oddly dressed middle-aged couple looking directly at us. They both smiled and then she gave a nervous little wave as they made their way towards us. They approached like long-lost friends, she perspiring freely with a large fur coat draped over her shoulders, while he wore a heavy brown tweed suit.

'Ee . . . lads . . . it's good to see thee! Jolly Jacks . . . does our hearts wonders 'avin our Navy in port . . . Just like being at home.'

He was a jolly red-faced man, and he shook our hands warmly.

'Come on lads . . . let's go and have a celebration 'sup' . . . now, you'll join us for a pint or two?'

His wife, Muriel, muttered something about '. . . hopin' it's cooler in the lounge,' as she pulled her fur coat tightly around her shoulders.

During the subsequent conversation while we 'supped' our drinks, it transpired that he was '. . . in scrap metal business from Hartlepool . . . and not doin' bad an all! Lot of money to be made if you know 'ow.' Bill and Muriel had been in Cannes for several days and were on holiday for two weeks.

Pincher Martin had by now rediscovered his confidence. He was leaning forward in his chair, two bottles of lager and a full glass on the table in front of him, grinning at everything that either of them said. The look on his face said, 'We've landed on our feet!'

The Grand Salon was furnished with many large, well-padded armchairs, settees and coffee tables, which were scattered throughout the luxurious surroundings. At the far end of the room were the huge curtains, draped in folds of heavy and expensive fabric, which concealed the stage from view. I smiled at the thought of Pincher's face when he saw those gorgeous girls, all naked and painted in gold.

He, of course, was in his element. Bill, with Muriel's support, kept ordering more lager, delivered in batches of six. She lay back on the settee, perspiring heavily with her fur coat still draped over her shoulders. Bill was also sweating freely in his Yorkshire tweed as he supped his beer and savoured the thought of all that scrap metal piling up in Hartlepool. They were a warm-hearted couple who, while enjoying Cannes, both knew that '. . . Next year it'll be Blackpool, if we have anythin' to say about it.' Meanwhile they were determined to make the best of it, especially now that they had found 'Jolly Jack'. The Grand Salon was their luxurious 'backdrop' but we were their contact with reality and home.

When I was on my third lager, Pincher looked at me and frowned. He leaned forward, breathing lager fumes over my face, and spoke quietly under his breath.

'One more and that's yer lot, Will, old son . . . we don't want no tears now, do we?'

And having said this, he broke open his ninth lager and smiled kindly at Muriel as he fumbled the empty bottle back on to the table.

'You lads must come and have a bite to eat at Majestic afore thee goes and sails off . . . eh . . . what about it?' Pincher grinned from ear to ear, winked at me and downed another lager.

'Mind you, it'll have to be tomorrow, 'cos shortly we'll be on our way. We're havin' supper with a Froggie metal merchant . . . and by gum, 'e's payin!' he added with a laugh.

Before they left, Bill loaded the table with another batch of lagers and gave us his room number at the Majestic. Then, with true Yorkshire warmth, they both wished us goodbye.

Pincher sat there with a great big stupid grin on his face.

'Will . . . me old fruit, you . . . you've cum oop bliddy trumps!

110

Besh "Baron Shtrangle" I've 'ad fer years . . . and years.'

And then he downed another lager. As he did this, I noticed that there were signs of activity within the Salon. People were beginning to move their chairs and settees to face the stage, helped by fussing waiters. Clearly they were getting ready for the show. I managed to swivel Pincher in the right direction in spite of his occasional lunges to capture the remaining bottles of lager. He was looking decidedly vacant as I explained to him that we were about to see a variety show.

'Bliddy hell, Will . . . what yer onner about . . . ehh?' said Pincher as he poured more lager, most of which splattered over his right foot.

The curtains opened and the orchestra burst into life. Pincher stared glassily in the direction of the music with a look of incomprehension and irritation on his face. For comfort he grabbed another bottle of lager, and this time filled up his left shoe while the rest went down his bell bottom trousers.

'What yer got me int . . . inter . . . you craf . . . craft . . . y lill' sud?' He grinned stupidly.

My 'seadad' had just completed this garbled sentence, when he rose unsteadily to his feet, swaying dangerously from side to side and began to spew neat lager from his open mouth. I grabbed him by the shoulders and pointed him in the direction of the distant neon sign which read 'Messieurs'. Pincher staggered forwards as I steered him from behind toward the faraway sanctuary. Every two or three paces he would belch forth more lager. Chairs and settees were scrambled clear from our erratic advance, the occupants back-peddling furiously with their feet – rather like beach-peddleos at the seaside – as we cut a swathe through the 'fleet' towards the far end of the Salon. Cries of '. . . Merde . . .!' continental gestures and further colourful French expletives preceded our ignominious exit,

111

which seemed to take forever.

By now I had the assistance of increasing numbers of horrified staff including the Salon Manager. He was gesticulating wildly and repeatedly shrieking,

'Citron et café noir! Alez, Citron et café noir!'

I pushed Pincher Martin through the 'Messieurs' door and I waved the Manager away to get the taxi, momentarily wondering why he was stating the bloody obvious. Of course we needed a taxi, a 'fast black'; or his 'citron noir' as he called it. It was quite plain to everyone that we needed a taxi to get Pincher back to the ship.

The lavatory was empty except for an elderly woman who emerged from one of the cubicles.

'Oh . . . Pardon, Madame,' I apologised, as Pincher belched another broadside. Madame, magically armed with a mop and bucket, was sounding off regular 'Oo là làs,' as I continued to apologise. Then I realised that she was very much at home and was clearly part of the establishment. I got Pincher bent over the nearest wash basin, where he continued getting rid of the remaining fourteen bottles of lager.

'Citron et café noir est très bon . . . oui?' said the Frenchwoman encouragingly as she continued swishing around Pincher's feet.

Pincher had now collapsed on to his knees and was clinging to the edge of the basin with both hands. I untied the jumper end of his 'silk', the other end being under his collar and round his neck, and secured it to the taps. His head was now safely strapped in position over the basin. Meanwhile the Manager and three or four waiters had rejoined us and were all excitedly babbling away in rapid French. It was then that the 'penny' dropped. One of the waiters entered carrying a cup of coffee.

'Ici, le citron et café noir, Monsieur!' he announced, triumphantly. Floating in the middle of the steaming black coffee, lay a large slice of lemon. Citron!

Somehow, I got the coffee down Pincher's throat while he was still on his knees and strapped to the taps. The Manager had stopped clucking like a French hen, and had accepted my profuse apologies. I thanked the French 'Messieurs' attendant lady and cleaned up Pincher as best I could while he sat groaning and mumbling incoherent apologies.

Twenty minutes later, I was in charge of a shaken but upright Pincher Martin.

'I'm ... shorry, Will, I'm ... I'm ... sho ... shorry, Will,' he mumbled all the way to the door.

As we emerged a little unsteadily but discreetly from the 'Messieurs', I looked longingly towards the stage as the orchestra came to the end of its dramatic finale. I was just in time to see a flash of gold-painted legs and thighs disappearing behind the stage curtains to the appreciative applause of the audience. The naked girls had come and gone.

With as much dignity as possible we descended the imposing Casino steps into the warm Mediterranean night, escorted by the two gold-braided doormen. They had summoned a taxi, otherwise known to 'Jolly Jack' as a 'fast black'. And would you believe it – it *was* a black Citroën!

Canteen Messing

Life wasn't all beer and skittles, as they say. The mundane aspects of daily life had to be attended to, but even they had their amusing moments.

Canteen messing had its merits – that is if the Leading Hand of the mess was an exacting and balanced fellow and the mess contained a reasonable number of 'would be' Mrs Beaton's. We didn't do the cooking, but we prepared everything which was sent up top to be cooked in the main galley by the chefs. I use the word 'chef' with some reservation; they were ship's cooks but liked to be called chefs, and only a fool would fail to treat each one as though he had just completed his Cordon Bleu apprenticeship in haute cuisine. It was wise to address the Petty Officer Cook as though he were a master chef who had reluctantly abandoned his position in Paris to cook for us. If you didn't show respect, they boiled and burned your food on *every* occasion.

Each morning after breakfast, the Leading Hand of the mess would detail two sailors to be the cooks of the mess for that day. In a well-run mess this was no arbitrary decision, and the choice would be made taking a number of factors into consideration: the caterer's planned menu – he was an appointed member of the mess who kept the mess accounts and was responsible for our diet – the culinary talent available, and an equitable sharing of the weekly tasks.

We would be sitting round the breakfast table drinking our tea and having a fag.

'Today we're on a figgy duff and clacker for dinner,' would say Harry, our Leading Hand of the mess. 'Will for the "awning" and Fatso for the figgy duff. Any problems?'

Our first task was to scrub out the mess. This we did on hands and knees, strenuously scrubbing the corticene deck with soft soap and water, then scrubbing and bleaching the pine table and benches. And when the mess was clean and tidy, we rolled out the oilcloth table-cover and commenced our culinary arts.

The secret of 'clacker'-making lay in the quality of the pastry 'awning' which covered the large baking tray. The pot mess ingredients were usually the same for 'clackers': four cans of tinned meat or stewing meat from the ship's butcher, sliced carrots, marrow-fat peas, onions, three tins of beans and finally three tins of tomatoes, otherwise known as 'train smash'. All this was topped up with cold, watery, powdered gravy. It was then that one's artistry was brought to bear in the making of the pastry for the 'awning'.

I had won fame for my pastry-making for two reasons: unlike most 'awnings', mine were not grey and rubbery, and the mess had given me their vote of confidence. Hence I became Will, the 'clacker' king. This had been achieved through my simple powers of observation. I had noticed that other messmates didn't wash their hands after scrubbing out the mess, and consequently the grey scum which still clung to their hands, became part of the ingredients as it mixed together with the flour and the lard. I also noticed that they squashed, mashed and beat the grey pastry to death. The resultant product vaguely resembled a well worn, grey overcoat which had seen better days. When cooked, parts were similar to a burned biscuit while other parts locked the jaws together like a huge mouthful of chewing gum.

Not only did I wash my hands – in the manner a surgeon 'scrubs up' for an operation – but I also mixed the ingredients delicately with a large fork until they had reached a pastry-like consistency. Only then would I gently pat it and delicately roll the pastry into an awning covering, to be eased over the tray's contents and supported by several old cups. My fame spread, and from time to time sailors would be sent by their Leading Hands to learn the secrets of the clacker, but my messmates, jealous of their clacker king's pastry, would tell them to 'piss orf and make their own.'

Fatso Giles, on the other hand, had majored in figgy duff. He adored the leaden quality of his mum's recipe. Using flour and great lumps of suet, which had to be fined down in his podgy hands, he would knead away ecstatically, then dump in lashings of sultanas and raisins, which stared back at him out of the duff

115

like crow's eyes as he scrunched them into a gooey mass. And
when he had moulded his football of delight, he would wrap it
in muslin, tie the knot and lower it lovingly into the fanny. The
mess craved for Fatso's once-per-week giant figgy duff.

But having prepared our delicacies, the show wasn't over till
the 'Fat Chef' had sung. There was more to be observed and
weighed in the mind before we parted with our prepared dishes,
and before a golden clacker and steaming figgy duff would grace
our table come dinner time. We would carry our works of art
carefully up near-vertical ladders to the galley, then stand at the
door watching the various 'chefs' going about their business.
They moved in among their oil-fired ranges, which were littered
with trays and 'fannys', ready to boil to a pulp or commit to the
heat of the fiery oven. And we would carefully note which 'chefs'
wore white gloves.

Those with white gloves were under treatment for the 'clap'.
Those without had possibly just recovered. This same treatment
was also meted out to wardroom stewards who had acquired
the same malady. It sometimes occasioned innocent wardroom
visitors to applaud the custom of servants wearing white gloves,
'especially in these days of falling standards,' – which usually
made the ship's officers choke on their soup.

Venereal disease was endemic in many parts of the
Mediterranean in those days, and naval medical science had
deemed that the wearing of gloves would somehow prevent this
unsociable ailment from spreading throughout the ship. Another
point of view, shared by disciplinarians, was that the humiliation
of being seen in white gloves would cure the problem at its source.
If it didn't, at least they would know who had got it. Even though
we thought that these views were stupid, we weren't going to
chance our luck. Hence we would select the glove-less 'chefs'
who weren't 'going to the ball', saying quietly in their ear, 'Chef,

me old mate, you always do our specialities proud,' and hand him the treasured dishes.

My other pastry speciality was apple pies. Somehow I managed to get the right amount of baking powder into the recipe without the pies exploding, which made them light and fluffy and earned me another bow to my illusory 'toffological' status.

The title of 'toffology' rate was awarded to anyone who spoke without a regional accent and whose voice might be likened to a BBC announcer. This attribute automatically accorded the owner an honorary Ph.D. in the eyes of the more gullible and trusting sailors on the lower deck. This, therefore, made him the fount of all toffological knowledge, which was hard to define but was usually pretty esoteric. It was an awful responsibility to have to carry, especially owing to my itinerant, sketchy and fragmented education. When the subject was particularly obscure, however, I could get away with a fabricated answer which allowed me to adjudicate with tact between those in dispute. But it was often a minefield and could embrace the most arcane subjects imaginable.

One morning at breakfast Geordie said pleasantly to Jock, 'Pass the golden syrup, mate.'

There was a heavy Highland pause as Jock looked across the table at Geordie and pointed to the can.

'That's nay golden syrup, mon . . . it's trickle,' he replied dourly and with Gaelic conviction.

'There's nowt about treacle on the label . . . it's golden stuffin' syrup,' said Geordie, with equal Northern conviction.

'I'm telling you, mon, I ken it's *trickle* . . . and if you's want it . . . you ken it too,' said Jock, now starting to rise from the other side of the table.

Meanwhile Harry, our leading hand – a man of some education and discernment – who enjoyed my mythological status as a toffologist, said innocently,

'Let Will, decide. He's our toffology rate.' He grinned wickedly and added, 'He's bound to know.'

All eyes focussed on me; Jock resumed his seat, Geordie unclenched his fists, and Harry sat back and relaxed, pregnant with anticipation.

'Aaah,' I said, uncomfortably, 'that's an interesting one . . .' and watched Jock's eyes narrow and Geordie tense.

'It's not quite so simple as you may think,' I said, stalling while searching for a mutually honourable answer.

'In the West Indies, it's called molasses . . . and they make rum with it,' I said desperately. A flicker of interest crossed their faces as they pondered the possibility of turning our can of . . . call it what you will . . . into rum. But they were not satisfied yet.

'However, you are both absolutely right,' I said, and then quickly continued.

'Hamish McTavish, an early distiller, introduced molasses in 1745, and referred to the molasses as 'trickle'.' Jock smiled and Geordie glowered.

'But when it was exported across the border to England, the consistency of 'trickle' was more commonly referred to as syrup . . . and because of its golden colour, people south of Hadrian's wall, came to use its more common Saxon name of syrup. But Scotsmen have always known it as trickle. But to an Englishman, it's golden syrup.' I concluded nervously, with as much conviction in my voice as I could muster.

It was a close run thing, but honour was satisfied and there were nods of agreement around the table. Harry smirked knowingly and winked, and once again had had his fun at my expense.

Operational Seatime

We did, however, have our more serious moments within the ship, and that was when we went off to sea to carry out operational exercises.

Sea training within the fleet in those days was, in the main, divided into three parts: weapons and sensors, fleet manoeuvring, and seamanship. By today's standards, the former were crude combinations of mechanical and electrical contraptions. The sonar had been enhanced before and during the near-fatal battle of the Atlantic, as had radar, with British inventiveness and the might of American technology and know-how. The latter two qualities had always been essential elements to success.

Our weapons comprised a single 4" gun, a few bofors, an anti-submarine 'Squid' mounting and depth charges aft. As an anti-submarine frigate, our primary weapon was the Squid, which fired depth bombs 250 yards ahead of the ship. They were set to explode at the estimated depth of the target submarine, and this was established by the 'Sword' sonar, which passed the depth to the bombs in the Squid mounting. The depth charges had become obsolescent with the introduction of ahead-throwing weapons and the depth charge was retained as a back-up.

Much of our time during exercises at sea was spent chasing our own target submarines, S and T class, in the exercise areas off Malta. The tactics and expertise had mostly been formulated during the latter years of the war. Ace hunter-killer groups, led by men like Captain Walker – the ultimate anti-submarine commander – had provided the foundation of expertise and knowledge upon which we based all our anti-submarine training.

We operated the sonar from the Asdic office, a small compartment at the back of the bridge, and a team of three manned the equipment. This comprised a range recorder, a bearing recorder and the First Operator. The latter was the key man in the team and controlled the sonar transducer, which was housed in a dome and poked out under the ship.

We kept watches in the semi-dark, packed tightly together on seats in front of our equipment, listening on headphones to the never-ending 'pinging' transmissions. It was a snapshot of the *Cruel Sea*, hour after hour of 'pinging' but without the danger or the fear. Our target was one of ours and she was determined not to get caught, since there had always been great rivalry between surface ships and submariners.

We listened and watched for the telltale bleep of an echo and the accompanying mark on the ionised paper in each recorder. And when we gained contact, the ship came to life. The Captain rushed to the bridge and the anti-submarine officer closed up, squashed behind our three-seat bench. The Navigator manned the bridge plot and the Squid was loaded with dummy bombs. Each time the First Operator heard the sonar echo bounce back off the submarine's hull, he thumped his control button as he crossed and re-crossed the target. This registered on the recorders, so that range and bearing were shown. By now the Captain had swung the ship hard on her ear to point at the target and bring the Squid to bear.

As the range shortened, the bleeps came faster and faster.

'Change to scale 15,' said the Asdic officer.

'You've lost it. Cut right,' – followed by the familiar bleep of a regained contact.

'He's turned toward,' cried the sonar controller.

'Doppler slight to mod high . . . range 1800 yards. Bearing drawing left,' he reported in clipped tones, his rising adrenalin being heard over the 'mike'.

'Port fifteen, midships . . . steady. Revolutions 80,' said the Captain, peering over the compass in the direction of the unseen target ahead of the ship.

'Doppler changing . . . Slight to mod low . . . altering away . . . range 600.'

'Revolutions 110. Steer by Asdic,' said the Captain to the Quartermaster. Then, 'Action Squid,' to the controller; and simultaneously turning to the gunner's mate, 'Stand by one grenade.'

'Range 300 . . . doppler low . . . bearing steady . . . H.E. on bearing!' cried the controller with urgent excitement. This was quickly followed by two muffled bangs as the Squids soared forward into the air.

'Instant echoes,' reported the controller, and added, 'Carrying out stern sweep.'

We were over the top of the submarine and the gunner's mate tossed his grenade into the water below. This explosion told the submariners that we had carried out our attack.

That was a classic attack. It certainly didn't happen like that all the time, and I can hear the submariners saying, 'Too right!' The water conditions during the Mediterranean summer more often than not militated against gaining contact. As the heat built up during the morning, the surface of the sea became warmer as well. This warmth penetrated down and formed a temperature layer, which caused the sonar beam to bend downwards and thus reduce the detection range. In these conditions, the submarine dived beneath the layer and was very difficult to detect except at close range. But just to tease us, the submarine would pop up above it and then pop below. These were the times when it was best to keep clear of the bridge, for 'Bungy' Williams would often go berserk. That was when the Navigator wore his haunted look.

Lieutenant Ogilvy was our Navigating Officer and lived

dangerously under the large shadow of the Captain. At that stage of his career, it has to be said, he wasn't a very lucky Navigator. He frequently havered and dithered, not sure whether to stay on the bridge wing or stand by the pelorus. There was an air of indecision about him, which manifested itself in vague or hedged replies and nervous ticks.

'Where are we, Pilot?' the Captain would ask.

'Ah . . . yes, sir . . . just checking,' he would reply, and then hurriedly disappear to the chart table or the bridge plot; there he would curl himself into a ball, just like a hedge-hog, and stare fixedly at the chart, praying for inspiration while he fiddled with a pair of defective dividers, which were useless for measuring distance. Then, after a decent interval, he would return to the bridge.

'We're nearly there, sir. Not quite . . . but shortly.'

These answers infuriated Bungy Williams, who would bear down upon him saying,

'Nearly *where*, Ogilvy? And what's *shortly*?' And Pilot would rush off back to the chart table muttering incoherently to himself and start again.

Poor Ogilvy was also responsible for the operations room and the bridge plot, and these were two key elements of the system when we had lost contact with the submarine. Ogilvy knew that the only way he might avoid awkward questions from the Captain was to keep moving. Thus he was in continuous motion between the operations room, one deck below the bridge, his chart table and the submarine plotting table, which was housed next to the Asdic office behind the bridge.

Everything was fine so long as our 144Q sonar maintained contact with the submarine, but the moment we lost contact was the moment that Ogilvy's organisation had to start performing. He would be expected to propose the most likely area in which to search, giving a range and bearing based on the last known position of the submarine. This was also a signal to Ogilvy to speed up his movements from position to position, rather like musical chairs. The Captain, meanwhile, would be yelling into every bridge microphone, calling for Ogilvy to establish a datum and propose a search. But the Navigator was never long enough in any one position to establish anything.

A point came when the Captain cracked, lost his cool and wanted blood. Contact with the submarine had been lost for ten minutes, during which time the Captain had been screaming for Ogilvy to tell him where the bloody submarine was. The only reply he had had was faint and nervous.

'Just checking, sir.' And the Captain yelled back.

'Where are you, man?' he bawled, only to be met with silence.

Ogilvy was unfortunately caught on one of his quick sprints from the operations room to the bridge plot. Bungy spotted him out of the corner of his eye, moving fast from left to right, and pounced, all fifteen stones of him, on to Ogilvy's back. Together they hit the bridge deck. Then Bungy sat astride his pilot, who lay on his back looking up in panic-stricken terror.

'Where . . . is . . . the . . . shitting . . . submarine . . . Ogilvy?' roared the Captain as he bounced in time with his words on Ogilvy's stomach. Luckily the First Lieutenant happened to appear on the bridge, and tactfully helped the demented Captain to his feet before Ogilvy was sick. The joke was, of course, that everyone knew that Bartosik *wasn't* trying to *save* Ogilvy from discomfort, he merely felt that it was all rather undignified; in the Captain's place he would have had Ogilvy shot.

When the day's exercising was over and the Navigator tentatively offered a course for 'home', there was the excitement of entering Sliema Creek to look forward to.

Entering harbour after a day at sea had its moments too. The destroyers and frigates usually berthed in Sliema Creek between head and stern buoys. These buoys were large enough for two men to stand on, and were roughly 350 feet apart. There were sufficient numbers of buoys strung down the Creek to accommodate something in the order of ten frigates. Ships were always expected to berth with their bows facing the entrance, so that they could leave the harbour quickly in an emergency.

Thus the ships entered the mouth of the harbour and would then turn at rest to point their sterns down Sliema Creek. Having done so, they steamed astern to the allocated berth between two buoys. If the Creek was empty it was a daunting task, but not too much could go wrong provided: you didn't run aground on either side, you didn't overshoot and park yourself on the roadway at the end of the Creek, and you didn't hit all the buoys on the way to your berth. On the other hand, if the Creek was partly filled, or even worse, full – the Captain needed nerves of steel.

Captains' of ships who were 'first-timers' had sleepless nights on passage from England to Malta prior to joining or visiting the Mediterranean Fleet. Like playing the piano, some people are naturals at ship-handling while others are not. The daunting reality was that in order to maintain proper steerage-way astern, most frigates' had to ring on six knots astern, point the ship and pray. Just like a car, wheel corrections are opposite to that of going ahead, and this exacerbated the problem for the first-timers. And if that were not enough with which to contend, all the ships that were already berthed in two columns down the 'trot' would have their booms, ladders and boats projecting out from the ships' sides.

While all this was running through the Captain's mind, the whaler and the motor cutter had to be lowered while the ship turned at rest prior to going astern. The motor cutter would chug off in the direction of the stern buoy, while the whaler would be towed from the boat rope, which was reeved through the bull ring in the bow, and the whaler's crew would subsequently tend to matters at the bow buoy on arrival. If the Captain had kept his cool, the ship would be ploughing astern towards its small 350-ft. berth between two buoys, clear of all obstructions.

During this exacting evolution, the bridge was not a good place to be. The Captain would be rushing from one side of the bridge to the other, trying to anticipate which ship, or which row of booms and ladders he was going to hit. Our Captain, Bungy Williams, though a heavy man, moved as quickly as a charging Spanish bull intent on tossing the matador; to be in his path was not a good idea.

When the worst of the nightmare was over and the ship lay at rest just off the berth, the buoys jumpers would leap from their boats to their respective buoys, secure stern line aft and 'picking-up' rope forward. Only when both were secured, would the Captain force a smile.

'Well done No 1,' which really meant, 'Thank God, that's over!' and off he would scurry to his cabin for a large pink gin.

Leaving harbour was 'easy'. Entering could be hell. Once secured to both buoys, however, the harbour had its compensations.

Chapter 6

The 'Polish' First Lieutenant

Wherever we went and whenever we were in harbour, we always gave cocktail parties. In the 1950s, the Fleet didn't spend much time preparing for war. The world had only recently finished yet another war 'to end all wars', and the Russian navy wasn't yet that strong. Though we exercised our gunnery and anti-submarine skills – curtailed by restrictions on fuel, one of our most important tasks was to show the flag. And when we weren't showing the flag, we still gave cocktail parties to each other. These, of course, were either social, political, or a mixture of both. When I say 'we', I mean it was the wardrooms of the Fleet which extended hospitality according to the whims or obligations of the Captain and his First Lieutenant.

Each Captain received an entertainment allowance – which wasn't that much – to contribute towards the cost of official receptions. The difference was met by the ship's officers on an equitable basis according to rank; thus the Captain paid the largest share while the Midshipman paid the lowest. Private parties were not subsidised by the official entertainment allowance.

In the main, the ship's company wasn't too much affected, except for the wardroom stewards and the duty part of the watch. The parties were usually held on the fo'c'sle or the quarterdeck, under spread awnings with decorations made out of neatly

126

wrapped signal flags strung between the guard rails and the awning ridge ropes and illuminated with a backbone of overhead coloured lights.

Joseph enjoyed his cocktail parties. They were splendid platforms for exercising his charm, enlarging on his personal views and influencing higher authority; he was a good-looking man with presence, and was adored by the ladies. It was particularly noticeable that senior officers' wives found him hard to put down. He moved smoothly among them like an ice-skating 'maitre-d'; his charming compliments and accompanying smiles were returned with modest giggles and fluttering eyelashes. And while he pirouetted from group to group, he signalled, like a tic tac man at the races, for glasses to be filled and petits fours to be passed.

I should know, for I was often there. He would 'invite' Woolly West, Alderson and me to dress in our best and carry trays loaded with iced drinks among the guests. His 'invitations' were difficult to resist and, to give him his due, we would be promised a 'make and mend' the following day. Joseph's briefings were always the same.

'Tonight you vill have the honour to be serving the important people,' he would say with a perfunctory smile,

'But don't talk to them, Villis, unless they ask you the question,' he would add sternly as an afterthought, and for my special benefit. On one occasion he had caught me chatting happily, drink tray in hand, to a large motherly figure who turned out to be the Commander-in-Chief's wife.

We used to enjoy the parties – though we didn't let on to Bartosik – and as the drink took its toll, and the Petty Officer Steward's effectiveness diminished in inverse proportion to the secret drinks he had downed, Woolly and I would take a quick slurp of whatever was on the tray as we ferried our way to and from the pantry. We were wise enough not to overdo it, but usually by the end of the evening we would be grinning uncontrollably at everyone we served.

There came the occasion when some of the officers' wives, including Joseph's wife and sister-in-law, came on holiday to Malta. The First Lieutenant organised a cocktail party and we were hauled in to help serve the drinks.

It was a jolly affair and all was going well, except that throughout the evening I had been worrying about the Daily Orders. I had typed them earlier, but I hadn't got Joseph to sign them before the party had started. Thus I couldn't distribute them until he had done so. I had them to hand, however, waiting for a suitable moment to catch him. I looked around, and then I noticed that he was not on the quarterdeck: 'Good,' I thought, 'he's nipped off to his cabin. I'll go and catch him now.'

When I got to the officer's cabin flat, Joseph's door was shut. I knew that I had a decision to make. Bartosik took pride in his twenty-four hour availability on all matters relating to the efficient running of the ship. In working hours he had a constant stream of officers and senior ratings knocking at his door, wanting approval and advice for decisions to be made. He had become fed up with the constant 'knock, knock' at his door – which was mostly open in any event – and had had a brass plate made which said, 'Don't knock – Come in.'

I had already done the course and knew that it wasn't quite as simple as that. Each day I had to get his signature for Daily Orders. When the door was open, it was easy. But when the door was shut it wasn't. If I knocked he might open the door, take me by the ear and say: 'Villis, vot does the sign say?' and hold my face close to it. On the other hand, I had once courageously pulled the door open with a bang and found him clad only in his vest.

'Get out at vunce, Villis!' he had shrieked, as I rapidly retreated to the ship's office.

It was all a matter of judgement. Did the sign really mean what it said at that particular moment?

It was obvious. The First Lieutenant was *dressed,* because he was attending his own cocktail party. Q.E.D., I could go in without knocking. I hauled the door open and stood there staring. A woman was lying on his bunk and he was bent over her muttering some words. Joseph turned round and I slammed the door shut. The door immediately shot open.

'Villis, it's quite all right,' he said anxiously, 'my vife's sister is feeling not vell'.

'That's all right, sir, I quite understand' I said, and slammed the door shut. And then I grinned.

It shot open again.

'Villis! I order you to say 'hello' to my vife's sister,' he said between clenched teeth, pushing me forward to shake hands with the bemused, supine woman, who was wondering what the hell was going on.

'She's not feeling so vell,' shouted Bartosik, furious at having to explain why he had a woman lying on his bed, albeit fully dressed.

'Now get out!' he yelled and I fled.

As I hurried back to the quarterdeck, it didn't take much to divine the First Lieutenant's greatest fear. He would be worried sick that I would tell all my messmates that I had caught Joseph in flagrante delicto, or, as the sailors would put it, 'on the job'.

It transpired that his sister-in-law was pregnant. She had come over faint and had been taken by Joseph to lie down, since his wife at the time was in deep conversation with Captain Bonham Carter, a man of no mean influence. There was every likelihood that his wife had been briefed as to what to say to the

Captain, and that was not an opportunity to be missed, sick pregnant sister-in-law or not.

Joseph was right to worry. I did tell them all, and the story made their day. But I told them the truth, which was funny enough on its own. Also I forged his signature on Daily Orders and nobody seemed to notice. Nevertheless, it was noticeable that Bartosik was more circumspect in his attitude towards me for several weeks or so. He kept giving me quizzical looks.

The Mandolin

Once again we were off to show the flag. This time we headed north to Sicily, the land of the Mafia and shady deals.

There wasn't much entertainment in the town of Port Augusta in those days. There were plenty of bars after the Mediterranean pattern, where one could sit outside and watch the hot, sticky, slow-moving world pass by. Inevitably, the more determined sailors were able to locate the back-street dives, where there were other pleasures to be had besides chianti wine, but which were more frequently accompanied by the penalty of 'clap'. It was a sleepy Sicilian harbour town, where the going was tough and the people had to fight for a living in whatever way they thought best.

We were anchored off the town about a half mile from the landing jetty, and by 8 o'clock in the morning the heat of the sun had made the decks without awnings hot underfoot while the sweat trickled freely down one's back. Our motor cutter was plying to and from the shore, taking the postman to collect the mail, collecting supplies of fresh vegetables and fruit and bringing off the occasional shoreside official.

The Captain usually used the motor cutter for his official calls on the local mayor or whomever – dressed formally in his 'ice cream' suit with sword and medals. His personal fast motor boat, the 'skimmer', was a temperamental beast, which always seemed to be under repair, with two or three ERAs trying to make it work. When it did, however, it went like a bat out of hell, and made a fine sight kicking up the spray going into the plane. Too often, though, the Captain would take off majestically in a cloud of foam only to come to a lonely halt half way to the jetty as the engine cut out. Wisely, he usually used the motor cutter.

Jolly Jack always knows where to find 'bargains' wherever he goes. In Port Augusta, he listed the bargains as being cheap chianti, ouzo, the 'girls' in a certain quarter of the town, and . . . the mandolins. Mandolins came in all shapes and sizes and were made by the local craftsmen. They were attractive looking instruments, finely polished and well finished, and they immediately captured the imagination of our ship's company.

The locals knew when and where to sell their mandolins, and a favoured location for this was in the bars during the evening, when the ouzo and chianti had begun to take its hold. They waited for their customers to go critical on drink; then, armed with their mandolin, they would play Volare – the pop song of the time – and get all the jolly jacks singing. After a couple of songs, the next victim would be allowed to strum a few discordant notes on the mandolin, and the Sicilian would strike.

'Madonna! You play'a da mandolin like the grand musician, in one'a' week, you do it. No kiddin.' And then they would sell like hot cheese cakes on Sliema front.

The last liberty boat of the night would be full of singing sailors, strumming tunelessly as they rendered their version of Volare, so pleased to have got the knack of playing the mandolin so quickly. After five days in port, the ship was flooded with strumming maniacs, who practised incessantly during their spare time, and the jangling of mandolins could be heard even above the noise of auxiliary machinery.

The morning we sailed, the locals made their last determined effort to rid Port Augusta of all available mandolins. They came out to the ship in 'bum' boats laden with them and bartered with the sailors, high above them on the upper deck. Trade was slow because most of the sailors were by now 'stony' broke, but desultory trading carried on before we weighed anchor, mostly by sailors who had been under stoppage of leave or just hadn't gone ashore.

The transaction would follow a set routine: once having reached agreement (involving lots of shouting from both vendor and customer), a heaving line would be lowered with the agreed amount of money, and then the mandolin was hoisted inboard. One particular sale was transacted through one of the lower portholes, which was within reach of the 'bum' boat. The proud new owner, however, having grasped his prize, found that he couldn't get it through the 'scuttle' because the mandolin was too big. At that moment the ship completed weighing anchor and got underway with the sailor holding his instrument half in and half out.

In less than a week, mandolins started to become available on the ship's second-hand market. In most quarters tempers were thin and the mere plucking of a mandolin string would be greeted with shouts of outrage even by those who owned them. Prices plummeted and the bottom fell out of the mandolin market. The ship returned to Malta for a few weeks and during this period many sailors were seen to take their instruments ashore to sell to other drunken sailors in the bars or maybe to a dghaisaman in lieu of the fare on the way back to the ship. Within a month there were very few mandolins to be seen on top of the lockers in the messdeck, but 'Fatso' Giles was one of the exceptions.

Some weeks later we were on passage to Tobruk. Those who weren't on watch had had their supper and we were lounging around the messdeck table; some reading or writing letters and the rest spinning yarns. Our Leading Hand of the mess, Harry Teadon, was sitting back on the cushions with a hint of a smile on his face, and wondering how he might liven things up for his amusement. He enjoyed throwing a controversial 'bone' into the conversation and would then sit back to watch the fun, as prejudice, ignorance and make-believe heated the discussions to boiling point.

It was at this moment, during Harry's reflections, that 'Fatso' Giles chose to get his mandolin down from the top locker and wistfully examine his ill-gotten investment for scratches.

'It's still in perfec' nick,' he said laconically to no one in particular.

Harry spotted his prey in the instant.

'Why don't you sell it? I'm sure one of these lads will buy it,' said Harry, looking at us and knowing that the mention of 'mandolin' was a dirty word.

A derisive cheer went up among us and Fatso was told what to do with his bleedin' mandolin. But Harry's 'bone' had sparked a new-found hope in Fatso. Maybe someone would buy it. After all, it wasn't scratched.

'Two quid and it's yours,' said Fatso generously. 'Enough for my run ashore tomorrow night,' he expanded hopefully.

No one bit except the lad who told him that he would have it if Fatso *paid him* two quid. Then Harry played his master stroke. It was inspired and would really get things going in the mess.

'I'll tell you what, Fatso, I'll give you thirty bob for it on one condition,' said Harry, smiling. Fatso's eyes sparkled with new found hope.

'Honest?'

Harry sat upright and leaned forward across the table, his eyes twinkling with wicked anticipation.

'Yes honest,' he said, and continued, 'If you fit that mandolin over someone's head, so's he wears it like a collar, I'll give you thirty bob.' He sat back triumphantly to watch the fun.

Those sitting within range of Fatso hurriedly backed away out of range as he looked around for a likely target. Horace didn't move as he was more trusting than the others. He looked up and saw Fatso standing on the other side of the table, mandolin raised on high and about to strike. The only thing that saved him was the hammock rail. As Fatso swung it down, it touched the rail and glanced off Horace's head on to the seat cushion beside him.

'You bastard!' cried Horace, as he scrambled away out of reach, rubbing the side of his head.

Fatso was mortified as he inspected his now damaged mandolin, realising that he had botched his only hope of catching anyone unawares. The construction of the mandolins was very flimsy, much of the materials consisting of light wood panels, veneer and even bits of balsa wood. The damage was slight but beyond his ability to repair.

'Not good enough,' said Harry, as the tears streamed down his cheeks with laughter.

'It's got to end up round the neck, like a collar.'

It was then that I weighed the odds. I was broke and wouldn't be going ashore except to swim.

'Why not? 'Fatso,' I heard myself say, 'I'll do you a deal. You can fit it over my head for fifteen shillings, and not a penny less.'

His scheming little pig-eyes narrowed as he considered the situation. It didn't take him long to decide. Either he got fifteen bob or he was left with a 'dead' mandolin.

'You're on,' he said, as our mess began to fill with sailors from

134

other messes who had got the 'buzz' and wanted to see the outcome.

Harry placed thirty bob on the table in front of him and sat like Nero, waiting for the entertainment to begin. As contestants in a ring before the fight, Fatso and I sorted out the procedure and the rules. I was to kneel on the floor, protecting my eyes with a blindfold, and he would count to three and then strike. Rather like the condemned man, I made a last request:

'But not too hard, Fatso.'

'Don't you worry, Will, it'll be just like a tap on the head. You won't feel a thing.'

Duly blindfolded, and kneeling in the position used for Samurai executions, I heard him count 'One, two. .' and then the bastard hit me.

I came round, so they told me, ten seconds later. I was supported by two messmates and was wearing a mandolin neatly around my neck like a large collar and tie. The sound of laughter gradually broke through my dazed condition as I gazed around me at a messdeck full of convulsed sailors amid cries of: 'Well done, Will. It was great!'

Apart from a slight headache for an hour, and a bump the size of an egg, I didn't suffer at all; and anyway, I was fifteen bob the richer, if not much wiser.

The Captain of the Heads

We continued to make our way round the Mediterranean ports as the months wore on and the restrictions on fuel allowed. We used less fuel on passage at economical cruising speed than we did when carrying out fleet manoeuvres and other fleet exercises, and so after three or four weeks rotting in Sliema Creek, we were sent off on 'show the flag' visits. It was during one such visit that I crossed Bartosik's path yet again.

He was standing behind the 'defaulters' table, his hands resting lightly on the surface, and there was a thin, ominous smile on his face.

'Ordinary Seaman Villis, ve both know that this is not the first time that you haf given me the difficult problems. I think now, I vill give you the *difficult* new duty, yes?' This wasn't a question; it was a statement.

'From tomorrow you vill be the new captain of the ship's company heads.' He said this confidentially, and I imagined in a manner that the Prime Minister might use when honouring a backbencher with the prospect of knighthood on the morrow. He was in fact, appointing me to the duty of ship's lavatory cleaner, known throughout the Royal Navy as the 'captain of the heads'.

'The toilets are very bad looking and vill need much work. Ve vill see you do the job good, yes?' He concluded with his charming continental smile.

The Coxswain paused and looked expectantly at the First Lieutenant, rather like an inquisitive chicken, trying to divine whether he had finished. Then, satisfied that justice had been done, he 'sang' out loud and clear, 'Salute, about turn, quick march.'

Under the circumstances, the Coxswain was well satisfied that I was to be incarcerated in the heads for six months; he had been unable to frame a suitable charge that would have stuck, so instead, I had been invited to 'request' for a 'duty change'.

I had just lost a very 'cushy number' as the First Lieutenant's writer. This entailed working in the ship's office, typing the 'Daily Orders' at the end of each day, and also acting as his 'runner'-cum-general-dogsbody. Thinking to milk the system, I had decided that I would get myself a 'blue' station card. These cards were issued only to sailors who had special day duties, which on occasion required them to work in the evenings. Holders of the card were therefore excluded from Duty Watch; they were entitled to go ashore every evening having finished their work. This appealed to me, but I also thought that it was my due. No more Duty Watches, so I could shove off ashore whenever I liked. I'd managed to achieve my aim by going to the Coxswain's office and telling him a small white lie.

'I can't be in a Watch, Swain, cos 'Jimmy' often needs me for typing out of working hours. He'd go bonkers if I wasn't available.' While this was true, the First Lieutenant certainly had no knowledge of my proposal.

The Coxswain had looked at me searchingly and not a little suspiciously, but somewhat reluctantly had agreed:

'Very well, Willis, if that's what 'e wants, so be it.' And off I'd gallop with my beautiful blue station card and somehow or other the Coxswain had forgotten to check that it was okay with the First Lieutenant; thus I had happily lapsed into a false sense of security.

My current predicament had occurred because 'Jimmy' had found out that I had conned the Coxswain. Bartosik would never have sanctioned a blue card; certainly not to me of all people. Anyway, one evening when we had anchored off Monte Carlo for several days, Bartosik had sent for me. I was dressed in my Number Ones and all ready to go ashore.

'Ah, Villis, tell me, did you have the good shore run last night?'

I tensed, sensing danger. There was no way that Bartosik was asking me this question out of interest for my welfare.

'Er . . . yes, sir, it was very pleasant. I had a walk round the town and really enjoyed studying the architecture,' I lied.

'So you like the buildings of Monte Carlo, no?' He didn't wait for my answer; he wasn't interested.

'I see that you are off vunce more to study the architecture tonight,' he said with studied sarcasm. Again, he wasn't looking for answers; at least, not quite yet.

'Then tell me, Villis, since the ship is in two Anchor Watches, how is it that you haf two days studying the architecture? You don't like to do some evening duty, maybe one day to help?'

His voice had an edge to it and had risen an octave. He was smiling but his blue eyes were icy. The Coxswain was sent for and the game was up. That was why I was now the new Captain of the Heads.

After Both Watches of the Hands at 0800 the following day, I made my way slowly and with heavy steps to my new workplace, the ship's company heads.

The layout of the 'heads' was very simple and very basic. On the ship's side there were ten semi-enclosed, raised lavatories; to use them, one had to climb several steps before opening the two small metal doors to enter. Once inside and seated, the partitions between each 'trap' barely came up to one's midriff. Thus, when all ten 'traps' were full of seated occupants, it looked like a race meeting, with all the horses boxed for the start and the jockeys mounted ready for the off.

As I entered the heads, I was greeted by the sound of a shouted order.

'Attenshun in the 'eads. Cap'n Will's rounds.' This was followed by a loud derisive cheer from the ten fully occupied 'traps', whose temporary 'owners' stood to attention with grins on their faces and their trousers round their ankles as they saluted.

'You bastards!' I thought, as I tried to rid myself of the stupid 'lemonlike' grin on my face. 'I've got to get out of this job – fast. But how?'

My first day was hell. the smelly heads seemed to be

permanently full of sailors who came and went in a continuous stream. They used it not so much for its designed purpose, but as a gossip shop and stop-over for a quick fag. They sat in cosy proximity in the 'traps', so's not to miss out on the far-fetched stories about last night's run ashore.

'Bloody hell, you should'a seen 'er. Legs all the way up to 'er arse! No, honest.'

That was typical of the many and varied intellectual conversations which graced the insalubrious setting. And while they were actually occupying the traps, stubbing out their fag-ends willy nilly, I couldn't get on with the job. It was a 'catch twenty-two' situation. They wanted the 'heads' to be 'shiny-bright' while they chattered constantly on their bums.

That night, as I lay in my hammock wondering how to avoid being closeted as a spectator in the ship's company heads for the next six months, I had a brainwave. It was 'dodgy' but he just might agree. Tomorrow I'd go and 'put it' to the First Lieutenant.

Next day after both watches, I went up to Bartosik's cabin and coughed timidly at the already opened sliding door. He was a distinguished looking man, close to his mid-thirties, with black hair and fine-cut features. His bearing and mannerisms were those of the confident naval officer; he was at ease with both his superiors and his subordinates. His undoubted charm was that of the aristocratic continental. It was the popularly held view on the lower deck that he had the ability to 'charm the pants off any woman, and probably had'. Nonetheless, he was a difficult man to understand. Bartosik's aristocratic Polish background was attuned to dealing with 'serfs' and officers. The 'serfs' were there to obey and get on with the work; his subordinate officers were there (under the threat of immediate and dire retribution) to ensure that his orders were carried out to the letter. Most of the lower deck liked him; all of the officers feared him, and at times this included the Captain.

Like all First Lieutenants, he used his cabin as an office. As usual he was going through his Ship's Standing Orders. Bartosik loved 'Standing Orders'. Ours seemed to grow like the Doomsday Book and increased every week; they were already three inches thick. Furthermore, in most Ships of the Fleet, Daily Orders were no more than one page of typing, outlining the days events and the times at which they would take place. This was usually followed by a few notes, giving general information and the 'Jimmy's 'do's' and 'don'ts' of life. It was really rather like a formal ship's newspaper which had to be obeyed. But Bartosik's Daily Orders were designed for the heavy reader. Quite often they contained three or four pages of extracts from different sources, which included: The Articles of War, King's Regulations and Admiralty Instructions, Mediterranean Standing Orders and any other such orders as came to mind. The extracts all contained severe threats, and I'm sure that he was an avid reader of Voltaire, who had remarked on Admiral Byng's execution, 'Pour encourager les autres.'

I stopped my dreaming and returned to the present. The First Lieutenant looked up from his desk and eyed me.

'Yes, Villis, vot is it that you vish to say?' he asked, as he continued turning the pages of his voluminous orders.

'Well, sir, I've been thinking . . . ' I didn't get any further.

'That's very good, Villis. I like that you think.' He smiled and then waited expectantly for me to go on.

'Well, sir, . . . what if in, er . . . say, three weeks' time . . . that is . . . when you do First Lieutenant's Rounds, . . . you, . . . er . . . say . . . find that the Ship's Company heads is the . . . best you've ever seen?' I was struggling with my words because his irritating smile had broadened the more he heard me struggle.

'Vell, Villis, that would be a 'fezzer on your bonnet' and vill be looking good.' He then leaned his head quizzically to one side.

'There is something else, no?' I took a deep breath, then 'shot' my words as if from a machine gun.

'Then if you were very, very pleased and you thought that it was the best in the whole Fleet . . . and . . . '

Like a boiler starved of fuel, I ran out of 'steam' and stopped. Bartosik was leaning backwards on the two rear legs of his chair; he was studying me with amusement and he was enjoying himself.

'Then vot, Villis?' he asked, now reeling me in like a fish about to be landed.

'Would you er . . . give me a new job . . . and . . . and change my duty to Bowman of the motor cutter, sir?' I blurted out. At last I'd said it. I felt utterly relieved at having finished, whatever his answer, 'yes' or 'no'.

He and his chair descended rapidly to the upright position; both feet were planted firmly on the deck. His smile vanished and his face had become set, his brow slightly furrowed in concentration. He sat looking pensively at the bulkhead in front of him. I thought the silence would never end, and then he spoke – not to me but to the bulkhead and with pointed finger, which beat in time with selected words, chosen for emphasis, so that I might never doubt his meaning. 'So, it is the *deal* that you give me, *yes?*'

Momentarily, I thought this was an angry accusation but he continued in an even voice.

'But Villis, you must *understand* that I will be a very *exacting* judge. If you fail, maybe I vill *hang you* in the heads, *yes?*' The description was vivid and not beyond belief. With his next utterance, Bartosik's expression mellowed.

'Ven I see the reflection of the First Lieutenant's face in the

141

toilet, on the seats, on the deck and in the bulkheads . . . only *then* vill I honour this *deal!*'

I slid down the shiny handrails of the near vertical ladder from the officers 'flat' in one swoop and without touching the steps. I was jubilant as I ran aft, down the main passage towards my lovely 'smelly heads'. The 'game' was on.

My plan of action had already been formulated in anticipation of the unlikely event that 'Jimmy' would agree to my deal. Later in the forenoon I went up to the Paintshop and chatted up the ship's painter. He was a chum of mine and he agreed to 'make me up' a sign that day; it would be ready for tomorrow morning at 'Both Watches.' After that, I went to the stores and signed for a variety of cleaning materials for the heads. There were a couple of items in amongst these which I deemed very necessary for my plan. It pleased me when the stores rating commented.

'You wanna' watch it with that stuff, Will', could do you a lotta' damage!'

My final call was to the Bosun's locker, where I collected five fathoms of one inch sisal rope.

Armed with my newly painted sign and other goodies, I 'fell out' from Both Watches and made my way to the heads in high spirits. As usual, I was greeted by the usual merry throng of sailors who were settling themselves down in the traps ready for their morning gossip, fag or whatever.

'Morning, lads, you'll have to be quick today, 'cos 'Buffer' says that 'Jimmy' wants me to shut shop for a little while. It's so's I can have a good clean up without you lot here'. I'd lied happily on the Buffer's behalf.

Having put up my notice, which said, in bright red capital letters, 'SHUT FOR CLEANING', I locked the door from inside and told them to 'hurry up'. I let them out moaning in ones and twos, until they'd all gone and the ship's company heads were in my sole possession. Then, I set to. An hour later, after a number of unsuccessful cries of distress from the other side of the locked door of 'Come on, Will', let us in, mate. I'm dying to go!', I stood back and surveyed my handiwork. Seven out of the ten traps were roped off and firmly shut. On each of the doors I had placed a cardboard notice which read 'BEWARE, cleaning ACID on seats!' Of the three 'stand-up' urinals, two were closed off and also had signs saying 'Neat ACID, Beware splashes!' I then opened up for business.

I knew that I had to gauge the timing of my total plan with care. Nothing too outrageous or sudden. It would have to be a cleverly timed campaign; a sort of creeping paralysis which 'snuck' up on them as the days went by. They should be given to believe that my best endeavours were directed toward their comfort and welfare; I wanted them to feel that it was an honour and a privilege to enter my domain and that indeed they were lucky to get in at all. But this would take time.

As the days passed, they gradually came to accept that in order to 'go', one had to queue outside in the passageway, each waiting his turn until one of the three traps or the single urinal became vacant. No smoking was allowed in the heads, owing to a sign which declared, 'Inflammable Cleaning Materials in Use!' In addition I gradually increased the hours in the day when the heads were totally out of bounds owing to 'Intensive Cleaning'. Initially it was for one hour a day, but by day seven it was up to four hours.

It was my policy that at least seven out of ten traps were permanently coated in acid. One particularly cocky sailor, who said that I was 'talking bollocks . . . there ain't no acid,' had jumped nimbly over the rope into the trap and sat down. His scream was apparently heard in the galley and on the upper deck. Thereafter they would even double-check the three authorised traps. That was the first and last time that my word was doubted.

But they couldn't fault me. I was always polite and solicitous and made sure that I continued to give them the impression that I was working in their best interests. The day would come when they would crap in total luxury; and then they'd thank me.

The refurbishment and major refit of the ship's company heads had by now become the all-consuming topic of conversation throughout the messdecks. They were, much to my surprise, largely learning to live without it during the day. Those that didn't make it during working hours either used the Petty Officers' heads or waited until 1630, when I 'knocked' off. Nevertheless, I did have some misgivings. It meant that some sailors had to adjust a lifetime habit, by performing at the end of the day rather than the beginning.

The day of reckoning drew nigh and the evening before I had worked right through until 0100, with only a short break for supper. The 'buzz' had spread throughout the ship.

'You'd better 'ave a crap before 0800, 'cos it's Will's big day. They'll be shut all mornin.' And so they were.

By 1100, when Rounds were due to start, everything gleamed and sparkled: the floor shone, the enamelled paintwork looked like the Royal Yacht's ship side; the toilet bowls glistened, the brass porthole 'scuttles' shone like gold and all the toilet rolls (each individual sheet marked 'Government Property') were brand new. The air was sweet to the nose and the whole place had taken on the appearance of a lavatorial palace; it had never seen better days.

Ship's Rounds started up forward, and thirty minutes later I could hear the shrill whistle of the Coxswain's bosun's call as the First Lieutenant and his entourage approached. I was smartly dressed in a freshly pressed shirt, put on only when I'd finished cleaning; my shoes were polished and I was wearing my best 'divisions' hat. I'd even used a dab of aftershave, having also liberally sprinkled it around the head's beforehand. Now I was suffering butterflies in my stomach as my destiny approached. Would I pull it off?

Bartosik entered and immediately came to a halt. As always, he was immaculate and wearing the white gloves he wore for Rounds, not for medical reasons. He stood quite still by the entrance, taking it in with his hawk-like eyes and forming an overall impression. His face was inscrutable and he said not a word. It was with relief that I saw his face slowly break into a beaming smile. He looked directly at me. He was positively oozing goodwill from every Polish pore as he held up both hands in an expression of delight.

'Villis, this is now the vunderful heads that you haf' done!' he said as he commenced his tour of inspection.

The First Lieutenant inspected every trap and every urinal, one by one. His head lowered into the depths of the lavatory bowls, and at each and every one he exclaimed exultantly,

'Vunderful. I see my face!'

The entourage, including the Messdecks' Officer, the Coxswain, the 'Buffer' and other hangers-on, followed him round the compartments like members of the cast of HMS *Pinafore*, keeping at a respectful distance and nodding in agreement every time that Bartosik exclaimed aloud in admiration. When he had come to the end of his inspection, still smiling, he addressed me personally with a final remark.

'Villis, so clean, you vill eat your dinner off the floor!'

The Coxswain stiffened, looked at me, and then back to Bartosik in search of confirmation. For one awful moment I thought that the Coxswain would repeat the order.

' . . . Eat your dinner off the floor.'

But happily, the Coxswain read the First Lieutenant's smile correctly and the danger was over.

On the Monday I said farewell to my 'palace' and joined the motor cutter's crew as Bowman for a spell. Meanwhile, good old 'Joseph'! He'd honoured our deal.

A New Suit

We steamed through the Sea of Marmara and entered the waters of Istanbul. The Flagship opened fire: puffs of white smoke billowed in time to the GI's call.

'If I wasn't a gunner I wouldn't be here'.

Bang! Then followed by another . . . and another, until the salute was done. The shore battery, impatient to reply, made its presence known; high on the fort a smoke ring bloomed – a pause – a bang, repeated, as each answering gun echoed the previous one across the flat blue sea.

In the early 1950's the Royal Navy still boasted a Mediterranean Fleet. It made a grand sight entering harbour in line ahead and in two straight columns. We young sailors would be 'fallen in' on the upper deck in our gleaming white suits, the guards and bands would be paraded, the Royal Marines splendid in their pith helmets, the multi-coloured flag pendants flying at the yard and the Sunday white ensigns streaming full at our sterns. For our backdrop, the ancient city of Constantinople lay bathed in the early morning sun. We steamed slowly towards our appointed anchorages to the barely audible 'Hearts of Oak' played in the flagship by the Royal Marine Band.

This was what the Royal Navy was all about, and one of the reasons we had joined. The excitement, the pomp and the circumstance, the romance; all so very different from the drab post-war circumstances which prevailed at home.

But it is at just such emotional, dreamlike moments that the harsher realities of life often have a nasty habit of bringing one back to reality. Not that I could say that Joseph Bartosik always dealt in realities. They were more like incredible surprises.

All First Lieutenants worth their salt, are fanatical about their ship's appearance. Our First Lieutenant was worth his salt. No sooner had we entered any harbour than he wanted a 'touching up' party to go over the side. If necessary, he would have us painting in the rain, blowing a gale and even at night – especially if he knew that a senior officer would be passing our ship early next morning. But his all-time best occurred while we were still glowing with reflective pride, having just anchored off Istanbul.

No sooner had the Fleet anchored and squared off the upper deck, the boats, booms and ladders, than Bartosik wanted one paint stage over the side. The Admiral in charge, however, had signalled that the rig on the upper deck was to be 'Number 6's until such time as the 1200 salute – for a Turkish dignitary – had been fired.

Nobby and I were on the messdeck, having changed out of our No 6s, when the Buffer arrived at the door.

'Sorry about this lads,' said the Buffer with an apologetic expression, addressing Nobby and me.

'You'll 'ave to get *dressed* into yer whites,' he continued, while taking his cap off and uncomfortably scratching his bald head.

'I needs a couple of hands over the side now, 'cos Jimmy wants the rust marks covered straight away.'

We both looked at the Buffer as if he were mad and then laughed.

'Pull the other one, Buffer,' said Nobby, 'We'll be up in our overalls as quick as we can.'

'Fraid not. Rig of the day's No 6s . . . and that's what he

wants,' said the Buffer grimly, his hands in the air and his head hung low in resignation.

'Jimmy told me, if you spoil yer suits you can 'ave another one . . . free issue like. But only if yer gets paint on 'em,' said the Buffer in an incredulous but conciliatory tone.

Nobby was always quick to spot the opportunities in the worst of situations. To my amazement he smiled at Buffer.

'That's all right Buffer, someone's got to do it. Might as well be Will, and me.' Nobby gave me a warning look which said 'Keep yer mouth shut, Will.' Then I knew he was up to something.

We were over the side for an hour. The Buffer came up forward and peered down over the flare, checking that the job was in hand, and then left us to get on with it. By the time we had finished we were splattered in grey paint, and that included our caps. The Buffer said 'Cor blimey' and sympathised when Nobby told him the pot had slipped out of his hands. Nevertheless, he praised us for being 'good lads' and sent us away below to shower and get a cup of tea, also adding that he wouldn't be needing us for the rest of the day.

'You've done yer whack and I'll see to it you'll get new suits,' he said grandly. And later the First Lieutenant kept his word and agreed.

What neither Buffer nor Joseph knew was that Nobby and I had managed to dress ourselves in No 6s with the help of our messmates, using worn out and torn articles of clothing which were good for nothing but rags. We had even been able to find a couple of battered caps and two pairs of near sole-less shoes to wear. The tricky part of this operation had been to get up on to the upper deck and over the side before the Buffer had had time to see us dressed like scarecrows. It happened that our luck was in. Once over the side and hidden from view, we had been able to smother ourselves in paint and hide our scarecrow appearance.

Later, we were issued with an entire new outfit, and Nobby even claimed for a watchstrap and pair of underpants, saying that the latter were ripped while climbing up the stage rope.

That evening Nobby and I went ashore and had a thoroughly rotten time trying to find a place where we could get 'big eats', comprising sausage, eggs, chips and tomatoes. It was even worse than our attempt in Athens. At least there, we had ended up with two boiled eggs on a plate, followed by a packet of crisps on another plate, followed by two raw tomatoes on yet another plate. They hadn't been able to hack the sausages.

After our abortive meal, Nobby had joined a queue of Turks, thinking it was for a belly-dancer show, but it turned out that they were patiently waiting their turn to mount two overworked prostitutes. We shoved off fast. Then we listened to the wailing of Turkish music in a seedy bar while we drank some foul-tasting beer, followed by black treacle coffee, and finally we caught the 2100 boat back to the ship. Ah well, you can't win them all.

Chapter 7

Colourful Characters

O nce more we ploughed our way back from the Eastern Mediterranean towards our home port for a period of ship maintenance and repair. We called in at Crete, however, and visited Suda Bay for several days so that the ship's company could enjoy swimming from the deserted beaches and climbing the hills before settling down to mundane maintenance in Malta.

Towards the top end of the bay lay the forlorn rusting wrecks of naval ships sunk during the battle of Crete. Their torn and battle scarred remains projected clear of the water and rested there in sombre silence as monuments to the dead. We rowed our whaler in silent tribute close to those tortured rust-brown sides. No wise-cracks, no jokes, as we pulled slowly away in silence and awe, but for the measured dipping of our oars as each of us was lost in thought at the hell they had suffered not so many years ago.

Later that day the breeze increased and settled into a steady force 4 – just right for a cracking sail.

'Right lads, lets 'ave all yer old clobber in the sack. We'll barter these old clothes fer 'nosh' – chickens, fruit and the like,' said Dowson, who was a real tough nut. He had decided that we would sail the whaler up the deserted bay to the small fishing village in the distance.

Dowson, an ex-London barrow boy, did the bartering with

the 'natives' – a friendly bunch of gnarled fishermen with their black-shawled wives and chattering children, who in no time were running around laughing gleefully wearing sailors' battered caps and oversized boots. They waved us goodbye as we sailed away laden with scrawny chickens, fresh eggs and fruit, looking forward to 'big eats' for supper.

Once more back in Malta we settled down to ships' chores and each day we sought diversions to stem the tide of boredom. We were forever chipping decks and screens to fight the onset of rust, applying red lead, yellow chromate and grey paint, scrubbing, sweeping and washing down. But in amongst the humdrum activities there were frequent sparks of humour, which always occur when two or more jolly jacks are brought together. Life was never dull for long among such a rich, diversified and colourful gathering of sailors.

Horace, for instance, was an ex-*Ganges* boy who persistently misunderstood. Horace wasn't his real name; he had been nicknamed by some messdeck wit early on in the commission. He was a slow-speaking and thoughtful lad. Horace deliberated over the most trifling of matters. His movements were slow, and it would take him several minutes to decide which boot to put on first. If you asked him a question, he would consider his answer. Horace would sometimes turn up for the Middle Watch dressed in oilskins to meet the gale only to discover the weather was fine and his Watch wasn't due until the morning.

The jokers caught him twice with the time-honoured leg pulls. He went to the paint shop to fill the emergency navigation lights with red and green oil, red for the port light and green for the starboard. Then he thought he was colour blind, because he couldn't see the difference.

When he said that he wanted to smoke a pipe, they sent him

to the Coxswain's office to apply for a 'pipe' licence. He obediently called at the sickbay for a medical, and afterwards applied to the Chief Stoker for a fire-fighting test – lest his pipe flare up and get out of hand. He filled in a questionnaire drawn up by the lads. Finally, he attended First Lieutenant's Requestmen for permission to smoke. Horace went innocently through the charade, and no one ever let on. I've often wondered, though, whether the joke was not on us and that Horace was merely keeping us amused.

He found it difficult to get into his hammock at night. He would do little practice jumps while hanging from the hammock bar before taking the leap; and sometimes would sail over the top, missing his hammock altogether. And when the sea was rough and the ship was rolling, he was in real trouble. One night he tried, and shot over the top on the down-roll, bouncing off the fellow in the next hammock before hitting the deck.

Several days later his back was still hurting from the fall. Horace had already been to see the sick berth attendant (SBA), who had given him some ointment and told him to 'Come and see the squadron Doc when we get into harbour.'

He did so and told him, 'I gotta sore back when I got in me 'mick, and it hurts . . . just about here.'

The doctor examined the bruises as Horace lay on the table, then said with mock severity, 'You know what caused this?'

Horace looked up at the doctor inquiringly

'You jumped into your hammock with alacrity, didn't you?' said the doctor severely, and with a straight face.

Horace, lying prone on his stomach, swivelled his head at the doctor, giving a look both indignant and hurt.

'I never got in me 'ammock with no one. I hate that sort of thing.'

The doctor explained what he had meant, but Horace had

152

misunderstood and left in a huff.

By no means were the colourful characters confined to the lower deck. There were still plenty of eccentric naval officers in being during those days and the stifling desire for total conformity had not yet taken its toll of individuality.

Captain Myers was Captain (SM), and was in charge of all the submarines in Malta. He was Captain of the submarine depot ship, HMS *Forth*, which was mostly berthed in Msida Creek. She was a repair and support ship for the submarines and they berthed alongside her. Directly opposite was Whitehall Mansions, which was the Wrens' Quarters in Malta.

The submariners had often used their initiative, with the help of powerful periscopes, to watch the girls across the Creek getting ready for bed. The Wrens were aware of this, and most of them took precautions to close the curtains, but some enjoyed titillating the sailors and would give them a thrill from time to time. Once this came to the attention of the 'Queen Bee' – the Senior Wren Officer, the game became more difficult. She complained. Thereafter, all periscopes had to be blindfolded so that the girls could dance naked in peace. The show, however, wasn't completely stopped because sometimes the blindfolds were removed – and the amateur strippers would occasionally perform by appointment.

'Crap' Myers was a very experienced submariner, and had been awarded the VC during the Second World War. He was variously described as an eccentric, a dangerous nutter, and a very hard man. Without doubt he had a great sense of humour – so long as you were not the butt of it – and he was well liked by his men and no one could question his courage. Captain Myers was one of those men who invariably looked and growled like a bear. His language seldom left much to the imagination.

All those who served under him, including his wife, could expect to be bitten and mauled whenever he was thwarted or displeased. Many a sailor trembled in his presence at the defaulters' table, but if the misdemeanour tickled his fancy, he might let the man off with a warning. One thing was for certain: you could never be sure what he would do or how he would react.

It was by chance that I came into contact with him. I met a certain pretty teenage girl at the Under Twenty Club one evening. She told me that she was a nanny and worked for a naval Captain's family somewhere in Birkikara. After I had known her for several weeks, she invited me to come to supper one Saturday evening. The Captain and his wife would be going out to dinner and we would be on our own, baby-sitting. This struck me as being a wonderful opportunity to try to get to know her better. It meant, however, that I would have to go in uniform, because it was all too difficult to go to the Under Twenty Club to change, then go all the way back to Birkikara.

I bought a small bunch of flowers on Sliema front, then boarded the gear-groaning bus for Birkikara and lust. The old Bedford buses were an educational experience to ride. Each had its own shrine above the driver's head and the Maltese passengers would gaze at it frequently, silently praying for a safe and uneventful journey. After each bus stop, and as the driver engaged his first gear, many would cross themselves and mutter brief incantations as the bus pulled away on its next leg of the course. Whenever a priest boarded the bus, devoted old ladies, dressed in black shawls, would rise to offer their seats to him. Quite often these spiritual gentlemen were both young and fat. They would take the nearest seat offered and sit down without a qualm, possibly rewarding the donor with a perfunctory sign of the cross. There was one occasion when I had stood up for an old lady and she had promptly offered the vacated seat to the priest. I wasn't having that, so I sat down again before he could leap in, but the old lady continued to refuse to sit in it while the priest was standing.

The house wasn't difficult to find. It was several miles out into the scorched countryside, built directly on the side of the narrow road, and only separated from it by three steps leading up to the front door. The high garden walls abutted on to the house, giving complete privacy both to the house itself and to the grounds inside; everything was built in cream-coloured Maltese stone and it looked as strong as a fort.

I had been told to arrive at 7pm, for she said that Myers and his wife would have left for their dinner party by then. Having banged the large knocker, I waited expectantly – clutching my flowers and idly dreaming expectant thoughts.

A growling bear of a man half-opened it.

'What the fuck do you want?' he said culturedly, eyeing me suspiciously between the gap.

He was dressed in his white uniform, shorts, socks, white shoes and shirt. His shoulder straps had four gold rings and he was clearly the Captain.

'I'm sorry, sir, have I the right house?' I asked stupidly, stalling for time and wondering what to say.

'Who sent you, and what are you after?' he growled at me, pawing the door impatiently.

I sighed with relief as I saw her approaching through the hallway behind him.

'Captain, this is Hugh Willis . . . I told you . . . I invited him to supper,' she called and smiled reassuringly at me as I stood frozen in the doorway, flowers at the 'shoulder'.

'Oh it's Fanny you're after!' he grunted, 'you'd better come in.' And he turned on his heel and marched off down the passage.

'I'm terribly sorry,' she said, 'but their dinner party's off. He

155

had to work late . . . some crisis or other . . . and his wife's hopping mad.'

My designs on seduction had fled from my mind. It was now a matter of survival under the scrutiny of this bear of a four-ringed Captain. I had a beer before dinner which I hardly dared sip, while being cross-examined by Captain Myers. His wife was charming and worked hard to draw his fire, knowing that I was now the victim of his pent-up anger. But after a time we sat down to dinner and the wine mellowed his mood. He then became interesting and chatty and told amusing stories about naval life in general. By the end of the evening I was sorry to leave, even though my style had been unexpectedly cramped.

My next visit to Birkikara was under much less stress. Neither the Captain nor his wife were present and I enjoyed the novelty of baby-sitting without the supervision of a senior naval officer. Sadly, my new-found girl friend had to return to England shortly thereafter because her mother was ill.

Lieutenant Cosby was a confident junior officer. He was a most competent aviator, who flew Sea Furies and he had been sent to HMS *Loch Scavaig* to acquire his bridge watchkeeping certificate. Aviators referred to seaman officers as 'fish-heads', but had to learn the seamen's nautical 'tricks' to further their own future careers. This was common practice, since when the 'flyboys' aviation days were over, they would often return to the fleet and continue their careers at sea to achieve command of ships.

Cosby was employed on the bridge as a second officer of the watch and also in carrying out general seamanship evolutions. Cosby's main problem was that he didn't do a lot of listening. For each of these evolutions there was always an experienced seaman present. Unfortunately Cosby's logic told him that since he was an officer, he would naturally know what to do, because *he* was in charge. One such occasion occurred when we were moored at the head of the Grand Canal in Venice.

'Cosby, I vish that you vould hoist the motor cutter by the fo'c'sle vindlass and inform me ven this is so,' said our Polish First Lieutenant.

'Very good, Sir. No problem . . . I'm on my way.'

We duly rigged the boat's falls through the various deck blocks and took three turns round the windlass on the fo'c'sle in readiness to hoist.

Cosby then proceeded to give all the appropriate commands until the motor cutter had been hoisted to the davits' heads, when he cried out: 'High enough.'

So far, so good. It is, however, at this moment that the boat's crew secures the boat with life-lines so that the weight is transferred from the windlass to the davit head. Only then can the order, 'Light to, off turns!' be given.

Cosby thought otherwise and took a short cut. The boat petty officer turned white and screamed, 'No Sir . . . ' and the intrepid aviator, bursting with confidence, commanded 'Off turns I said . . . '

At this point the sailors backing up the boat's falls promptly dropped them to the deck.

Gravity had the last word. The falls paid out, screaming through the blocks, and two tons of motor cutter hit the heavily polluted waters of the Grand Canal with an almighty splash. The coxswain and bowman had somehow managed to jump clear on the way down, and the stoker miraculously appeared from underneath the shattered remains of the boat's canopy.

To add further to the confusion, the Chief Bosun's Mate, a balding sparrow of a man, who enjoyed a great sense of drama, cried out from the upper deck.

'Hang on . . . I'm on my way!' and dived head first into the murky waters.

The sense of occasion had got the better of the Bosun, because he had somehow forgotten that he was a poor swimmer. It seemed that he might have remembered on the way down, because by the time he was halfway to the water, he changed shape and resembled a twittering, crumpled ball of feathers as he hit the water.

The First Lieutenant had heard the crash and appeared on the upper deck just in time to see the boat's crew rescue the Chief Bosun's Mate who was coughing up neat canal water and being dragged to the after ladder. All of them had to be given anti-biotics immediately, the shattered boat had to be recovered (and subsequently repaired) and a slightly less confident Cosby was told that his leave was stopped for a month.

Within a week, however, Cosby's confidence had returned with renewed vigour. Apparently the motor cutter incident had been a misunderstanding. He had really meant: 'Off turns . . . *when* I give the signal.' And we hadn't waited for him to finish his sentence.

He was not only a confident officer, he was also very persuasive. Cosby convinced the First Lieutenant that he should be given a chance to prove his metal as cable officer on the fo'c'sle. Two weeks later he took up his position forward for our entry into Sliema Creek. We would be securing between two buoys, head and stern.

This entailed disconnecting the anchor cable from the starboard anchor as a bridle for the buoy. The port anchor was left ready for letting go in an emergency. Thus the starboard anchor now had no cable and was held in position only by a large bottle screw slip.

Getting between the buoys was a tricky manoeuvre, made

worse on the day by the strong wind, and the ship began to drift on to the adjacent shore. But never mind! Cosby was to hand, looking even more confident than ever. He knew that he could save the day by letting go an anchor.

The ship continued to drift towards the shore and the bridge gave the order to 'let go' the anchor. Cosby seized the heavy sledgehammer and removed the pin from the slip in a trice; he then gave a mighty blow to release the anchor and save the ship from disaster.

It was unfortunate that he had chosen the starboard anchor. It shot out from its hawse-pipe and splashed cable-less into the water. But in his enthusiasm he hadn't noticed that the anchor wasn't attached to anything because he was looking up at the bridge with a 'didn't I do well' smile on his face.

'Starboard anchor gone, sir,' he shouted proudly between cupped hands.

And so it had.

The Last-Minute Touch Up

Our Captain was also a colourful character. *Loch Scavaig* had become due for its annual harbour inspection, which was to be carried out by the Flag Officer, Flotillas. We endured weeks of preparation and the day finally arrived. The Admiral was due alongside in his barge at 0900, and would be accorded full ceremonial. The ship's company was fallen in on the upper deck and the guard paraded on the quarterdeck. I was proudly armed with my bosun's call, and was one of the selected piping party.

Last-minute preparations and final touches were still taking place ten minutes before the barge was due to arrive. With minutes to go, everyone was there except the Captain, who was waiting in his cabin for the Admiral's approach to be reported.

'Villis, go quickly . . . Tell the Captain, the Admiral's barge is now in sight,' said Bartosik.

When I got to his door, I knocked and looked inside. He was struggling to do up his tunic collar, straining to bring the metal clips together, but being thwarted by the size of his large neck.

'First Lieutenant's respects, sir. Admiral's barge is approaching,' I said dutifully.

'Willis, never mind that, come quickly . . . Help me do this up,' he gurgled, his face getting redder with every tug.

He stood with his head leaning back as I grappled with both ends of his collar around his throat. Bungy William's face was now crimson, and it must have seemed – had there been an onlooker – that I was strangling my own Captain. Somehow, I managed to engage the clips and Bungy choked his way past me, gasping for air and whispering 'the Admiral's coming!' He sounded as if his throat had been cut.

With the Captain in the lead, we galloped down the starboard side towards the quarterdeck, spying the Admiral's barge on the beam. We had only one more obstacle to overcome before reaching the quarterdeck. The after ladder rose on to our deck through a cutaway section in the quarterdeck awning, and Bungy approached this at speed.

Too late, he saw the forgotten pot of silverine paint – used for a last-minute touch-up – and planted his left foot right in the middle. He fought bravely to keep his balance, but fate and gravity were against him. The Captain, arms outstretched above his head like a drowning man, lingered for a moment, then fell headlong on to the quarterdeck awning. He was a heavy man and it bulged and shook like a trampoline as he bobbed about on it, paint pot still stuck to his foot. I watched him elegantly kick it free and saw it arch over the side to splash alongside. I took his hand and hauled him clear.

The Captain's timing was immaculate. He took up position facing the top of the gangway just as the Admiral was piped on board. His left shoe and trouser leg, however, were gleaming with silver paint and his footprints marked the green-painted quarterdeck, indicating the route that the Admiral would take.

It wasn't clear whether the Flag Officer, Flotillas was struggling not to laugh or was truly concerned.

'Williams, my dear fellow . . . What bad luck. Last minute touch-up?' said the Admiral with a suspicion of a smile.

Funnily enough, we had a good inspection after the Captain had changed and calmed down. There were those cynics on our messdeck who had a theory.

'The Skipper done it on purpose – to take the Admiral's eye off the ball.'

The First Lieutenant's inquisition at the end of the day was quite another matter, and I'm sure that Joseph thought that 'Villis' was in some way responsible.

Self Improvement

I had been conscious of my almost non-existent academic qualifications ever since I had failed to be accepted into both Sir John Cass and the Merchant Tailors' schools. *Ganges* had further emphasised my shortcomings when I had failed to join the stream of advance class boys (AC), and, due to my poor maths, had been classed as a 'hewer of wood and a drawer of water'. Nevertheless, I had passed the educational examination for Leading Seaman at *Ganges*, and academically, this would also hold good for Petty Officer. It didn't amount to much though, and merely meant that I could write plain English and had the ability to do simple mathematics.

Woolly West was the one who inspired me to start doing

something about my lack of qualifications. He had started to study for the higher educational test (HET) in his spare time. He having been an AC boy at *Ganges*, had goaded me by saying that I was too idle to bother. That did it. So I chose to do English, history and navigation. I knew that I wouldn't have a hope in hell of passing mathematics or mechanics, whereas I knew that I could study navigation on board.

The educational qualification required for an officer was to pass four set subjects in one sitting, and these were: mathematics and mechanics, geography, history and English. This was my ultimate goal, but I knew that this would not be possible until I was sent to school for a full-time course. Bartosik didn't have that in mind.

Anyway, after three months of studying, we took our examinations, and two months later we were informed that we had both passed our set subjects. Woolly had got his mathematics and English, which qualified him academically for warrant officer and the special duties list. I was cock-a-hoop with my passes, and it gave me the confidence to start thinking about my future. Maybe I wasn't as thick as I thought I was; maybe one day I might become an officer. Joseph Bartosik didn't think so.

'Villis, you vill never become the officer,' he said to me one day at his 'request' table, I having just requested to go ashore on a month's educational coaching course. He did, however, reluctantly allow me to go on it prior to the next HET examinations. The naval schoolmasters did their utmost to help, but a month wasn't long enough. I failed hopelessly at maths and mechanics but I did pass English and history and achieved a first class pass in pilotage and navigation. To be fair to Bartosik, he did make one observation.

'Villis, you never fail to give me the big surprise.' Twelve years later, however, under very different circumstances, I sat opposite

Captain Bartosik, who was the President of the Board and awaited his verdict yet again.

Private Moments

I had met Charles and David at the Under Twenty Club. They both served in HMS *Liverpool,* a Town Class cruiser, and the three of us often went around together when our ships were in Malta. One evening over a beer or two in the club, they told me the following story about one of their more colourful shipmates. I had already met this character at the club, and wondered at his eccentric dress and manners.

He was the sort of chap who always wore a cravat with an open neck shirt when in plain clothes. He preferred to walk with a stick – which had at first caused him problems when going ashore in uniform, though now he left it ready for use in the club. He seldom smoked, but when he did he would use a cigarette holder. It was made in two parts and he screwed it together with a flourish, then tapped the cigarette on the table before inserting it into the holder. His manners were impeccable and he always shook hands.

I can't remember his name, but it was something like Aubrey Featherston de Witt; he was an ordinary seaman doing his national service. De Witt was also born of wealthy parents and his background was unimpeachable. Furthermore, he had been educated privately and bore all the hallmarks of an upper middle-class education. He was, however, ingenuous beyond belief and oblivious to the realities of his new-found environment. Naval connections in high places, a horror of joining the Army, and good fortune had decreed that he should serve his two years in the Royal Navy.

Inevitably he became an easy target among his more worldly-wise messmates. They pulled his leg unmercifully; but somehow, they never seemed to be able to penetrate the illusory world in which he lived. They filled his hammock with potatoes, waiting with glee to watch him unlash it before climbing in; but when he discovered what they had done, he was amused.

'I say, chaps, you've made me a potato pie bed.'

Then, without further ado, he emptied the potatoes all over the deck, and swung into his hammock without another word. The Leading Hand of the mess made the culprits clear up, while Aubrey watched disinterestedly from the comfort of his hammock.

Most of the jokes that were supposedly at his expense continued to backfire among the perpetrators. One day they poured some oil into his boots and then waited to watch the fun. He put on his left boot and feeling the sticky oil, promptly pulled it off and poured the residue on to the deck. In keeping with the spirit of the jape, he then plonked his right foot in a puddle of oil, stirred it around, and marched up and down crying loudly.

'Me Man Friday with big left foot'.

It took the pranksters an hour to clean off the footprints, and later they were made to pay for Aubrey's new socks and boots, which amused him no end. Thus thwarted, his tormentors decided to adopt a new tack. They knew that Aubrey took offence whenever they used obscene language, particularly so when it was directed at him. They also knew that Aubrey's sensibilities were deeply shocked by the lack of privacy in the adjacent heads. Sitting about his business in midriff-high trap, with messmates on either hand making ribald comments, was not Aubrey's idea of a secluded convenience for his private moments. Much to his delight, he had discovered a small heads up forward which had head-high cubicles and protected him from prying eyes. Since this discovery, he had chosen to make the long trek forward for his daily 'george'.

They noticed that Aubrey was now only to be seen in their heads for an occasional pee. Speculation had it that he was either heavily constipated or that he was 'crapping' during the Middle Watch. It wasn't long before someone tailed him to his morning sanctuary and the new plot had been formulated.

They selected a witty Irishman to compose the words. He used a marlin spike to etch a short ditty about Featherston de Witt into the layers of paint on the bulkhead at the end cubicle – Aubrey's favourite in the forward heads – and then made the words stand out with a black pen.

The following morning all eyes were on Aubrey as he departed for his morning ritual. But that was the last they saw of him for several hours. He didn't return to the mess and wasn't to be seen at both Watches of the Hands. It was not until dinnertime that the full story of Aubrey's tangle with the captain of the forward heads became known.

Apparently the plot had gone like a dream – initially, that is. He had gone to the end cubicle as planned, but after a short pause had shot out through the door in a hurry. It seems that he had rushed to the fo'c'sle locker and demanded the loan of a chipping hammer. The lockerman described Aubrey as being very agitated and said that he had refused to tell him what he wanted it for.

The next part of the story was related by the indignant captain of the forward heads. Sharky was not only proud of his heads but enjoyed his 'quiet number' up forward. So far as he was concerned, 'No bastard was going to spoil it either.' It seems that the first he knew about it was as he was approaching the heads. He heard the hammer banging away 'like some maniac had gone mad inside.' The banging came from the forward cubicle, which was locked. Sharky had evidently gone spare and hollered,

'What the bloody hell's goin' on? Stop that, you bastard, and open up'. But the hammering had continued and no one had replied.

Then Sharky lay on the floor and looked underneath the door. 'The bleeder was chipping my bulkhead as though there were no tomorrow. I yelled at 'im ter stop. But all he said was 'I'm sorry, old chap, but I really must get this filf cleaned off first,' and carried on bangin'. Apparently the gap was too small for Sharky to crawl under, and 'Anyway, I weren't goin' in wiv a madman, was I?' concluded Sharky defensively.

The Messdeck Petty Officer was called and he ordered Featherston de Witt to open up immediately or else. The hammering continued briefly and then the lock was undone and Aubrey emerged smiling, chipping hammer in hand. He refused to tell the Petty Officer anything except that he had just removed some filthy graffiti. When they looked inside the cubicle, they saw that he had chipped an area 6 inches square down to the metal. He was relieved of his offensive weapon and marched aft to the quarterdeck.

Aubrey was brought before the Officer of the Day. He was charged with 'Wilful damage, conduct prejudicial to good order and naval discipline,' and because Aubrey refused to reveal why he had done it, was given Commander's Report.

The subsequent proceedings and events which took place filtered down to the messdeck during the following days. Aubrey had been arraigned in front of the Commander, but still refused to explain. Only when the Commander pressured him further, did Aubrey say that he would tell the Commander, but only in private. This was very irregular but I suspect that the Commander's curiosity got the better of him. The Divisional

Officer and the Master at Arms were invited to withdraw, and Aubrey bared his soul.

The 'defaulters' table' was reconvened and the Commander re-considered the merits of the case.

'While I sympathise with your situation, de Witt, I can't have you take the law into your own hands. Say every one did what you did?' said the Commander, probably visualising hundreds of sailors hammering his heads to bits.

'One day's stoppage of leave,' said the Commander and before the Master at Arms could repeat the sentence, Aubrey piped up:

'I'm awfully sorry, sir, but that won't be convenient tonight, I'm dining with Uncle.' The collective look of incomprehension around the defaulters' table, was complete.

'What uncle?' asked the Commander in amazement.

'The Flag Officer, Flotillas, sir. I shall of course, be delighted to do my punishment tomorrow, or whenever it is convenient to yourself,' said Aubrey reasonably, and with deference.

Aubrey went to dinner with his uncle that night. Later he related the incident in the club. He was frightfully matter of fact and thought that '*Liverpool*'s Commander's an absolutely spiffing chap.' He wouldn't, however, say what was written on the bulkhead, other than to remark that 'It was really quite rude'.

By then, the verse had been distributed round the ship, and from memory went something like this:

> Poor Featherstone de Witt
> Can't have a shit
> Till his bum is quite hidden
> In his own private midden

Royalty in the Creek

There was a time, for a number of weeks when we saw quite a lot of Royalty. Princess Elizabeth and Princess Margaret were on holiday in Malta. Philip was Captain of HMS *Magpie,* and quite often, after completing daily exercises off Malta, we would find ourselves berthed astern of *Magpie*. This gave us a grandstand view of the royal visits.

On completion of the daily exercises at sea, the ships would enter harbour one after another. The Princesses would be waiting in the Commander-in-Chief's green barge for the *Magpie* to make her sternboard to her berth. Once *Magpie* was secured, they would go aboard and no doubt enjoy a gin and tonic or two in the wardroom. They must have been very happy carefree days for Elizabeth since she was usually laughing with her husband and her sister. Anyway, after a few days, we became quite blasé about our tenuous connection with the King's daughters, and even our First Lieutenant stopped camping on the quarterdeck lest the green barge should be seen in the distance. The messdeck attitude towards the Royal family was warm and friendly. There were no axes to grind or bitter resentments; the King was an integral part of our daily lives, if only from the frequent reminder that we were ruled, punished and guided by King's Regulations and Admiralty Instructions.

Though times were harder, the attitudes of the British people were so much softer then. They didn't have to suffer the loud-mouthed anger of minorities and anti-monarchist vitriol which is nowadays stuffed down our throats. There was more spontaneous acceptance among our people. Envy and 'entitlement to so-called rights' didn't figure as they do today.

Our only other contact with Royalty occurred when Lord Louis Mountbatten became the Commander-in-Chief of the

Mediterranean Fleet. So much has been written about him –
including the good and the not so good – that there can be little
more to contribute other than a sailor's fleeting eye-view.

On taking up his new command, he visited every ship in the
Fleet. Our turn came on a hot summer's day while we lay at our
berth in Sliema Creek. He hadn't come to inspect the ship; he
had come to talk to the ship's company. He made it clear by
signal that he wanted the minimum of ceremonial fanfare. In
other words, it was to be an informal visit. The fact is, however,
that no ship's Captain can comprehend an informal visit by his
Commander-in-Chief. Bartosik was nonplussed and didn't
approve.

Mountbatten was piped aboard, shook hands with the
Captain, and was straightway taken to Bungy's cabin while the
ship's company was stood at ease to await his return.

I stood there, reflecting that on the morrow I was to take part
in the finals of the Mediterranean Fleet sports day. I had reached
the finals for the one hundred and twenty yard hurdles, and I
was champing at the bit to get ashore so as to do my last training
run.

Five minutes later we heard the 'still' which presaged his return
to the quarterdeck. He strode into the middle of the neatly lined
sailors and mounted the white, scrubbed teak grating. He was
dressed in bush jacket and trousers, his chest covered with
ribbons, sparkling shoulder straps of gold and silver, and his
cap ablaze with 'scrambled egg'.

'Stand them at ease,' he ordered the First Lieutenant. Then
with outstretched arms, he beckoned us towards him.

'Gather round, I want to see your faces'.

His voice projected a magnetic presence. Confidence oozed
from him as he scanned the gathering around him and surveyed
our faces from the height of the bollard grating. His opening

question immediately commanded our full attention.

'What have you done with Screech, where is he?' he asked with a hint of a smile.

Screech was our mongrel terrier and the ship's mascot. He was a character and had a mind of his own, going ashore whenever he felt like it, and cadging a lift from the ship's dghaisaman. He possessed a fine set of sea legs in rough weather and was never sick. It was a guinea a minute to watch him go up the near vertical ladders when the ship was rolling heavily. Screech would start with a flying run on the down roll, nearly make it to the top, then back peddle almost to the bottom before catching the next down roll and going airborne as he flew clear of the hatch.

He had, of course, been confined to his hammock for the Admiral's visit.

'Go and get him,' said Mountbatten, pointing to a sailor at the back. 'I can't allow absentees, he'll want to hear what I have to say.'

Whatever tension there may have been dissolved instantly as the sailors roared with laughter and loved his common touch. He told us of his intentions and ambitions regarding the Fleet; he attended to Fleet domestic issues, addressing matters of concern, and we felt that he was taking us into his confidence in everything he said. And now and then he would add seasoning to his words.

'Oh, by the way . . . where's Frogmore? Put your hand up, Frogmore'. Somewhere in the crowd an astonished Frogmore hesitantly raised his hand.

'In future, lad, you must practice your high diving in harbour rather than at sea'. Once again we laughed and wondered at his inside knowledge. Frogmore had been balancing on the bridge wing, fiddling with a knotted halyard to pull it clear, when over he had gone into the sea. It had been a gloriously sunny, calm day, and the ship astern of us had recovered him by whaler within five minutes.

We all thoroughly enjoyed watching the look of amazement on the faces of those he picked out for comment.

'Where's Willis? Ah, there you are. Mind you win tomorrow, and don't knock down any hurdles,' he grinned.

When he had left the ship, conversation was centred entirely upon his ability to convince us that he was taking a personal interest in the day-to-day affairs of *Loch Scavaig*. There is no doubt that he made a very good impression upon the ship's company; it didn't matter that he had got his brief from the Captain while we waited on the quarterdeck. What did matter was that he had taken the trouble to have our Captain prepare a brief and had used it to such rewarding effect. The sailors thought that he was great and anyway knew nothing of the jealousies of those contemporary senior naval officers who envied his connections and his panache. He may not have been a great tactical naval commander, but he certainly knew how to capture the imagination of a ship's company.

Chapter 8

Commission's End

For a while things had been rather quiet for the Navigator and he hadn't been subjected to any manhandling by the Captain since the incident of the lost submarine. We were returning to Malta from a visit to Aqaba and Port Said, however, when he managed to bring their relationship to the boil again.

I happened to be keeping the Middle Watch in the Seaguard (the Radar Office, a little cubby-hole just forward of the funnel) and my task was to report new contacts to the O.O.W. on the bridge using the intercom. Additionally, I passed regular ranges and bearings of all contacts on my radar screen, via a sound-powered handset, to the plotter in the Operations Room. That night there wasn't much shipping in our vicinity and the Watch was going along quietly and without hassle. Shortly after 0200, when one of the lads had just brought me a welcome cup of 'kye', I spotted a faint radar echo 28 miles ahead of the ship.

This surprised me because under normal conditions our 277 radar usually picked up larger ships under 25 miles, but more often just over 20. Must be a bloody large ship I thought as I picked up the 'mike' and called the bridge.

'Bridge, Radar Office. Contact bearing 280, range 28, over.'

The O.O.W. and the Operations Room acknowledged my report without comment and I thought no more about it. After three further reports to the Operations Room, they informed the O.O.W. and me that this particular contact was stationary. I studied the contact closely and realising that it was now far larger than any ship could possibly be, I reclassified it as being land.

'Rubbish,' said the O.O.W. down the intercom. 'Are you sure that it's not a rain squall?' he asked, full of doubt, because a rain squall on a windless Mediterranean summer's night, and without movement, was pretty unlikely.

'It's land, sir, bearing 281, range 25 miles' I replied.

By the sound of his voice, the O.O.W. was now a worried man.

'We're not due to pick up Malta until the morning watch, at about 0700.'

Like all good O.O.W.s', when in doubt he called the Captain and the Navigator to explain this phenomena.

The Captain, dressed in his green pyjamas, went up the bridge ladder two rungs at a time and quizzed the nervous O.O.W. They discussed the facts as the Captain paced up and down while waiting for Ogilvy to make an appearance. He was obviously skulking in his cabin, desperately wondering how to explain that Malta had shifted itself some fifty miles to the east during the Middle Watch.

Suddenly I heard the door of my cubby-hole being unclipped as though by someone desperate to get in; as it swung open, there was the Captain, dressed in Sherwood green pyjamas, holding Ogilvy by the scruff of his – standard issue – striped pyjamas. The radar office wasn't big enough for three people – two maybe, but not three. The Captain, a man capable of making quick decisions, instantly appreciated the situation and grabbing me by the scruff of the neck with his free hand, yanked me off my chair on to the funnel deck. Meanwhile, still holding Ogilvy by his collar, he propelled him on to my now vacant seat and held him by either ear with his face hard up against the radar screen.

'Tell me, Ogilvy, how did you manage to do it? We're five bloody hours early, Ogilvy. That's fifty sodding miles at ten knots, Ogilvy. We're not due to enter harbour until 1000, Ogilvy. We've now got to skulk, like a French frigate, over the horizon for five hours.'

The Captain released his ears and stormed out of the Radar Office, leaving Ogilvy slumped in the chair. I was really sorry for him and hid behind the funnel until he had collected himself and left the office, a chastened Navigator. It's a tough old existence!

The VIPs

Three weeks later we were sitting in Malta doing nothing very much when we were detailed to sail to Athens. We were to spruce the ship and to embark some important VIPs. *Loch Scavaig* had been chosen to take the British Ambassador, his wife and a guest, Sir Malcolm Sargent, on a five-day tour of the Greek Islands.

The ship was hurriedly painted prior to our departure and we were still in a flurry of activity as Joseph Bartosik went into organisational 'over-drive'. Cabins in the officers' upper cabin 'flat' were allocated for the guests and Joseph also detailed three young sailors to be their cabin hands.

There was 'Woolly' West, that studious, smart and intelligent young sailor, who tended to know it. There was Jamey Alderson, the small, thoughtful and nervous boy, who was permanently in fear of doing or saying the wrong thing. And there was me, the often too-clever-by-half First Lieutenant's irritant.

'You vill have the great responsibility and privilege to look after our guests. I shall be votching you very carefully,' said Joseph, who always thought that working for our betters was a privilege.

'Woolly'West had been allocated the Ambassador, Sir Geoffrey Norton.

'Vest, I vish that you take very good care of the great man.'

Alderson, chosen for his nervous and harmless disposition, was told that he had been given a delicate responsibility.

' . . . Take the great care of the Lady Norton . . . Like your mother.'

I had been allocated to Sir Malcolm Sargent.

' . . . Vot is it that you know about the classical music, Villis?' he asked me with a thin smile.

But having a sketchy education, I kept my mouth shut for a change. Anyway, he didn't wait for an answer but went on to tell me that Sir Malcolm was the BBC Symphony conductor and ' . . . the gentleman who vill play the vonderful promenades . . . in London.' The three of us spent the next two days cleaning, scrubbing and painting while we were on passage to the Piraeus, the port of Athens.

We anchored off Piraeus and our motor cutter went in to fetch the distinguished guests from the jetty. We were dressed up in our best uniforms, standing by on the quarterdeck, a lowly element of the reception party. The 'Still' was piped, the Guard came to the 'present arms' and everyone saluted as the Ambassador came up over the side, followed by his wife and Sir Malcolm. They were all whisked away and we were called forward to carry their luggage up to their quarters. The Ambassador and his wife had a large suitcase apiece but Sir Malcolm had three large suitcases. This was my first indication that he was a man of sartorial splendour.

While the guests were being entertained in the Captain's cabin, we set about unpacking their belongings and stowing and hanging their clothes. I think I counted thirty shirts, six lightweight suits, dinner dress and a box of stiff wing collars,

175

several dressing gowns, numerous pairs of casual trousers and shorts, three bathing costumes, some ten pairs of shoes and two umbrellas. Additionally, he had a dressing case filled with expensive toiletries, silver-backed hair brushes and tortoise-shell combs. Sir Malcolm, I discovered, was an immaculate and very dashing conductor.

Having stowed away all his kit, I went to see how my two messmates were handling their unpacking. Woolly West had finished and was looking bored, so we went along to see how young Alderson was faring. He stood there as though hypnotised by a snake, and in the same spot we had left him some forty minutes previously. The case lay on the bunk unopened.

'What's up? Why haven't you put the clobber in the cupboards?' asked Woolly.

Alderson stood like a dormouse about to be gobbled.

'I can't,' he said, 'Look inside and see for yourselves.'

I opened the suitcase, lifted the lid and laughed with glee.

'Is that what's frightening you?' I said as I pulled out a heavily armoured set of ribbed corsets and waved them over my head.

'Thank you, boys, I think I'll take those,' said Lady Norton standing in the doorway.

'I'll finish unpacking myself.' She said this with a smile and considerable *savoir faire*, while shooing us out of her cabin.

I met Sir Malcolm later that day. He was dressing for dinner and I was returning his polished evening shoes to his cabin.

'Ah, so you're the young man who's looking after me. What's your name?' He was brushing his jet black hair, which was parted down the middle; as he spoke to me, he looked in the mirror, a brush in either hand, and swept the brushes through his hair for the entire course of the conversation. He continued this double-handed sweeping action, asking me questions about my age, where I came from and what my job was in the ship. Sir Malcolm was friendly and not the least bit patronising, and he made me feel relaxed. He was of medium height, slimly built and with a long narrow face that was sun-tanned and smiled frequently as he spoke. I liked him immediately.

During the course of the next few days I came into contact with him regularly and he was always 'chatty' and at ease.

'What's he like, Will?' asked my messmates.

'He's very pleasant . . . and friendly, and not at all snooty . . . ' I replied, not quite sure what I meant.

'He's a toff,' said Fatso, and looked at me for confirmation.

'Well, . . . I'm not quite sure what you mean . . . He is a 'toff' but not in the way that you think,' I answered.

'Is he all right?' asked George.

'Yes . . . he is,' I said with finality. And that was that for the moment.

Two days later the First Lieutenant announced that Sir Malcolm would address the ship's company on the lower deck in 2 mess during the 'dog watch' that evening.

There was a hushed response, then they all looked at me.

'I think he'll be good,' I said, knowing that they would pass judgement on my opinion later, and added: 'Honestly, he's all right.'

The First Lieutenant brought him to the mess and formally introduced him in his inimitably aristocratic Polish manner. Sir Malcolm was dressed casually – without tie – but immaculately casual, wearing a shot silk suit and an expensive cravat.

'Thank you, No 1, I think I've got them now,' he said with a smile as Bartosik reluctantly left him to the mercy of the peasants.

'I've come to talk to you about music. What a difficult thing to talk about without a gramophone or even an orchestra to support me. So instead, I think I'll tell you some funny stories . . . musical stories. By the way, this is not compulsory. Anyone who would rather do something else is welcome to go,' he said provocatively. Not a soul moved.

He stood looking at us with a confident smile and then pointed his finger at a sailor who sat quietly, legs crossed.

'What sort of music gives you pleasure?'

The sailor gawped and the others laughed.

'All right, you then,' he said, pointing at another fellow, who instantly stopped laughing and turned red.

'It's difficult isn't it? How to explain what you like, I mean,' he said, now sitting on a nearby bench and leaning back against the table, relaxed, arms outstretched and palms upturned.

He held us spellbound for nearly an hour, with colourful anecdotes about the London Symphony Orchestra; about humorous happenings during rehearsals and when playing before grand audiences. He related his experiences at the Promenades – an annual event which Sir Malcolm made internationally renowned – and many of his stories were delightfully told, with a wicked dry sense of humour, and with himself often the butt of the joke. He possessed an easy charm and was never patronising. When he had finished, he got a tremendous round of applause and when he had gone, I didn't hear anything but praise. My messmates were full of praise and told me that, 'Such a toff, could come down for a 'wet' of rum any time he wanted.' And in those days, that was some compliment.

Our whistlestop tour of the unspoiled Greek Islands included Milos, Khios, Sifnos, Leros, Rhodes, and Kos. The ship's company went on 'banyans' while the Captain and his guests did the cultural tours. When we were in Rhodes, the Captain made the mistake of bringing off his guests in the last liberty boat, full of sailors high on ouzo and singing every verse of the 'lobster' song – which leaves nothing to the procreative imagination. Neither the Captain nor Lady Norton were amused and the First Lieutenant mustered the rabble on the quarterdeck until there wasn't a squeak to be heard.

We returned to Piraeus to land the VIPs at the end of their 'cruise'. That morning Sir Malcolm told me that I was to come and see him before he left, since he had a 'little something' to give to me in appreciation for looking after him. I dashed off below, full of anticipation and reckoned that such a man as he would slip no less than a crisp, white five pound note into my hand as he departed. What a 'toff!'

Having packed all his bags and checked that he had left nothing behind, I lingered in the officers' flat waiting for Sir Malcolm to make the presentation.

'Ah, there you are, Willis,' he said with his usual smile, as he approached from the Captain's cabin.

'I want you to know that I appreciate the way you took care of me.' And so saying, he withdrew a brown envelope from his pocket and handed it to me.

'Whenever you come to the Proms, Willis, I want you to promise me that you'll come back stage and see me. Don't be put off by the doorman. Just say that Sir Malcolm wants to talk to you.' With that, he shook my hand, wished me the best of luck, and was off.

So was I. I ran like hell to the messdeck, clutching the brown envelope and thinking of the fabulous run ashore that it would provide. When I was seated at the mess table, with nosy messmates gathering round to envy my fiver, I ripped it open and pulled out the contents. I couldn't believe it! In my hand was a full frontal black and white photograph of Sir Malcolm Sargent resplendent in evening dress with his baton poised – no doubt, to commence Elgar's 'Pomp and Circumstance'.

At the bottom of the photograph was a clear white strip, in which he had written 'To Ordinary Seaman Hugh Willis, with my best regards. Sir Malcolm Sargent.' I picked up the envelope and frantically searched for the fiver. It was empty.

The whole mess erupted into uncontrollable laughter as they watched me sitting there, my mouth open in disbelief.

'You said he was no ordinary toff, Will,' said Nobby, between fits of laughter.

'You were right Will, he were a bleedin' skint toff.' And then I saw the funny side of it and consoled myself with a cup of tea.

The sequel to it still makes me cringe to this very day. Harry Teadon, being a bit of a musical buff, offered me thirty bob for the picture – and I took it. The Captain, quite rightly, had told his guests not to give us money . . . instead, a token. And that's what dear old Sir Malcolm did. I hope he has forgiven me for selling his picture; I regret it.

The Cultural Run

A week later I had some more culture. Most youngsters are blind to things cultural. They are too busy thinking about all the joys of self-indulgence and leisure. They need to be guided, encouraged and even led gently by the nose down the cultural path; to have their appetites whetted with wonders from the past. While it's true that you can't make the 'horse' drink the water, it can often be persuaded to do so with a cupped handful of cool water gently applied to its lips.

Joseph Bartosik was less subtle than that. If the plebs had to be inculcated with culture – and I doubt he was convinced that they should be – he would march them to a fire hydrant and connect them at maximum pressure. Anyway, I suspect that it was the Squadron Padre who persuaded a reluctant Joseph to accept the consular invitation for a busload of young sailors to visit the temple of Diana at Ephesus. At the time we were visiting the Turkish port of Izmir, which in 1951 didn't boast much more than a few cafés selling treacle coffee in thimble-sized cups. One could also hire a hookah for a smoke.

'Villis, I don't care if you do vish to study the sailing in the boat. You vill enjoy the lovely temple, and so vill all the others,' said the First Lieutenant after I had tried to convince him that my education would be served better in a sailing boat.

We boarded the clapped-out bus – each of us provided with a bag meal – dressed in our number 6 suits and already looking hot and miserable. The padre was a dumpy fat man, dressed in an ill-fitting lightweight suit and wearing large tortoiseshell glasses. He wore a loose fitting Panama hat which sat askew on his head and he fussed around looking like a nervous barn owl.

'Oh what a privilege we have been offered,' he kept bleating heavenwards – hopefully to his own Deity rather than the pagan Diana – while rubbing his podgy hands together with glee.

As the ancient bus coughed and jerked through the agony of its double de-clutching, I surveyed its drab interior. The slatted wooden seats were designed to ensure that the passengers would be in no danger of dozing off during our two-hour journey – mostly down dirt track roads, probably built by Alexander the Great on his way to Persia.

The driver of this antique bus – looking every bit the archetypal Turk, with generous, drooping moustache and red fez – was hunched in his seat embracing a huge steering wheel. To lend colour to its interior, the deckhead of the bus was painted purple, while the wood-ribbed flooring harboured a scattering of animal droppings and variously shaded chicken feathers. Through the dust-caked windows I could just make out the parched countryside, where the occasional hint of green attracted dozens of hungry goats. We seemed to bump along for ever in our four-wheeled hell, until at last it came to a halt.

181

As I crawled out of the bus into the blazing heat of the midday sun, feeling like a half-baked potato, I saw that we were situated on a sandy hummock which fell away to a shallow valley below. The guide was already there, wearing sun glasses, sensibly dressed in shorts, and standing in the shade of his large umbrella. He was a member of the British Consular Staff and had come in his own car. He wasn't stupid.

The religious 'owl' promptly attached himself to this pathfinder for the Empire and hung on his every word as we reluctantly followed them down the hill in crocodile formation. Our white suits were stained with sweat marks and rapidly became covered in dust and dirt as we made our way along pitted paths which were strewn with rocks. We trudged in silence except for the padre's increasingly frequent pleas to our guide:

'Is it far to go now?' he would ask as he wiped his brow with a dust-stained and soggy handkerchief. The ground flattened out and we walked a further half mile before our guide came to an abrupt halt, apparently in the middle of nowhere.

He closed his umbrella and pointed it dramatically at half a dozen dirty rectangular stones, which lay flat on their sides in the middle of a cracked and dried-out swamp.

'Behold, gentlemen,' said our guide, 'the Temple of Diana in all its glory.'

Twenty-five bedraggled, hot and steaming sailors stood with their mouths open. Even the padre looked as though he thought the guide had lost his head.

Our pathfinder, however, was a man of considerable imagination and archaeological enthusiasm and he proceeded, under the cover of his large umbrella, to bang on about Diana.

'The beautiful goddess of the moon, armed with her bow and arrow, goddess of the hunt, and once the Greek virgin Artemis, who made childbirth a wonderful pleasure for women, and whose temple you now see before you . . .' he drivelled in wonder, while swaying his umbrella musically in time with his words.

'If the fat cow shows her bleedin' face 'ere, she won't be a virgin for long,' said one disillusioned tar, while another speculated that the guide had mispronounced goddess of the 'hunt'. Ten minutes later, after further uncomplimentary and critical discussion had taken place among the sailors, we started to make our way back to the distant bus. Those who hadn't already eaten their corned beef sandwiches now removed them from the crumpled bags and munched the crispy warm remains on their way up the hill.

Three hours later we climbed the gangway like a bunch of mute black and white minstrels. We were greeted with cries of:

'Look out! here come the culture vultures. 'How'd it go then?' asked those who had wondered secretly whether they had missed out on a good 'piss up' at the temple.

'It were bloody great, mun,' answered Geordie, who had spent the whole day moaning.

'We 'ad a vestal virgin apiece and my bastard was dead keen on '*unting*', and followed this with an obscene mime.

'Mind yer, Will's luck were out . . . his were in the family way,' he added laughing at the look of disbelief on their faces.

'But as fer that cow, Diana . . . the bitch never showed up.'

The following day, I was on the quarterdeck when Bartosik happened by.

'Villis, the padre tells me that it vos a vonderful day in the country that you all had.' He was smiling wickedly as he said it.

'Ah well,' I thought, 'maybe I'll appreciate culture when I'm older.'

The six-week summer cruise had been great fun but now, once again, we were returning to our home port and most of us were looking forward to three or four weeks in Malta.

The Smuggler

The flag-hoist dropped away from the starboard yard in HMS *Peacock*. She had executed the order to 'Proceed independently in accordance with previous instructions.' Our ship increased speed and broke away to port, to clear the line of ships within the column.

'Hands fall in on the upper deck for entering harbour,' crackled out over the ship's Tanoy system, and a moment later, 'Close all scuttles and screen doors. Close all Red and Blue openings. Special Sea Dutymen to your stations.'

Our ship, HMS *Loch Scavaig*, was about to enter Grand Harbour, Malta. We had just returned from our cruise in the Eastern Mediterranean, and we were due to carry out maintenance and repair in the dockyard. We had been given a berth in Frenchman's Creek, and this was handy for getting ashore in the evenings. One either caught a rickety bus to Valletta, or a Maltese dghaisa across the long stretch of the harbour.

I was looking forward to going ashore that evening to the Under Twenty Club in Valletta. It had been established with the primary object of keeping young servicemen away from the dubious delights of the 'Gut', a once notorious street in Valletta. Although the club was run on conservative lines – by a retired Army Major – it offered three magnetic attractions.

First, as a member, I was allowed to stay the night in one of their small cabins and it cost only two and sixpence; secondly, we were allowed to change into plain clothes while staying at the Club, and this was a luxury normally enjoyed only at home. But the biggest and most powerful attraction was the presence of girls. They were the daughters of servicemen and civil servants who were based in Malta. Their parents were generally happy about allowing them to use the club because the Major 'stood

184

for no nonsense'. He had eyes in the back of his head, and he needed them.

After we had secured the ship 'fore and aft' to buoys in Frenchman's Creek, I had dashed off below to get showered, changed and ready for the 1600 liberty boat.

Hurriedly I stowed my plain clothes into my 'pusser's' naval-issue green suitcase, adding a spare shirt, shaving gear and other bits and pieces. I collected a packet of twenty State Express cigarettes from my locker – the allowance for one night's leave – grabbed my suitcase, and rushed off to the Quarter Deck to catch the liberty boat.

The late afternoon sun had not yet lost its heat, and I felt the trickles of sweat run down my back as I walked towards the dockyard gate. As I approached the main gate, I was signalled into the 'Search' Room by a Maltese dockyard policeman. It was routine procedure to pick one or two sailors from every group that landed. The Police Sergeant, standing behind the table, looked at me in a friendly manner as I flipped open the case for his inspection.

'Glad to be back from your travels then?' he grinned, whilst feeling through my belongings. He had removed my trousers and the shirts before we both saw them lying there, scattered in the bottom of the case.

Six packets of cigarettes lay exposed! My stomach churned. Slowly, he picked up the packets each in turn and opened them. Each packet contained one or two tired, sorry and bent cigarettes.

'What's this then?' he asked as he fixed me with an accusing stare.

'I can explain,' I said, frantically mustering my scrambled thoughts. I realised what had happened. When going ashore, I always took a *fresh* packet of cigarettes. On returning in the evening, I emptied out my pockets. It was my habit to throw the old packet – if any were left – into the suitcase, which was stowed on the top of my locker. During the six-weeks summer cruise, I had acquired all these odds and ends.

I tried to explain but the more I tried, the more confused became my story, and the more complicated it sounded. Worse still, I knew that the dockyard police played everything by the letter of the law.

'You're 10 cigarettes over the limit.' He looked at me questioningly.

'But Sergeant, they're all bent and stale – nobody would smoke those,' I pleaded.

Rules were rules, and reluctantly he told me that I would have to return to the ship, and that a Dockyard Police Report would follow in due course. I felt utterly miserable, knowing that I wouldn't be going ashore for some weeks to come.

Two days later the report arrived and I was charged with smuggling. King's Regulations and Admiralty Instructions were quite clear about the matter. It was a serious offence in the light of the jealously guarded Duty Free privileges enjoyed by the Royal Navy. However, I consoled myself with the thought that I hardly looked like the last of the big-time smugglers, and that they would realise that it was unintended.

I stood rigidly to attention in front of the Captain's defaulters table.

'Off Caps!' said the Coxswain.

'Ordinary Seaman Willis did smuggle 10 cigarettes contrary to King's Regulations . . . '

The charge was read out in all its pomp and legalese; the evidence was given by the First Lieutenant; the Dockyard Police Report was studied and my version of events listened to without sympathy. The Captain, Commander 'Bungy' Williams, surveyed me from time to time with a grim expression as he listened, read and deliberated.

'This is very serious, Willis. This is an offence which warrants detention, where you would be confined in prison!' His glowering face subsequently relaxed a fraction, but my blood ran cold.

'However,' he continued, 'On this occasion I will take into account your age and that your actions were thoughtless rather than premeditated. Fourteen days number 11s.'

My relief was instant. Moments earlier I had been vividly imagining that I had been destined for the dungeons of Malta. It had a bloodthirsty history studded with dreadful sieges, knights fighting off invaders, and all manner of people being walled up alive in the fortifications. Thank heavens I had got off lightly with only No. 11s. The punishment involved stoppage of leave and lots of extra unpleasant work, but it soon went by and I didn't give it much thought until two months later.

I was writing a letter at the messdeck table, going through the agony of thinking of something new to say to Mum and Dad. I had done the bit about, 'How are you . . . ? The weather's fine here and I went ashore to the pictures last week . . . ', when suddenly I had an inspiration. I recounted the 'smuggling' saga as a light-hearted and humorous story. It must have filled quite a few pages and I was pleased to turn this unfortunate incident to my advantage. Some weeks later Mother wrote back commenting: ' . . . I've told you before, you should be more careful in future . . .' and that was that. But it wasn't.

Six weeks later I was sent for by the First Lieutenant, Bartosik. I stood at the door of his cabin as he addressed me.

'Villis, I vish to know vot you have been saying viz your home writing. The Captain vill see you in his cabin and vishes you tell him.'

I hadn't got a clue what he was talking about but it sounded serious. As a young sailor, it was frightening enough to be brought before the Second-in-Command of the ship, especially Bartosik. To be called upon to explain oneself in the Captain's cabin was almost unthinkable. The Captain of a ship was not unlike 'God' to the young sailor. He possessed total power over all things affecting our lives. He lived in the 'holy of holys' and his cabin and quarters were in another world. It was daunting.

Bartosik prodded me through the door into the Captain's presence. He sat there, large and resplendent in his white 'bush' jacket.

'Ordinary Seaman Villis, sir,' said Bartosik accusingly.

'Right, Number One, I think you had better stay here and listen,' said the Captain ominously. He heaved himself to his feet, grabbed a pencil and pad from his desk, and pointed me in the direction of a luxurious arm chair.

'Sit down, Willis.' His voice was disconcertingly genial and his tone was almost coaxing. It was an awful invitation. How does one sit in the presence of God? I glimpsed the First Lieutenant out of the corner of my eye and felt that he agreed with this sentiment so far as I was concerned. I sat gingerly, as though expecting the seat to burn my arse, and then crouched lightly on the very edge, screwing my face into what I believed was a look of earnest concentration and deference.

'Tell me, Willis, what did you actually say to your father? That is, about your little misdemeanour?'

Captain Williams was a big man with a heavy face, supported by two or three double chins, and he was very red; no doubt all this was helped on by the large gin and tonics he was reputed to drink. He forced a smile as he asked me this question.

'Er . . . which one, sir?'

The Captain was puzzled for a moment, and then established that we were talking about the ' . . ah . . . occasion when you accidentally took too many cigarettes ashore.'

'You see, Willis, I've had a letter from the Admiralty asking me to clear up a misunderstanding . . . ' He wriggled uncomfortably in his chair and continued. 'It seems that your father wrote to the Prime Minister, Mr Winston Churchill.'

My eyes widened in disbelief and they must have looked like cricket balls. The Captain was now warming to his theme. 'Saying, that *I* was going to send *you* to *prison!*' His expression was pained and his eyes too widened in disbelief.

The silence was explosive. I went numb and very nearly lost my balance as my buttocks, barely touching the chair, searched for the edge.

'But that was a joke, sir! He couldn't *really* have written . . . or said that to Mr Churchill.'

Captain William's face hardened for a moment and then relaxed. He returned to his coaxing tone.

'*What* was a joke, Willis? What did you *actually* say in your letter?'

It was like a nightmare revisited. My father was always writing to someone about something, and it was always to someone important. Quite often he didn't get replies, other than an acknowledgement to the effect that the matter was being brought to the attention of . . . Most people ignored his eccentric letters. Mother was always on guard, but he used to write them secretly in the garden shed. Once she happened to find out only when she read the letter in the local paper. On that occasion he had proposed that all the 'yobs' in Southend-on-Sea should be deported to Tristan da Cunha, armed with knives and automatic weapons, and left to get on with it. And the *Southend Standard* had printed it.

In a strangled voice, I tried to reassure him that my father was eccentric; he was always writing *funny* letters, and that anyway, I couldn't stop him.

189

'All I did, sir, was to write a *funny* letter to my parents and . . . it wasn't meant to be taken seriously.' Too late, I realised that I was digging myself into a hole.

'Well, Willis,' his face became crinkled again as he delivered his message between clenched teeth, 'Winston Churchill, the Admiralty and . . . *especially I* haven't found it *funny.*'

The seat beneath me felt red hot. I was crouched like someone taken short and about to relieve myself.

'In future you are not to write '*funny*' letters to your father. Is that understood?' He rose to his feet, pointed at the door for me to go, and then seemed to remember something.

'Oh . . . and Willis,' his features had relaxed into their more comfortable lines. He was smiling, like a naval edition of Mr Pickwick, as he cooed, ' . . . you will remember to write to your father, telling him that it was only . . . er . . . a joke. Sending you to prison, I mean.' His voice, once more, was becoming impatient.

'Go to your messdeck and write it now . . . and show it to the First Lieutenant *before you send it!*'

Grim-faced, Bartosik marched me to the door.

'Ve vill do this, sir. I vill stand on him vile he does it!'

I have often wondered what he told 'My Lords, Commissioners of the Admiralty' that might have assuaged the fears of the Prime Minister and reassured the electorate that smuggling was, whilst still taken very seriously, not always a prisonable offence.

Fleet Regattas

The Fleet Regattas were renowned throughout the Royal Navy for their fun. The delightful weather, the crystal clear water and the beautiful Mediterranean settings were made for such events.

They were eagerly anticipated and the organisation for the Regatta started many months beforehand. The Fleet Navigating Officer would study the long-term programme and choose the venue; a sheltered bay was required which would accommodate twenty or more ships.

Between the wars, the battleships must have made a grand sight anchored in line, but now the Mediterranean Fleet boasted only an aircraft carrier, though it had four cruisers and all the destroyers and frigates. The ships were anchored for the occasion in parallel columns to form the course, each column being about one and a quarter miles long.

Both Marmaris and Navarin bays were ideal and were isolated from human habitation except for the homes of fishermen and a few tiny villages which were tucked away from view. The areas were wooded and the golden strips of sandy beach were deserted and perfect for swimming and 'banyan' parties on the shoreline. But most important of all, the water was calm and crystal clear.

Each ship provided about five or six crews, made up from the various Departments within the ship. The premier event was that which was raced over a one-and-a-half mile course, and was awarded double the number of points for a placed position. The aim of every ship was to win the coveted 'Cock of the Fleet' trophy by accumulating the most points overall. This entitled the winning ship to display a gaily coloured cockerel at the masthead when entering harbour, a trophy very much sought after by every ship's company.

On the day of the racing a properly organised Fleet tote for laying small bets was run by the Flagship and communicated over the radio to all ships in the bay. Every race was followed by 'chucking up' parties in motor boats, mostly in pirate rigs, some dressed up as witches and old hags, flying flags and streamers, banners and blaring horns, klaxons, buckets and saucepans or anything else that would make a terrible din to encourage their ship's crews. The vast majority, who couldn't find space in the boats, packed the upper decks to watch.

Now once again we were looking forward to the annual Regatta, and training had already started in preparation for the day. Crews would take it in turns to use the whalers early in the morning and when work was over. I was very proud to have been selected as the bowman for the racing whaler's crew and we trained every spare moment available. Our squadron was well into this routine and the training was progressing well except for one minor hiccup.

Unfortunately, it so happened that about ten or more members of the various whaler's crews in *Loch Scavaig* had managed to misbehave and were under punishment for various offences. This included three members of my own crew, including me. We were under punishment for a period of ten days immediately prior to the Regatta. This was wrecking our final training sessions. We had to do extra work on board and therefore had little spare time in which to train in the boat. Something had to be done, but only one man could solve our problem and his name was Bartosik, our First Lieutenant.

With ten days to go, and before the big event was to take place, I went to see the First Lieutenant. I had rehearsed what I was going to say most carefully with the crew, all of whom agreed upon the outcome.

'Will, you're bleedin' mad. He'll tell you to get stuffed'.

With those encouraging words still ringing in my ears, I knocked timorously on his open door.

'Villis, vot do I owe for this pleasure of your call?' he asked in his usual mocking tone and wearing his faintly amused smile. It augured well.

'Sir, as you know, I'm in the racing whaler's crew . . . ' He saw my hesitation and filled the gap.

'Villis, I am vell pleased with that. Vot you vish I should say?' he asked as he leaned back in his chair, weighing me up with his intelligent blue eyes. He knew I had something in mind.

'Well, sir, three of us are under punishment in the racing whaler's crew ... and it's interfering with our training,' I finally blurted out, already appreciating that it hadn't sounded too good. But I knew one thing for sure: Bartosik wanted that 'Cock' flying at the masthead and our crew counted for double points.

'Villis, the punishment vos vell deserved, no? So vot should I do. Tell me?' he asked, but this time his voice held a trace of doubt and I had now caught his full attention.

'Sir, all I'm asking is that you defer our punishment until after the Regatta ... Sir?'

He looked at me in silence; then raised his right hand to his chin, three fingers clenched, chin resting on thumb, forefinger vertical on cheek. Sitting thus in silence, and occasionally tapping his cheek with his forefinger, he weighed my proposition.

'I think I know the better vay.' he said evenly, 'Ve vill cancel the punishment for everyone who is in a racing crew.' And he nodded his head in agreement with his own decision.

'But you vill all train in the boats ... every minute of your time, till the day of the Regatta, and ...' he pointed his forefinger like a gun at my face – 'If you don't vin your race, Villis ... I kill you!'

I couldn't believe our luck. Not only were the racing whaler's crew free men, but everyone in the ship who had volunteered for the Regatta had had their punishment cancelled, not deferred. Bartosik had come up trumps again, and when I broke the news I was the most popular man in the ship ... amongst those under punishment.

The first race was to start at 0900. Competing crews from

each ship were towed to the line by their motor cutters, each filled to capacity with cheering supporters. The coaches screamed last-minute tips to their crews through megaphones above the noise from the yelling men, the churning of the water and the motor boat engines.

They cast off the tows and rowed to the start. The committee boat, filled with self-important officials and megaphones, nagged them into line and sorted out their positions. The starting thunderflash exploded and they were off. The roaring cheers which marked the 'off' carried across the water to the columns of spectator ships, whose nearside decks were packed with cheering sailors, banging their saucepan lids like crazed natives on the war path.

Twenty sleek 27-foot grey whalers thrust away; blades whipped, dug and strained for the lead as they heaved on their dipped oars, each row of splashes marking the haul with blobs of white flecked foam. And as some caught their stride, their striking rate reduced as they settled in to their pace and slowly gaps appeared as they pulled ahead and others lagged astern.

And so the races continued throughout the morning. By midday, our squadron was clear ahead on points. *Peacock* and ourselves were drawing ahead of all the ships within the fleet, and our squadron was leading for the Squadron Cup as well. By mid-afternoon it was becoming more certain that the coveted 'Cock off the Fleet' would be won by *Peacock* or *Loch Scavaig*. The tension was running high in both ships and by the time the last event – the racing whalers – drew nigh, *Loch Scavaig* was one point in the lead.

We battled neck and neck, every inch of the one-and-a-half mile course. At halfway we were still even, neither boat drawing ahead more than a foot or two. I don't recall hearing the deafening cheers, the klaxons, the ships' sirens and cacophony of saucepan lids as we crossed the finishing line, not knowing which of us had won. The committee boat decided in favour of *Peacock* by the narrowest margin, and we had lost the Cock of the Fleet by a quarter of a point. Our squadron, nevertheless, had won by a very large margin over all the others, so honour was well satisfied and afterwards Joseph smiled instead of shooting me.

After supper, and in accordance with the long established Regatta custom, all the boats got underway filled with 'pirates' and armed with sacks of potatoes, stirrup pumps and buckets. The aim was to attack anything that moved on the water – other than one's own squadron – and also to make passes at the 'enemy' ships at anchor. The latter responded with fusillades of potatoes, high powered jets from fire hoses, gash buckets full of slops and anything else that came to hand as the marauders passed by. The brilliant searchlights and ten-inch signal lamps lit the Fleet and illuminated the bay – which was alive with all manner of craft. Within an hour the bay was filling with sailors swimming aimlessly amongst the battling boats, most of whom had been tossed in the water during their engagements.

As the evening progressed, the tempo and the daring increased, and there were moments bordering on madness. By now, hundreds of sailors were swimming among the ships and boats without a thought of the danger. The Wardrooms of the Fleet joined in – having downed their dinners, port and brandies – in among the thick of it, some driving their 'skimmers' like bullets, firing green and white flares into the sky and jumping into the sea with the rest of them. It was colourful chaos and must have looked like the battle of Matapan.

Drink was not to blame for these sailors' high jinks. The sailors entitled to a tot of rum had drunk their tot many hours before at midday. In those days there was no beer issue. Drink could

195

not be stored away for later use, except by senior ratings, who were sometimes issued neat rum. Grog went flat after several hours.

This regatta madness couldn't happen in the Fleet today. Admirals and politicians would be hung, drawn and quartered by the press once the media had caught a whiff. The Royal Navy naturally mirrors the social mores of the times, and we live in ultra-correct times today. It amuses me to wonder, however, what the health-and-safety bureaucrats, plus the hoards of 'nanny' state do-gooders, would have had to say about such disgraceful, wondrous goings on. I can hear them exploding with self-righteous indignation – and I'm sure they would be right by today's stifling standards – but by heavens, such annual events did wonders for our morale. Thank God no one was drowned and none were seriously hurt – no doubt largely through the absence of drink and drugs. I wouldn't have missed it for the world.

I remember that during the previous regatta, Prince Philip had made fast attacking runs past our ship's gangway in his 'skimmer', and that we had doused him with water from the hoses as he passed within a foot of our gangway doing twenty knots. Even Royalty could occasionally be irresponsible in those days. And our Captain, Bungy Williams, appeared on the quarterdeck – uncharacteristically 'one over the eight'. He was armed with a Verey pistol and, to hoots of delight from scattering sailors, discharged a red flare down the length of the quarterdeck, rocketing aft under the low-slung awning and disappearing out over the stern. Like it or not, sailors loved their 'skippers' to suffer the occasional human frailty, and I'm sure the same holds true today. But already the bells were beginning to ring the changes, as we shortly discovered.

In 1952, at 2200, the terse signal from the flagship called the celebrations to an immediate halt:

'All men out of the water and all boats to return to their ships. Douse all searchlights and signal lamps. The festivities are to cease forthwith.'

Mountbatten, the recently appointed Commander-in-Chief, was not amused. He summoned all the ships' Captains to repair on board the flagship in the morning. They all got a bollocking and that day the Fleet was ordered to carry out 'general drills'. We were, in the naval vernacular, hauled up with a round turn and two half hitches.

After the Regatta, the Fleet departed to their various destinations to show the flag on the way back to Malta. We were instructed to proceed independently to Malta, since we had to prepare for our departure for England. Our foreign commission was nearly over and it was rumoured that we had been detailed to escort some old tub of a ship back to UK.

But we reckoned that we had had a good innings in the Mediterranean during the past two years. We had visited Venice, where the young free-church padre had fallen into the evil smelling Grand Canal during a 'get-to-know-your-sailors' run ashore; we had sailed through the Suez Canal, where the Egyptians on the bank had bared their bums as we passed by; we had seen the 'gilly gilly' men perform, and spent a week anchored off Aqaba – among sharks and barracuda – while we watched over the uneasy peace on the border between Jordan and Israel. Some of us had done the trip to the ancient city of Petra – each sailor riding a donkey – and marvelled at its wonders. We had visited ports along the coast of North Africa from Tripoli to Tangier, and we felt that we now knew the customs and the Mediterranean coastline quite well; and we certainly had some stories to tell when we got home.

Chapter 9

Home and England

Two years and more had dissolved into memories and we would be on our way home in a matter of a month. To us unmarried youngsters, the time had passed quickly and it hardly seemed possible that we would return to our families as young men of twenty in place of the callow youths that had joined the ship two and a half years before. The excitement mounted and conversations seldom excluded some reference to the family, the eight weeks' leave which was due, and the 'rabbits' – presents – we would buy for our loved ones at Gibraltar on the way home.

The married sailors talked of nothing else than an imminent two-year shore job. This, they hoped, would be their due, but some would be bitterly disappointed. They dreamed of becoming a 'barrack stanchion' and of going home each night. While many lived in the Chatham area – that being our port of Division – there were still plenty of sailors who lived in Scotland and the North of England. They prayed for a draft to some nearby, and probably obscure, establishment, many of which still existed but were shortly to be closed as the defence reviews increased. Hopes and ambitions were rife.

Our dreams of a fast passage home were doused when the rumour proved true and the Captain announced that we would be towing a 'landing ship tank' (LST) back to England. That meant that the passage could take anything up to three weeks, depending on the weather, before we reached Chatham. In fine weather we would make eight knots but as the sea increased during a gale, it could drop to three knots or less. Additionally, it meant that we wouldn't be stopping at Gibraltar for 'rabbits' – which were cheap. This too caused immediate gloom among the ship's company.

The voyage home was slow, frustrated by early autumnal gales in the Bay of Biscay. Nonetheless, our first sight of England sent a shiver of anticipation through the ship. We sighted Portland Bill at about six miles on a grey and overcast morning as we headed for the Nab Tower and Portsmouth to deliver the LST.

Tugs relieved us of our wretched tow and we made our way alongside Fountain Lake Jetty for the weekend, prior to sailing for Chatham. Excited families from all over the country had come to greet their husbands, boyfriends and sons. They quickly filled the ship, going down to the freshly scrubbed messdecks to the accompaniment of animated conversation.

'Haven't you grown!'

'Oh my God, you've got a beard!' while embarrassed sailors would reply,

'Hush, Mum,' and grow quite red. Wives with children would exclaim proudly,

'You don't remember your dad. This is him,' and the child would stand cross-legged and stare shyly at his feet, while Dad gave a nervous laugh,

'He had bloody better,' while thrusting a giant teddy bear into the boy's arms and picking up the struggling youngster.

But the burst of emotions soon found their more comfortable level. As I looked across the table, answering Mum's questions while Dad sat gazing at me in wonder, my ears were invaded with other fragments and snippets of nearby conversation:

'You know that Doris got married?' and 'Albert's bought a

car.' Then to my right, 'You'll never believe it but . . .' and another comment full of promise, 'Now that you're home, we'll get one.' All these words were buzzing in my ears as I struggled with my thoughts.

And Mother, the practical one as ever, said:

'I'll take you down to Dunns. We'll get a nice sports jacket, a Harris tweed. I expect you'll need some flannels too.' Meanwhile Father grinned.

Marcus had lent Dad the car. It was black and shiny, and the chrome on the bonnet and bumpers had been polished by Father for hours. We would go home in style and I wouldn't have to sit freezing in the back of the Morris Cowley.

'I wouldn't let Father come in the Cowley,' said Mother with her nose in the air.

'He wanted to, though. I thought the sailors would laugh and you would be embarrassed,' she said knowingly, and she was right.

I still had some way to go before getting my values in place. And then we set off to Westcliff on Sea in the 'limousine'. I revelled in the luxuries of home for a full weekend, thoroughly spoiled by them both. Brother John, now turned nine, was suffering boarding school and, remembering my unhappy times, I felt sorry for him.

The following week, after we had berthed in Chatham, we set about preparing *Loch Scavaig* to join the Reserve Fleet in the Medway 'trot', whence she would in time be committed for scrap. By now it was autumn and the weather was wet and cold. We were suffering all the associated discomforts. The ship transferred to dockyard power and went into an eerie silence. Gone were the comforting whirr and buzz of auxiliary machinery. Footsteps echoed down the cold passageways, running with condensation, and the messdecks were chill and grim. All bathrooms and heads on board were shut down. Steam from an ancient boiler provided limited hot water to the Dickensian shoreside bathroom, and another Stevenson contraption turned out to be the mobile galley.

The heads ashore were unbelievably squalid. Ten lavatory cubicles were situated in a windy building, built of brick with a corrugated iron roof. These turn-of-the-century lavatories were designed in such a way as to catch deposits in the channelled duct beneath a row of wooden seats – and thence float downstream by means of constantly running water flowing beneath the cubicles to the sewer opening at the far end. Thus, if you were stupid enough to use the cubicle nearest the sewer end, you were in danger of enjoying the privilege of nine deposits beneath you as you sat reflecting on the vicissitudes of life.

To have to undergo this indignity was bad enough, but the November weather was particularly cold that year, and one had to reach a state of desperation before going to the heads ashore. To have to go at night was due either to very bad planning or else to nature's sudden whim. Sailors, however, are usually able to turn the worst of situations into laughter. It so happened that November the fifth provided the inspiration we needed.

Nobby and I devised a plan to liven things up. Like the children we still were, we bought several packets of Brock's little bangers, each of which went off like a thunderclap. Then we armed ourselves with a like number of empty match boxes, and prepared ourselves ready to strike the following morning.

The heads 'rush hour' occurred at about 0720, allowing time before having to fall in for both Watches of the Hands. When all the cubicles had been filled with customers, Nobby and I took up position. When they were comfortably seated, we started to launch the 'bomb ships' from the top end of the lavatory waterway. We had established that we had just time to launch the fleet before the first one would explode, and we took a last glimpse of the Armada sailing down the gully before hurrying clear.

We had barely left the heads, when the first bomb exploded with a thunderous roar. It all happened so fast after the first explosion. There was an ear-splitting scream of distress, followed by a white-faced, stumbling sailor, his trousers around his legs, emerging from the heads' main door. Then more explosions came in quick succession as the lavatory emptied of startled sailors with their trousers at half mast or clutched in their trembling hands. Nobby and I watched them as they milled around in confusion, wondering what had happened or speculating among themselves about leaking gas mains and the build-up of methane in the pipes.

It was soon our turn to go home for eight weeks' leave. At first it was all sweetness and light. Mother took me to Dunns and bought me a 'gentleman's' sports coat, with two vents at the back and made of Harris tweed. Flannels, shirt and a conservative tie completed my county image for Southend-on-Sea, but we didn't really live there; we lived in up-market Westcliff-on-Sea, the home of middle class London commuters and wealthier Jews. The Gentiles were mostly frenetic commuters, working in London offices and suffering the twice-daily journey to and from town. The steam trains were notoriously dirty, crowded and late. The passengers politely squabbled over 'time-established' seats, glowered when another opened the window, read their papers in silence and arrived at their destination in crumpled suits. Father, still dressed in his pin-striped trousers, black coat, starched collar, bowler hat and black tie, described it as 'mobile torture on the way to hell!'

The Jews were, in the main, stockbrokers, tradesmen and shopkeepers, and hard-working opportunists with a ready eye for profit. They were mainly orthodox Jews, dressed in black Homburgs, with long beards flowing in the wintry wind. Many still paid sixpence to the paper boys on Saturday mornings to light their ovens and illuminate their dark Victorian halls; kosher Jews were not allowed to work or cook on the Sabbath. Except for business, they kept to themselves and to their own kind, for which they were often resented.

Times were hard and rationing was strict. Food was always plain fare, butter was a luxury and good meat hard to come by. Utility clothes were cheap and lacklustre, and luxury items of all kinds were costly and scarce. In short, material life was drab. Nevertheless, there was hope over the horizon. The politicians were now promising good times around the corner and the general mood of the country was on the upturn. We had a new Queen who was married to a dashing naval officer. The Coronation brought colour and novelty into our lives, and television – owned only by the few at first – was all the rage as a topic of conversation. It gave people an incentive to scrimp and save for this new entertainment and became a symbol of relative wealth: 'The Jones' have got TV . . . a twelve inch screen. Dad says we'll get one next year.' This was ritual conversation on the part of those who wanted to impress.

That year Mother persuaded Father to buy our first flickering, and occasionally temperamental, black and white set. It was an Echo, built in Southend. The television became the most prized possession in the house. It was accorded a God-like reverence, with pride of position on a polished sidetable in our lounge. Special rules were established. Father had to be present in order to turn on this complex electronic equipment; I was not to touch it, Mother initially fearing it would probably explode if tampered with by an inexperienced amateur.

My honeymoon homecoming lasted just over a week. It was

now winter with nowhere to go and I was running out of money.

Secondary Occupations

'Why don't you do something useful? Getting under my feet all day . . . lounging about,' said Mother, after what she considered to be a decent interval of pandering to her son.

'Get yourself a job . . . try the Kursaal . . . they're open all year round.' Mother was clearly concerned that I still had seven more weeks' leave before having to return to my ship. Anyway, I was getting hard up and needed more spending money.

The Kursaal was the premier fun fair-cum-slot machine emporium for Southend on Sea, and Mother knew the wife of one of the directors. I got on my bike – as was enjoined by a well known politician many years later – and pedalled five miles for a job. The grand entrance to the Kursaal was shabbily imposing in those austere days. Two doormen stood outside and two more stood inside behind the revolving doors. They were dressed in dark blue serge uniforms and wearing large peaked caps – almost certainly government surplus from the Army and Navy Stores – but with gold tassels and epaulettes added, which gave them the appearance of poorly paid Nicaraguan admirals.

The 'admiral of the fleet' wore an extra gold tassel and was helpful and kind. He was a small, grey faced man of about sixty, with a walrus moustache which was nicotine-stained in the middle.

'We gotta junior doorman post vacant,' he said, eyeing me up and down and apparently approving.

'If yer wants it . . . it's your'n for a fiver a week.'

Thereupon, he took me to the store and kitted me out with the uniform of office. Apparently, I didn't rate much of a rank, for my uniform didn't have any tassels. Furthermore, it was far too big for me. The trousers bottom hid my shoes and the jacket drowned me. The grease-rimmed cap – no doubt from brylcreem, which was the favourite of the day – was so large that when I turned my head too quickly, the cap didn't turn with it. I emerged from the fitting store looking like a poor man's Buster Keaton.

'Yer looks great,' said the walrus with evident pride. 'Come along with me, son. I'll show yers the gate.' It was clear that I didn't qualify for the grand main entrance . . . yet. As he walked me through the grounds of the Kursaal, he speculated and waxed warm on my chosen career.

'If yer does yer bit and works 'ard, yer could be promoted to the front entrance . . . within, say, a couple of years or so,' he told me, and with the same enthusiasm that a general would tell a soldier, 'there's a Field Marshal's baton in every knapsack.'

We arrived at my 'gate', which was on the far side of the grounds. It comprised a single rusty turnstile which opened on to a cul de sac overlooking shabby, run-down terraced houses displaying champion-sized weeds in their tiny front gardens. Apart from the occasional mange-ridden cat, nothing moved within sight.

'It's a bit quiet at this time of the year,' he said with remarkable understatement, 'but it'll give yer a chance to sort yerself out . . . you don't get the large crowds comin' this way.'

My heart sank to the bottom of my boots as I gazed at the houses of gloom opposite me with their grey unwashed net curtains.

'Seein' it ain't too busy, yer can 'ave an hour off fer dinner at twelve. Just close the gate and lock up. Then come fer a pie wiv me,' he said kindly, adding, 'watch out fer the troublemakers . . . good luck,' and disappeared round the corner.

Thank you very much, Mother, I said to myself, standing

there in my ridiculous outfit and feeling foolish. I stood it for two hours until twelve o'clock and didn't see a movement, let alone catch a troublemaker. Except for the occasional stirrings of a few net curtains in the houses opposite, I might as well have been on the moon. I was not cut out for the doorman's long vigil; there had to be something better.

I marched back to the main entrance, changed into my clothes, bade farewell to the astonished admirals, who told me I was missing the main chance, got on my bike and pedalled like hell for home.

Mother was disappointed at my lack of staying power and Father laughed till he hurt. He always did have a funny sense of humour. Anyway, that evening I read an advertisement in the *Southend Standard*: 'Stores Assistant Wanted. Apply in Person to Airborne, Southend on Sea.'

Once again I mounted my bike and cycled five miles in search of a job. The interview was conducted by the chief storeman with his clipboard in hand. He wore a white overall coat and on his upper lip was a thin, well razored moustache. He reminded me of a hospital doctor doing rounds on the ward. Both the coat and the clipboard were badges of office, and his collar and tie indicated that he was part of the established staff.

He took me on, knowing that I wanted to work during the remaining seven weeks of my leave. Meanwhile, it would give him time to find a suitable replacement. His three humpers and loaders were falling behind with their internal deliveries of stores and I could fill the gap. He explained that Airborne was a diversified company which produced and sold a variety of products including parachutes, Bata shoes, carpets, rubber dinghies and furniture materials. Each day the store received two big lorry loads of materials. I was to join his hard-pressed team of three, who were under considerable strain and couldn't keep pace.

The chief storeman then introduced me to his interesting staff. There was Harry, the 'gaffer', going on sixty, wrinkled, weather-beaten and wearing two days' grey stubble on his chin. His flat cap, held together with grease and grime, looked liked a permanent fixture, and a cigarette stub was lodged over his ear. Harry's two mates, Alf and Arfur, were younger editions, possibly in their early twenties – already looking as if they were approaching fifty. Both wore hand-knitted hats which covered their ears, and pinafore overalls that had seen better days.

'This is Hugh,' said the chief, checking his clipboard to be sure, and then he explained whence I had come. Harry looked puzzled, paused, then said,

'Oh, 'Ughie . . . I see. In the Navy and all.' I squirmed while the other two grinned and called, 'Allo, mate.' The chief, having satisfied himself that Harry now had the weight, scanned his clipboard.

'I think that's all. I'll be in my office, checking the stock.' With that he marched smartly off.

'Right,' said Harry, 'let's 'ave a cup a char while I gives yer the form.'

It took Harry half an hour over two cups of tea and a couple of Woodbines to explain the form. We sat on the outside wall-lift in its lowered position. It comprised a steel platform which could accommodate half a ton of stores, and which was raised by a handle connected to a chain, called a Weston purchase. It went up the outside of the factory building to the loading doors fifteen feet above. In order to raise the load, one turned a handle on a wheel attached to the chain. The gearing was such that twenty turns of the handle raised the platform no more than six inches. For the platform to be raised to the upper floor opening, it required some 600 turns.

Harry explained to me that the first lorry came at 0900, and that it took until dinner time to get the first lot of goods unloaded. The second delivery arrived mid-morning, and was raised in the afternoon.

'That's 'ow it works, 'Ughie,' said Harry, nipping his second Woodbine and placing it behind his ear.

'Mind yer, we stops fer the cuppa char when we gets 'ot,' he added firmly in a trade union voice. Harry said that the distribution of work was simple. One of us turned the wheel with another at stand-by, while the other two sat at the loading door up top, looking down, legs dangling over the edge. The two 'wheel' men below did ten minutes turning then ten minutes watching, and so on. Or so I had thought him to say. After Alf had done his ten minutes – with lots of pauses to catch his breath – he was replaced by Arfur, while Alf went up top to dangle his legs with Harry; but I carried on. Then after Arfur had done ten minutes of puffing – but not much progress – he was relieved by Alf. It was then that I looked up questioningly at Harry, who was a permanent dangling fixture up top.

'Yer gettin' the 'ang of it, 'Ughie. Practice makes perfec',' said Harry, and waved encouragingly from his high perch, with Arfur now smiling beside him.

''Arry's got war wounds. I fink someone shot 'im,' said Alf confidentially, as I swung on the wheel. 'Sometimes it's bad, but uvers it's worse,' he added with a wink. They knocked off for tea twice in an hour, but after one stop, I didn't want any more. So I carried on turning the wheel.

'Gor Blimey, sumfing's gorn wrong,' said Harry indignantly as he looked at his fob watch on the end of its chain. We had completed our morning's work at 1100. He struggled mentally for a moment or two, and then turned to me.

'You've been turnin' too bleedin' fast,' said Harry accusingly.

'We ain't got nuffin to do fer an hour an' a half!' he continued indignantly. 'We 'ad better ave a cuppa.'

Harry chewed his lips, licked the stubble on his upper lip, scratched his chin and slurped a mouthful of tea.

'Harry, we could start on the afternoon load, maybe get half of it done before dinner,' I suggested helpfully.

Alf and Arfur shuffled their feet, gave me a look of withering scorn, and spat expertly at an empty can on the ground. Harry looked at me wide-eyed.

'Don't never say nuffin' like that again, 'Ughie,' he said, almost in pain. 'It's called the afternoon load 'cos we does it in the afternoon.'

Just then the chief storeman, head down and studying his clipboard, emerged from his office. The storeman looked up and saw that the lift was empty.

'My goodness!' he uttered in beaming surprise, 'you've finished the first delivery and it's only eleven.' Harry stood looking miserable, as though he had been accused of letting the side down. He was mentally struggling to find a simple explanation for this 'one off' misfortune.

'Yeh, well . . . it were a small load terday, chief, weren't it? And anyway, we got 'Ughie 'ere,' he said, giving me a furious look.

The chief storeman checked his clipboard and assured Harry that, 'if anything, today's delivery was larger than usual,' and praised him for doing so well. Harry looked as if he were about to throw up.

We started lifting the 'Afternoon Delivery' in silence. By dinner time we were half way through the second load, even though Alf and Arfur were obviously on a 'Go slow'. This made me mad and I turned the wheel with a vengeance, doing longer and longer stints – far more than my due. My anger had built up from the start. Harry and his mates had set out to use me as the workhorse, but the con had backfired. I looked up at Harry's dangling legs high above me, which were dancing and kicking in anger as he watched me working like a man possessed.

'You'll do yerself an injury,' he snarled in hope; probably he was toying with the idea of dropping a large box from above.

The hostility continued for a further day and a half. We broke the previous day's record and the chief storeman was a happy, smiling man. On the third morning, however, he wasn't smiling and he sent for me at dinner time.

'I've found a replacement for you. He's coming tomorrow,' he announced with measured seriousness.

'Has Harry been complaining about me then?' I asked flatly.

'Yes he has. He says that you've upset his team,' he said in a neutral voice.

'Well, that's it, then. I'll collect my money owed and go,' I said defiantly.

'No, no!' said the chief in alarm, 'I'm promoting you to be my personal assistant,' he said with a smile.

'I've told the new lad he had better pull his weight, along with Harry and his team. Harry now knows the score,' he said mysteriously, and left it at that.

The next morning he kitted me out with a clean khaki overall and issued me with my own clipboard and two standard issue pencils. I was in future expected to wear shirt and tie with my uniform, and would be allowed to eat my lunch – of sandwiches – in the office with the chief. From that day on I was to follow in his wake like a shadow, while he did the daily store checks, taking notes as detailed, and responsible for carpets and furniture cloths, including all the rolls of cut and uncut moquette. Additionally, I would be responsible for holding the store keys in his occasional absences on duty. Finally, and more to the point, my weekly pay rose by twenty shillings. I had fallen on my feet, as Pincher would say.

From that day on, Harry and I slowly became the best of friends. Later he confided that he had only been concerned with one thing: What would happen when I left? They would have been expected to work hard, which was all very well, but not while they were *permanently* employed. It was all right for me; I would be going back to sea, but what about them? By the time my six weeks were up, although Harry had nearly worked my relief to death initially, he and his team had gently slid back to their former routine and timetable. I had heard that the chief had been warned through union channels that his schedules were crucifying his workforce. It amounted to slave labour, and did he want trouble or peace? Those were the days of great union power. 'I'm all right Jack' was the often-heard cry and was to be so for many years to come.

Not So Much a Conquest

But life wasn't all work and no play. Imagining myself to be an eligible young man, and having taken a fancy to a girl I had recently met at a dance, I had invited her out on the Sunday. Afterwards, however, I realized that I hadn't been wise because nothing happened in England on a Sunday. Nothing was open and there was nowhere to go. The Lord's Day Observance fraternity still ruled the day and it was a 'closed shop' everywhere.

'She'll come for a drive with us in the car,' said Mother, and I winced at the thought. Mother was adamant and anyway, I had no better plan, so I accepted this dangerous offer.

Dad's car was a Morris Cowley, dated 1927 – artillery wheels and all – and even in 1952 it was a visual freak to behold among the young and impressionable youth of the day. I dreaded the thought of my new-found girlfriend – whose name I can't recall – sitting alongside me in the 'dicky' seat. It would be rather like riding double pillion on a wide motor bike.

When we were mustered for the start, Mother told Father to lower the hood – which covered the front bench seat only – 'It's not going to rain,' she said confidently. We cleared the town and found the familiar country Essex lanes, we two in the back wrapped in a large rug, 'To keep you both warm,' said Mother.

We hit the Billericay country lane doing 20 miles an hour and I could see that my girlfriend – her nose sniffily in the air – was suitably under-impressed.

We had gone no more than a mile down the deserted lane before Father casually opened the right hand door, climbed out slowly and made his way forward along the eighteen-inch-wide running board. Meanwhile Mother took charge of the steering from the left hand seat, her arms outstretched, her right leg extended to reach the accelerator, and her body sunk low in the process. She was now in such a lowly position as barely to see over the dashboard. Father, who was still up forward, had lifted the right hand bonnet and was tinkering with the carburettor while we progressed sedately down the lane at 15 miles an hour. My girlfriend – whose name I have definitely forgotten – was nervously drawing my attention to this odd performance, as though I didn't know what was going on. This was exactly what I had feared and I didn't want to know. Having satisfied himself that all was well in the engine room, Father then gave us the 'thumbs up' sign as he came aft to reassume command.

This was standard routine for Father and Mother while chugging along deserted country lanes; had I been alone in the back, I wouldn't have batted an eyelid. Father was always obsessed with the timing and constantly fiddled with the advance and retard levers. With my new-found girlfriend, however, I just couldn't cope. In silence we trundled along, and I tried to ignore the two cyclists who overtook us on the little hill.

Then what I feared most occurred; it came on to rain. Mother, knowing the drill, promptly hoisted the front hood into place and they disappeared from view. Father knew his drill too, and passed the large London umbrella through the window back to me. I unfurled the umbrella with my eyes shut and then tried to share it equitably with my now distant girlfriend. She had removed herself to the far side of the 'dicky' seat. In consequence, having tried at arm's length to put it over her head, it caught in the slip stream and turned inside out. This was not normal drill.

Ten minutes later, when I had managed to stream the now unbuckled umbrella, it stopped raining. Unfortunately, we were both pretty wet and her hair was looking dreadful, what with the wind and the rain. Mother then lowered the hood – thereby increasing our speed of advance by several miles an hour. She turned in her seat, smiled, and asked us both if we were having fun. As if in answer, the girl clutched frantically at her limp, wet hair and silently clawed it flat with her hands. I thought it unnecessary to tell Mother that we hadn't spoken for some while.

Father, meanwhile, who always wore his battered yachting cap in the car and looked as though he were about to round Cape Horn, yelled above the wind.

'We'll go home via the sea front as a treat.' I groaned, knowing full well that this would allow us to enjoy the full intensity of the rising south westerly wind.

As we approached the sea front, the lights turned red at the junction and we stopped. It was then that Father turned his head away from Mother and gave an almighty sneeze through the open window. Both top and bottom dentures shot through the air, landed and snapped a few more feet before coming to rest in the far-side lane. As Father leapt from the car, I saw with

213

dismay that his teeth lay grinning towards the oncoming traffic.

'Darling, don't use your hands! Pick them up with this,' said Mother – always worried that he might catch something – as she thrust a clean white hanky at Father.

I turned and looking behind us, saw that a queue of cars was forming in our rear; Father glowered, and stuffed his pipe aggressively between his toothless gums in a vain attempt to disguise his loss. He strode to the middle of the road looking rather like an angry, gesticulating Popeye, and dared any car to move.

They were all stopped *behind* us, but then the lights turned green and the oncoming traffic started moving towards his stationary gritted teeth. Father was now crouched protectively over his dentures; one arm outstretched to hold the cars at bay. With the other hand he scooped the teeth into his hanky and legged it back to the car with as much dignity as the circumstances allowed.

The lights now turned red and the drivers, impatient to be off, started to sound their horns and wave their hands in irritation, and it didn't help when Father wouldn't move off and kept sticking two fingers in the air.

An off-duty policeman, however, taking his mother for a quiet Sunday drive, untangled the traffic jam and we went on our way, beating into the teeth of an imminent gale along Southend sea front.

I never saw the girl again, but I did subsequently hear that she hadn't gone to work on the Monday.

The way to meet girls in those days was to go dancing. During my time abroad I had become reasonably proficient, confident enough to ask a girl for a dance, and so Saturday evenings were spent at Southend or Westcliff Palais de Dance. The rituals were much more formal in those far-off days – at least they were in the places where parents allowed 'decent' girls to go – and one had to understand that most young ladies expected proper behaviour in public.

Most of us were still callow youths and remarkably inexperienced. I was now twenty and still only fumbling. It would be another two years before I would take my great leap forward – having been given a push – and undoubtedly this had much to do with my Father's indoctrination and the warning signs in the Mediterranean. I was frightened to death of catching venereal disease. I had seen so many sailors, plus those in white gloves, who underwent discomfort and the indignity of regular visits to the sickbay. They all suffered stoppage of leave until they were cured. My father told me that he had once had an affair with an older woman when he was young, and before he was married. Afterwards it had frightened him rigid that he might have caught something nasty and he suffered for months waiting for his leg to drop off . . . or something. But that's not surprising, since Father had been brought up under the middle-class Victorian rules. Obviously they influenced their children in the moral strictures of the time, and Father had probably had his fair share of indoctrination, but that hadn't included detailed information.

He was hopeless at discussing the subject. The only time that he did so, he took me secretively to my bedroom, shut the door, sat down on the bed and struggled for words. When he did eventually get going, it all came out in a garbled rush and we were both embarrassed as hell. I kept interrupting, saying,

'I know all about that, Dad,' in order to shorten the agony.

The trouble was that every time I said it, he would look at me with a mixture of surprise, envy and disgust. It was as though I had been a practising pervert from the age of twelve.

Mother would have been much better at it, but she reckoned

215

that it was Father's job, and anyway, boys have to get on with it. Nevertheless, I knew that I had it in me to become an enthusiastic student of the art; but circumstances dictated that it would be a 'do it yourself' course. It makes me smile today, to think how utterly naive I and other youngsters were when compared to the modern-day lotharios. At twenty I was still groping around trying to discover the intricacies of unclipping a bra, while today they teach that at primary school. Not that modern youth would listen, but I now know it's all relative. I had just as much thrill feeling a cupped bra in the back seats of the stalls as those lads today, who choose to fill themselves full of pills during an equal-opportunity orgy.

It must have been about this time in my life that I first heard Mother say:

'You use this house like a bloody hotel.'

She accused me of coming through the front door, then out through the back.

'We never see you, except when you want food and a bed.'

It didn't matter that I was working all day, armed with my clipboard, counting rolls of uncut moquette.

'That's not the point,' Mother would say, sweeping past me and tossing her head.

So I thought I would kill two birds with one stone. I would take the current girl out for the evening, me on half pints and she on Babycham, and then bring her home for a nightcap of hot chocolate in our Cobham Road flat. It would be timed for 2200, when I knew Mother and Father would be in bed. We would sneak through the door, creep up the stairs, and make ourselves comfortable in the lounge. Then, bugger the hot chocolate, I would want to get on with my discovery course.

Timing was a critical factor; less so as far as the girl was concerned, but with regard to Father, quite critical. I knew that

Mother would be lying there tossing and turning.

'What are they up to in there?' she would be saying in an agitated voice to Father.

'They're squashing all my new cushions which I've just "poofed",' she would say in pique, then sit up and turn on the lamp.

'You know I don't like him in the lounge on his own.'

The room was always immaculate, everything in place, and she didn't like anyone using it; that is, unless one stood to attention in socks – no shoes – and didn't make contact with the bric a brac or furniture. Experience had shown that Father's tolerance factor, under Mother's persistent interrogation and commentary, was thirty to forty minutes. Could I solve the Chinese puzzle implicit in every bra strap before Father reached 'lift off'?

The mental pressure under these circumstances was hardly conducive to sublime seduction. Our conversation, held in hoarse whispers, comprised, 'Stop that!' and 'Oh come on,' and 'Shusssh, they're coming!' It sounded as if it were being broadcast on a loudspeaker against the background of the heavy, nerve-wracking tension within the house.

Suddenly it would be over. The door would open, the lights would come on – bright as Wembley Stadium – and Father would be standing there without his teeth and glowering in his green pyjamas.

'Do you know what time it is?' he would ask sharply, then remember to look at his watch.

Both of us would be sitting bolt upright, blinking in the light, dishevelled from the struggle, and she with one bra strap round her left ear.

'It's only ten-thirty, Dad – we came home for hot chocolate.' And then I would hear Mother in the background.

217

'Does her mother know where she is?' she would call out imperiously.

And that would conclude 'love's' passion for the evening. I would then walk her home in the cold, probably a mile or more, grope in the porch until an upstairs light came on, and take off fast when a deep throaty voice yelled,

'Where the bloody hell have you been all night, Mary?'

By the time that my leave came to an end, I was grateful to be returning to the ship and Mother was quite ecstatic. She was selling hats like hot cakes for Harry Denton in his shop in Southend. I had become bored rigid with my clipboard and uncut moquette, my amorous adventures were fraught with obstacles, and my conquests to date were nil.

The Reserve Fleet

I was very disappointed when I got back to Chatham. They sent me and a number of others to join the Reserve Fleet in the trot off Chatham. A whole load of destroyers and frigates lay stacked together between the buoys, already looking uncared for, with rust stains down the sides and grey covers over the guns and funnels. They were a forlorn, neglected sight and empty of life, like abandoned cars in a scrap yard which had seen better days, and one of them was a destroyer, HMS *Cambrian,* which was used as the accommodation ship. About a hundred of us were the minders for this sad collection of ghosts.

The only consolation was that I went home on weekend leave three weeks out of four, and Chatham wasn't a bad run ashore. They had a modern NAAFI club where we could stay ashore for the night in a single room. This meant that we could change into plain clothes and would be much more likely to find girl friends at the dances they held at the club.

Nobby Lawrence was the only other close friend from *Loch Scavaig*, and we both remained teamed up for our runs ashore. Now and again we used to catch the train up to London, and I had met a girl who lived in Wembley. It was a long way out of town and catching the last train to Chatham was always a nightmare of timing. One night I managed to miss the last tube train and bus, and found myself walking the deserted road from Wembley at twelve o'clock at night towards distant Charing Cross to catch the milk train. I was in uniform and reckoned that I wouldn't have any trouble hitching a lift. The occasional car had passed me but hadn't stopped, when to my delight a shiny new Jaguar pulled up alongside.

'Where are you bound for, Jack?' said a cultured voice through the open window.

'Charing Cross, if you're going that way,' I answered gratefully, as I peered inside.

'Jump in, sailor, I'm going right past it . . . your lucky night,' he said pleasantly, and opened the door.

The interior was luxurious and the leather seats gave off that expensive odour of quality. He was aged forty and dressed in 'black tie'. He chatted amiably about this and that, asking me questions about the Navy and which ship I was in. The roads were clear and I was just thinking to myself that it would be a fast ride to Charing Cross, when, without warning, I felt his hand on my knee. It shocked me rigid as I realized it wasn't an accident. He was continuing to squeeze my knee.

'You can cut that out, right this second,' I said in a strangled voice, pushing his hand away and wondering what to do next, since he was driving and was twice my size in any event.

'Hell man, no offence,' he said casually. 'If one doesn't try, one never knows,' he said reasonably, and gave me a sideways grin.

Thank goodness the journey was fast, and I listened in embarrassed silence as he philosophized wistfully about how one couldn't be lucky all the time, and there were bound to be bad nights when nothing turned up. And each time he made a point, he would look at me and say, 'Hell man, no offence,' and smile.

He dropped me outside Lyon's Cornerhouse, wished me luck in catching the train, and said, 'Hell man, I meant no offence. I just had to try.'

Lyon's stayed open all night for coffee and snacks and caught all the drifters who had missed their trains or had nowhere to go. Nobby was there waiting and hailed me over to his table, grinning like mad and still slightly high.

'I thought you'd be late, you dirty bastard,' he said, all teeth and still grinning.

'Did yer get a bit, then?' he inquired, wagging his finger in my face while I tried to hide my embarrassment.

'No Nobby, it isn't like that,' I said. 'You've got a dirty mind. She isn't that sort of girl,' I added, wondering where I had gone wrong before she had told me that I had better go.

To change the subject, I told him about my ride in the Jaguar and how the man kept repeating, 'Hell man, no offence. One doesn't know if one doesn't try,' and Nobby kept laughing till the tears rolled down his cheeks.

'Of course you would have to find a bleedin' toff in a Jaguar to proposition you,' said Nobby.

We caught the milk train later and from that night on, the expression, 'Hell man! No offence. If one doesn't try, one doesn't know,' became part of our everyday dialogue and was done to death in every conversation and any situation. But we always laughed.

I was still classified as a toffology rate in our new surroundings within the Reserve Fleet. There seemed to be no escape. One of the seamen was a particularly tough nut who was always in some sort of trouble or other. Conroy had a bullet-proof head and was only about 5'9" tall, but he was almost as wide. He possessed incredible strength, was a natural athlete and could do handstands on the upper deck guard-rails. His laugh was high pitched and shrill, like a girl's, and this was accompanied by a similarly pitched giggle. No one in the ship made the mistake of commenting on or laughing at his effeminate laugh. A big fellow in the 'Sailors' Return' had done that one evening, and came out of hospital a week later.

I found out that he had served with Captain 'Crap' Myers and that they had both got on very well. Hardly surprising, seeing they were both mad as hatters. Crap would challenge Conroy to do handstands on the guard-rails, right up forward on the fo'c'sle, when the ship was under way. Then he, as the Captain, would follow suit to prove that he could do the same. Conroy had been a Leading Seaman several times, but each time he picked up his rate again, he got busted.

Conroy wasn't a bully, however, but one walked on egg shells when addressing him or answering his questions, or even making a comment in conversation. It was best to remain silent and grin approvingly whenever you strayed into his territory. He was mad about soccer and used to play for a local team each Saturday. And then he got a letter saying that he was banned from playing in the amateur league, and he sat down and shed silent tears.

Apparently one of the opposing team, a big half back, had told Conroy that he giggled like a big mummy's girl on heat. They carried the half back clear of the pitch and the game was abandoned. I was foolish enough to walk into the mess when Conroy was dropping tears all over his letter.

'What am I gonna do, Will?' he asked me. 'It's my life, mate,' he choked.

I read the letter and noted that the final paragraph invited Conroy to give his reasons in writing and to explain his barbaric behaviour.

'You're a toffology rate, Will,' he said, now with a gleam of hope in his eyes, 'I can't write no good. But you can,' he added with finality.

'Get me pardoned, Will, and you'll never regret it.'

In reply to the amateur football board, I invoked his sick mother who was almost beyond help. She was being nursed by her loyal and devoted daughter, while Conroy earned what little he could to keep his mother's body and soul together. I continued, 'It was unfortunate that the big half back should have insulted both his sick mother and his sister when Conroy was on medication for depression.' Also that the pills he was taking were known to have side effects, and that at the time, Conroy had only vaguely been aware of his actions. The ship's sick berth attendant wrote out a bogus chit on headed notepaper, which we enclosed, and then we sat back and prayed that all would be well.

Several weekends passed by, and Conroy was nearly always to be found waiting for the posty every time he returned on board with the mail. He kept on asking me whether the letter would do the trick; he was a bundle of nerves, he went off his food, and I was becoming quite anxious lest the letter brought bad news. I was slightly comforted when he happened to say one day that no matter what happened, he knew that I had done my best for him.

The letter arrived and Conroy went mad. Thank God he went mad with joy this time. They suspended him from playing for two weeks, and added that this penalty was retrospective and that he had served his time. Once again he was free to giggle and laugh like a hyena on the soccer pitch.

Overnight I became his friend for life. He sang my praises and even tolerated me telling him that he should be careful from now on. All my messmates viewed me in a new light; everyone was incredibly polite and they went out of their way to fawn over me when he was around. It was eerie and I didn't feel comfortable, especially when I found out that he had spoken to all the others,

'If anyone touches our Will, he'll answer to me. Got it?' and then broke into a high pitched shriek of laughter followed by giggles. I even had to tell Nobby not to call me a silly old bastard in Conroy's hearing.

It was with a fair amount of relief that I heard that Nobby and I were to be sent down the river to Sheerness to join HMS *Wildfire* in the dockyard, to help out. It wasn't the last I saw of Conroy, me old mucker. A year and a half later I met up with him in Chatham barracks, and what a turn up for the books that turned out to be! In between times he had been rated Leading Hand and then back again to Able Seaman and back again to Leading Hand. It was quite giddying. Meanwhile I went to Sheerness with Nobby for three months.

Filling in Time

HMS *Wildfire* turned out to be a large, run-down Victorian building at the mouth of the Medway, and used over the past 60 or more years to accommodate sailors in between drafts or when employed in the dockyard. The building was an empty shell except for eight sailors, who now comprised the ship's company. The man in charge of us was a Regulating Petty Officer, who was also responsible for the maintenance and cleanliness of this old, three-story building lying at the water's edge within the confines of the Sheerness Dockyard. The yard itself was barely ticking over and its days were already numbered.

Within the building there were about a dozen long rooms which had been used as messes. Each had accommodated about a hundred men in the past, but now they were all empty and silent. Our job was to keep them swept and clean, making our way from one to the next throughout the day, and in the process becoming bored out of our minds. Each day we would set off from our small mess on the ground floor armed with dustpans and brushes, and wander aimlessly within this hollow shell of a building, all with bare wooden floors bearing the signs of thousands of boots and the daily scrubbings they had undergone over so many years. Each mess had large, overhead wooden beams, from which two long rows of hammocks had been slung throughout its length; and on each beam there were rows of deeply embedded hooks from which the clews were reeved, and which stuck out at intervals and marked each man's billet.

It was resonant with ghosts from the distant past; their voices and laughter hung in the echoing silence. We could visualize crowded mess tables, tea pots, fannys and shiny spittoons, and the kit bags and hat boxes lining the walls. Hammocks would have been neatly stowed in their racks, each one lashed with the regulation seven turns, with their clews and knettles tucked in. The bygone hopes, fears, loves and ambitions of their owners filled the air with a spectral presence as we laughed nervously and pushed our brooms.

Meanwhile, the RPO spent much of his time trying to find us. We would hear his voice echoing two floors below:

'Where are you? Willis, Lawrence? Come down here at once,' and we would scuttle away in amongst the warren of store rooms, heads and sculleries which graced every floor. When he did manage to find us, we would claim not to have heard him and he would stamp his foot in frustration.

The RPO was a small thin man with pinched features, just like a water rat, and he always wore his oversized cap hard upon his ears. He tended to strut rather than walk, which looked comical because his legs were so short. He was convinced that everyone was on the fiddle, even if no evidence existed; this was probably because he himself was always fiddling something. We would watch him going ashore with large paper bags filled with pusser's butter and sugar. It would only happen when his mate, a dockyard policeman, was on watch at the main gate. We had also found out accidentally that he was having an affair with the local NAAFI manager's wife. He would sneak out to visit her during the day. This was when the manager was selling buns, tea, cigarettes and razor blades to his thin customer base in *Wildfire* and the dockyard. The canteen was attached to our building, and while we sat watching the manager, having our stand-easy tea and buns, the RPO was bonking his wife down the road.

We didn't mind the fact that he was otherwise occupied. Someone had long since left an old battered table-tennis table on the second floor. Nobby and I got hold of a couple of bats and some balls, and we would play for hours when we knew that he had gone out on his bonking rounds or to the dockyard. He didn't do any work as far as we could tell. He wandered around in the dockyard calling on friends, drinking tea, or, when he was tired, went shopping in the town. But just to be safe, we frequently moved the table from room to room on the third floor. This usually ensured that we would get some sort of warning as he climbed, short of breath, up the stairs, trying hard to locate the distant source of the sound of the ping pong ball. At dinner time he would come into the mess as we were having our tot.

'I know what you two bastards are up to. Where is that bleedin' table tennis? I'm gonna have the bastard burned,' and then we would pour him a share of our tots, and give him a fag. He would take the offering, shaking his head saying,

'You two wanna' watch it. The officer in charge might call . . . unexpectedly like,' and then his face would go serious:

'Don't you go putting me in the shit. I've gotta' nice number 'ere,' and he would no doubt be dreaming of the NAAFI manager's accommodating wife.

It was a quiet number because the officer in charge, a tired passed-over lieutenant commander, lived ashore in Chatham and hardly ever turned up. Somehow, he always found a reason to be visiting Chatham Barracks, since *Wildfire* was classed as an out station. Nobody wanted to know about Sheerness – period. The town boasted one cinema, which showed long out-of-date, black and white films, a half dozen seedy pubs, and some ill-stocked shops, whose goods were all faded from the sun. The cinema was one of those old ones which occasionally had to stop the film to change the reel. It also had an out-of-tune organ which played at odd times, usually when something had either gone wrong or they wanted to change the reel. This monster organ would rise without warning, slowly emerging from the pit like a First World War submarine; it was usually mounted by an old lady who wore far too much lipstick and was draped in a black sequinned dress with a boa round her neck. The projectionist regularly flashed up handwritten notices on the screen such as: 'Would Mrs Bottomley please ring home immediately. Aunt Ethel is ill.' And I remember that one day they flashed a message that someone's house was on fire.

This gave Nobby and me an idea. One of our messmates was a stoker called Gould, who spent most of his time entering competitions offered by magazines such as *John Bull*. Gould was the most gullible man that we had ever met. He never won anything, but he was always checking the mail for the day when he would. This was too good an opportunity to miss. We called him by phone from the dockyard kiosk – both Nobby and I were good mimics – and told him that he had been short-listed as one of five potential winners. Gould was so excited that he wouldn't stop talking about it in the mess. We asked him when he would know, and he said that he had been told to keep his eyes and ears open for them to get in touch. He was not to contact them, otherwise he would be disqualified. Further instructions would follow and he had to be on the alert.

Several days later, Gould went ashore to the pictures. He made us promise that we would keep an ear open for the phone outside the mess, just in case the magazine rang with further instructions. When he had been in the cinema for about an hour, we rang the manager and asked for an important message to be flashed up on the screen: 'Stoker Gould. You are in the Finals. Further instructions follow by phone.' Both Nobby and I had then galloped over the road and waited in a shop doorway, hidden from view opposite the cinema. We saw him come out of the entrance like a madman and then tear off down the road at high speed towards *Wildfire*.

The leg-pull went on for another week and each time he would receive more instructions by phone. His final instructions told him that he was to be under the clock at Waterloo Station at precisely 7 o'clock on the following evening. He would be met by one of the magazine's beautiful models, who would take him to dinner at the Savoy for the presentation of the winning prize. As a means of recognition and identification, he was to carry a single daffodil in his left hand, and a copy of *The Times* under his right arm. When approached and challenged as the winner, he would reply:

'The daffodils are early this year, and so is the cuckoo.'

We helped Stoker Gould get ready the next day. We bought him his *Times* – the only one in the shop in Sheerness – and a daffodil. He borrowed my jacket and trousers and Nobby lent him a tie. We told him that we had ordered a taxi to the station, and we sat down waiting for it to arrive. No one else in the mess knew that it was a joke, and they were just as excited as Gouldie. Then I looked at Nobby and he nodded his head in silent agreement.

The trouble was that he wouldn't believe us when we owned up.

'You're just saying that 'cos yer jealous,' he kept on insisting, as we both told him the truth.

Eventually he believed us as we mimicked the voice and gave him all the details, including the message flashed on the screen. He was devastated and miserable with disappointment. So we took him ashore for big eats, followed by six pints in the 'Jolly Sailor' . . . by which time he had forgiven us.

Our final fling, before both being drafted to our next ships, was probably the cause of us being drafted away from *Wildfire*. The RPO had been particularly bad tempered for a number of days and we felt that he needed a shake-up. We believed that what was called for was something to occupy his mind. So we gave him a phone call from the good old dockyard kiosk. Our message was cryptic: 'The NAAFI manager knows, you know,' and then we hung up.

The RPO, white as a sheet, flew out of his office and wasn't seen until the next day. It was noticeable that he became more furtive than usual. He wouldn't visit the canteen and kept looking over his shoulder with troubled eyes from underneath his bulging hat, which rested heavily on his ears. He didn't bother to pursue the sound of the far off ping pong balls, and the strut had gone out of his walk.

Two weeks later Nobby and I were sent for by the RPO.

'Willis, you've got a crash draft to *Woodbridge Haven*. She's joining the Fleet Review at Spithead. Get yer bag and hammock packed.' Nobby was to join a destroyer based in Rosyth.

'Oh, by the way, Willis, your ship's based in Rothesay. Good for weekend leave, eh?'

He knew that both of us lived in the south and that we could say goodbye to weekend leave . . . that was, if we didn't want to spend the whole weekend travelling by train. He must have guessed that we were the culprits who had given him the fright of his life. It wouldn't be until five years later that I met my dear friend again; and the circumstances were very, very different.

Sad to say though, that was the last time I ever saw Nobby. We lost touch and I lost a friend. I often wonder what he's up to these days; still joking, I'll bet, and occasionally saying, 'Hell man, no offence. You don't know if you don't try.'

Chapter Ten

The Field Gun Crew

I arrived in Portsmouth Harbour Station the day before the
Fleet Review for the new Queen. The town was packed with
sailors and the ships were already in their allotted anchorages,
which stretched from Spithead down towards Yarmouth in the
Isle of Wight. The Naval Movements Petty Officer at the station
dismissed me with a wave of the hand and told me to catch a
dockyard PAS boat out to my ship. When I got to King's Stairs,
I saw a mass of milling sailors, all trying to find out which boat
to catch to their ships.

The harbour was full of boats plying to and from Spithead,
about twenty of which were queuing impatiently to get alongside
the King's Stairs berths. Chiefs and Petty Officers wearing arm-
bands were trying to establish some sort of order as they shouted
commands and referred to their clipboards, which carried the
boat routines.

In amongst our own matelots there were French sailors in
red pom pom hats, Portuguese looking lost, Italians talking ten
to the dozen, and guttural Germans smoking pipes. The babble
of conversation and confusion made a cosmopolitan spectacle,
and I knew that I was in for a long wait. Several hours later I got
aboard a dockyard MFV, which they said was bound for the
further end of the column where *Woodbridge Haven* lay.

As we rounded Gillicker point, the seemingly endless lines of ships stretched away into the distance: a long row of fat aircraft carriers, cruisers galore, and dozens of destroyers and frigates anchored neatly in columns. But only one battleship, HMS *Vanguard*, now remained to remind us of the past. Their decks and ships' sides were a flurry of activity as they touched up the paintwork, scrubbed the decks and polished the brasswork. The Solent was full of ships' boats plying to and fro.

The MFV's decks were packed when we set off, but as we called at ship after ship on the way, the decks thinned out until there were only a few sailors remaining. The skipper lowered his bridge window and bellowed:

'This is as far as I go. You'll have to thumb a lift the rest of the way.'

With that he went alongside the next ship and invited us to jump off. I could, however, just make out my ship about a mile further on down the line. The officer of the day told me to go to the bridge, where they would contact *Woodbridge Haven* by radio and call for their boat to pick me up.

I was tired and hungry, breakfast was seven long hours gone, and as I climbed up the ladder on to the bridge, I tipped my cap back from my sweating forehead.

'Put your cap on straight when you come on the bridge,' said Lieutenant-Commander Allan-Williams severely, binoculars in hand and standing by the pelorus.

'I know you . . . Willis . . . Collingwood Division. Failed your sixteenth week kit inspection,' he said darkly, then added, 'Not much has changed.'

He got the signalman to call the ship and arrange for a boat, and then carried on checking the anchor bearings, no doubt to ensure that the ship wasn't more than a foot out of position. Nothing had changed.

The Review was spectacular, even though we were fallen in manning the ship's side for hours. We caught a glimpse of the Queen and Philip as HMS *Surprise* eventually steamed up and down our distant anchorage. That night the Fleet was illuminated and fireworks filled the sky as the pageant continued, and it was to be another twenty-four years before the next Fleet Review graced the waters of the Solent; and then it would be a mere shadow of its former glory, as the intervening defence cuts had torn the Navy apart.

Meanwhile, little did we know it but Buster Crab was probably planning his dive beneath the Russian *Sverdlov* Class Cruiser when she would later visit Portsmouth harbour. He disappeared on the night of his dive and the newspapers later speculated for many years as to his fate.

The Fleet dispersed to their various destinations and we headed north for Rothesay. Once again I was faced with the challenge of being accepted by new messmates. As ever, the toffology rate who spoke rather posh was viewed with suspicion by many. Yet a lot of water had passed under the keel since leaving *Ganges*. I was now a confident seaman; I knew my stuff. I could hoist and lower boats, I was a good coxswain under sail and power, I had spent hundreds of hours at the helm of *Loch Scavaig*, and I could throw a heaving line like a professional. In fact, I was as good as, if not better, than many of them at seamanship.

As soon as this became apparent, I was quickly accepted, accent and all. My status immediately increased when the First Lieutenant appointed me as one of the two Coxswains of the motor cutter. This was a prestigious job which provided maximum exposure to the ship's company, since everyone used the boats. I worked twenty-four hours on and twenty-four off in harbour and at sea. It was absolute magic and I loved every minute of having my own 'command'.

Woodbridge Haven was a frigate, very similar to *Loch Scavaig*, and she was used as a target ship for submarines. The exercise area was off the Isle of Arran in the lower reaches of the Clyde and we would mostly day-run from Rothesay, then maybe anchor in Lamlash Bay overnight.

The submariners ran Commanding Officers' qualifying courses. They were called 'Perishers', and our task was to steam up and down and make it as difficult as possible for them to fire their torpedoes at us. Not unreasonably, they fired torpedoes without their warheads. Instead they were fitted with what they called blowing heads. At the end of the torpedo's run, compressed air would fill the torpedo head and float it to the surface ready for recovery.

As one of the motor cutter's Coxswains, it was my job to recover the torpedoes and bring them alongside the ship to be hoisted. It was a splendid test of seamanship in choppy seas, and usually we would have four or five torpedoes to recover each time the submarine fired. Whenever the sea was running, one had to manoeuvre the boat with great care. The torpedoes floated vertically but bobbed dangerously up and down two or three feet with each wave. If you got it wrong, the torpedo would crash through the bottom of the boat and sink you within a trice. Once the nose hook and belly band were secured, however, the torpedo was tamed by the tail and ready to tow back to the ship.

I also had the Watch in the sonar office, which was the same as in *Loch Scavaig*. Leading Seaman Spud Murphy was the TAS rating in charge of the sonar and I worked in the opposite watch. The ship was desperately short of qualified ratings since, as a mere target, we were at the bottom of the list of priorities. We had to train one signalman and a stoker to perform the duties of bearing and range recorders in my Watch, and Spud had to employ the sick berth attendant in his Watch. To begin with, it was a guinea a minute, but the teams soon settled down and before long they had got the hang of it.

During the submarine's attack, the ship had to behave aggressively and counter-attack. Thus we had to gain contact and home in on the submarine as it positioned itself to fire its torpedoes. The whole thing was rather like a one-man band as I coaxed and cajoled my operators on either side, held contact with the sonar, and called out the submarine's movements over the sonar broadcast. During all those months in *Woodbridge Haven*, I learned a great deal about sonar operating, something which was to stand me in good stead years later.

I took my Leading Seaman's examination and gained a first class pass. My only difficulty occurred when the examining officer tested me on lights for lighthouses and buoyage. When I sheepishly told him that I had passed my HET in navigation, he replied dryly that while he had been a navigator for ten years, *he* still had to refresh his memory regularly.

During the Glasgow holiday season Rothesay was alive with young girls who came over on the ferries to the Isle of Bute. During the long September weekends there wasn't a spare bed to be found in the island as they poured out of Glasgow and crossed the Clyde, knowing that there were lots of eager sailors lying in wait.

They held dances ashore every night, and the girls outnumbered the sailors by at least two to one. It was a sailor's paradise, only equalled by Londonderry, Newcastle or maybe Liverpool. But I wasn't to know that then. To me, Rothesay was heaven. And how I laughed when I thought about the RPO at *Wildfire* thinking that he had punished me by fixing the draft to *Woodbridge Haven!*

The months rolled by and the drafting authorities stole more and more of our sailors, sending them to higher priority ships. Even Spud Murphy went on his way and left me in charge of the sonar department. He was a first class TAS rating, while I was only third class. I knew little about sonar maintenance and the equipment down in the bowels of the ship in the sonar compartment. The week before Spud left us, he gave me a crash course on all sorts of bits and pieces: low frequency and high frequency alternators, how to change the brushes, high and low power inputs, how to seal the watertight dome for inspection and changing the transducer. It was all very 'Harry Tate', and when he had departed, I was left with the power to sink the ship.

Lieutenant Walker, the First Lieutenant, hadn't got a clue either. By default he was the TAS officer who was supposed to supervise my activities, but he didn't know an LFMA from a HFMA, whereas I did . . . just. He would come down to the sonar compartment, in accordance with ship's standing orders, and watch me do the dome seal test; and when I was halfway through and hadn't yet proved that the ship wouldn't flood, he would say in a bored tone of voice,

'Good. Carry on Willis,' turn on his heel and make his way up the vertical ladder.

Soon we were so short of men that the ship was recalled to Chatham to pay off and go into reserve. I had been here before and didn't look forward to joining that outfit again. We made our way south to Chatham and started the miserable task of de-storing, de-ammunitioning and putting the ship into a state of preservation.

I managed to find a load of sonar manuals, which vaguely indicated what I had to do to put the equipment into reserve. It was fun taking the sonars apart, hauling out the transducers and unbolting everything that looked as if it might unbolt. Eventually, after about two weeks, the sonar compartment looked like a junk yard, with all the bits and pieces strewn over the deck. I felt quite proud of myself, seeing I wasn't really qualified, and looked forward to the Reserve Fleet TAS officer's inspection.

I met him at the gangway and he seemed surprised that a third class TAS rating should happen to be in charge.

'How's it been going?' he said somewhat doubtfully as I led him down to the dome compartment.

'Oh great, sir,' I said as I opened the hatch, and he bent over to look down into the space below.

'My God! What the hell have you done?' he cried in disbelief.

'You've pulled the bloody lot to pieces.'

Apparently I had got the wrong manuals. Mine catered for the occasion when the ship was going to be sold off for scrap. He spent an hour with the First Lieutenant, who blamed the entire fiasco on me and I was told to reassemble the sonar under the close supervision of the Reserve Fleet Chief Petty Officer TAS. Furthermore, much of the work was to be done in my own time.

This was the last straw, so I put in a request to be drafted to a new ship. I told the First Lieutenant that I had done the Reserve Fleet bit once before, and that I really didn't want to do it again. He didn't share my view.

'Not granted. You'll be the last person to leave this ship,' he snarled which I thought was a bit much.

The next day I had to go into the dockyard to collect some spares from the store. Dawdling discontentedly on my way back, I happened to spot a notice which screamed out in large print: 'Wanted' and then underneath: 'Field Gun Volunteers'. It went on to say that volunteers should report to Chief Petty Officer Houghton in the Field Gun Office.

I had never heard of the field gun crew and had no idea what they did. So I chatted to one of my messmates who knew all about it. He told me that they trained for months in the barracks with the field guns, and then went off to Earl's Court for the Royal Tournament in London.

'They have a wonderful time up in London. They get more "fanny" than you can shake a stick at,' he said, full of envy.

The following day I said that I had to collect some more stores. I made straight for the gate that took me into the barracks and found the Field Gun Office. A Chief Petty Officer and two POs were inside drinking tea.

'Have we got a volunteer, then?' said the Chief Petty Officer, rising to his feet.

'Right, lad, come with me,' he said, and took me outside to where a large field gun wheel lay leaning against the wall.

'When I tell you, pick that up, put it on your shoulder. Then start running until I tell you to come back,' he said with a grin.

I picked it up awkwardly and just managed to get it on to my right shoulder, then broke into a stumbling trot down the road. I thought he had forgotten to tell me to come back, but thank heavens he hollered the recall from the distant office. When I stood in front of him, I heaved it off my shoulder and dropped panting to one knee, my head hanging low.

'Come on in and I'll take yer particulars,' he said with a smile, and I knew I was in.

The drafting Commander had made it clear to Captains that those accepted for the field gun took a very high precedence, and that only exceptionally would the Field Gun not get their man. Within a week my draft chit came through and I was to join in a couple of days. The First Lieutenant sent for me and I could tell that he was furious when I reached his cabin.

'I've a good mind to put you on a charge for leaving the ship under false pretences,' he said angrily.

'In any event, I'm going to have this draft stopped,' he added confidently.

He got rid of me the next day, after he had spoken to the Drafting Commander on the telephone. The First Lieutenant thought that the whole thing was outrageous.

'It encourages anarchy,' he bawled at me when he told me to pack my bags and clear off.

Some of us were lucky enough to join the crew five weeks early, and we spent those weeks getting fit in the gym under the close supervision of the physical training instructors. As far as I was concerned, I had landed on my feet and was very happy to be clear of the Reserve Fleet . . . and anyway, all the girls loved a field gunner, or so I had been told.

The Field Gun Crew

The idea for the Field Gun Crew stemmed from naval history; the Royal Navy had often sent some of its lighter guns ashore to support the army and when necessary to besiege forts and strongholds. Nelson, as Captain of the *Agamemnon*, landed sixteen guns, including three 12 pounders, four large mortars and five 24 pounder cannons from his ship in Corsica to besiege the citadels of Bastia and Calvi. They dragged and swung the guns up steep inclines, over chasms and across the most difficult terrain with 'sledges,' powerful blocks and tackles. It was a superb feat of seamanship demonstrated by his sailors on shore. It was at Calvi that Nelson was wounded in his right eye, as a result of which he would later wear that eye shield, which together with his empty sleeve, made England's most famous admiral recognised by everyone.

A little over a hundred years later the Naval Brigade had gone ashore in South Africa during the Boer War. Once again they had used their seamanship skills to drag and manhandle their 12 pounders across rough country, gorges and chasms with the aid of their blocks and tackles. They supported the army's artillery and their guns were much in evidence when the Boers laid siege to Ladysmith.

When the Royal Tournament was first held at Olympia, the Royal Navy decided that this history would be re-enacted by demonstrating these skills to the public. Years later the Royal Tournament venue was moved to Earl's Court which could accommodate many more people.

By the beginning of February they had recruited the full complement of fifty field gunners to start their training. We were billeted in our own separate quarters and had our own galley and dining room. The staff comprised the field gun officer, Lieutenant Kim, the Chief trainer, Haughton, three petty officers – including a sick berth attendant – and the chief petty officer rigger.

For a couple of weeks we continued with the gym and cross-country runs, prior to starting what they called 'bits and pieces' training. The object of the game was to move the crew, field gun and limber over a course which included two walls, one at either end, and over an imaginary chasm between them. The chasm was represented by the gap between two large, separated platforms; each platform had an integral ramp, angled so as to allow the equipment to be carried up onto the platform.

The first man to be sent across was called the first 'fly', and he had to swing himself across the chasm on the end of a rope. This hung from the 28ft. spar, which was projected over the chasm and rested between two crossed, vertical sheer legs. Thereafter, the men and equipment had to be hauled across the chasm on a wire rope to the far end of the track, and back again.

The total weight of men and equipment amounted to something in the order of two tons, and included the two-wheeled gun, the two-wheeled limber and eighteen men. As we traversed the chasm, crossed and went through the holes in the wall, the gun and limber had to be disassembled into parts, the wheels taken off and the barrel separated from the gun. The Chief Trainer told us that we would have to learn to do the entire course in under three and a half minutes if we were to stand a chance of winning – and by today's standards that was slow. Two teams were trained to compete with one another and the best team would run at Earl's Court against the Fleet Air Arm, Portsmouth and Devonport.

I was detailed as a right wheel number and would also be responsible for helping the gun over the wall. It all sounded pretty daunting.

Our 'bits and pieces' started one cold February morning. Chief Petty Officer Haughton started with the men who had to rig the large sheerlegs and the 28ft. spar. He made them rig the equipment in slow time until they were able to get the rig erected in preparation to carry the gear across the chasm. The rest of us stood around and watched, thinking about the tea and hot pies which were delivered at the 'stand easy' break.

One ex-field gunner called Kerr – a right tough-nut Geordie who had run in the team two years before – was telling us bloodthirsty stories of the injuries he had seen during his previous training. We listened goggle-eyed and felt a bit sick by the time he was done.

The riggers were on their third attempt at raising the sheerlegs when the whole thing collapsed and came crashing down. One sheerleg bounced off the other and then glanced off Lomax's head. He fell to the ground and lay moaning, with the blood pouring from the gash in his head. They got him to his feet and half carried him to a bench, where he sat white-faced and shocked.

Then I noticed that Kerr was kneeling at Lomax's feet as his head was being bandaged. He was staring attentively into his glazed eyes and tapping Lomax's knee, trying to get his attention.

'Can I 'ave yer stand-easy pie, mate?' asked Kerr caringly, as he looked up at Lomax's white face.

We were shocked by this callousness. How could he ask such a thing? Within ten days we were all just as bad. It was shortly after this incident that the Chief Trainer called me forward to witness the gun and carriage being launched over the wall. Apparently this was my scary job in between carrying the right wheel.

'Right, lad, they launches it up and over, and you throws yer body across it to stop it rollin' orf the wall your side, 'cos it's breech heavy to the right, and they gotta put the wheels on while you 'olds it.'

I didn't like the sound of it at all since the gun and carriage must have been about five hundredweight and the steel axles, without their wheels, looked lethal.

'Now I'll show yer once how it's done. It's gotta land between yer feet if you's want to walk in the future, and you gotta be quick to stop it rollin' . . . or else one of the axles will go through your belly button, or you'll be crushed under the 'ole bleedin' lot,' said the Chief Trainer with a friendly nod and a wink.

He then proceeded to demonstrate how it should be done. The gun was heaved up the wall from the other side at forty-five degrees by a grunting and groaning team of giants. The Chief grabbed hold of the trail lines from the other side and swung off them in the air; the gun came crashing down within an inch of his right foot as he threw himself forward to stop the gun from toppling to the right. Unfortunately he missed the breech, and the gun slithered off the wall and the axle impaled itself a foot into the ground between his right arm and chest. Chief Petty Officer Haughton extracted himself from his precarious position with dignity, jumped to his feet, dusted the coke clinkers from his jacket and squared his cap off.

'Right lad, nothin' to it, now you 'ave a go.'

Within a month, both teams were racing each other up and down the track. Racing was not quite the word, for we seldom achieved a clean run when something didn't go wrong. Our running times, however, were now under five minutes, but we still had to reduce it by a minute and a half. At the end of the day on the track, we were all exhausted and weren't interested in going ashore. We were fed like kings but there was no problem with burning off the additional calories.

Our weekly run ashore would mostly occur on a Saturday, since we only went home one weekend in three. We nearly always went ashore together, and this included all the trainers and staff. We would select a local pub and then sing the usual matelot songs till the pints ran out of our ears. The crews were a varied bunch and came in all shapes and sizes. The gun numbers were all giants, the wheel numbers lean and fast, and the 'flys' – who went over first on the spar – were tough and tiny. There was a number of field gunners from previous years in among us, and one in particular was a giant.

He was a gentle giant, whose strength and toughness were never in dispute. He seldom raised his voice, and though he always came on the runs ashore, he tended to keep himself to himself. He would sometimes be miserable for hours when he made a mistake in the drill. Not that he made any more mistakes than anyone else in training, but he was fanatically dedicated to giving of his best. We all were, but he seemed to show it more than the others.

And then my toffological condition returned to haunt me once again. He came to me in the mess, when it was quiet, and sat down beside me. He was clearly ill at ease and didn't know how to start. He shuffled his feet and then coughed.

'Will, I was wonderin' if you'd come ashore . . . and 'ave a drink wiv me?' he said with an embarrassed grin.

'I'd like to 'ave a chat sometime . . . that's if you don't mind.'

I met him early one evening, just after opening time when it was quiet. When I came into the pub he was sitting in a far corner, all hunched up and looking sad, but he mustered a lonely smile as I approached. After I had got us both a couple of pints, we made casual conversation about the day's training and nattered about this and that. Then during a pause in the small talk, he broke the silence and spoke.

'Will, I gotta problem, and I don't know what to do about it,' he said softly. His eyes were deeply troubled and he tapped the table nervously with his middle finger.

'I think I'm queer, Will,' he said baldly, and then leaned his large frame back in his chair in despair.

I went numb. Nothing else he could have said would have had a greater element of surprise or a more shocking effect. My knowledge and understanding of life hadn't yet equipped me to deal with such a situation. I wasn't yet twenty-one.

'What makes you think that, Mate?' I asked, fighting for time and searching for something helpful to say. He was biting his lower lip and not far short of tears.

''Cos I don't fancy women . . . not the least bit,' he blurted in two separate gasps. And then he lowered his head and shook, drawing in breath as he sobbed.

We must have talked for over an hour, although I was doing the listening most of the time. He told me that he had never done anything about it, he had had no physical relationship with anyone, but he knew that he was attracted to men. I was never in doubt during the conversation that he was talking to me purely as a toffology rate. This illusory 'persona' which he too had bestowed upon me apparently gave me the gifts of objectivity, understanding and wisdom. In his eyes I was a surrogate family doctor, or maybe the young village vicar; I didn't represent a threat. This experience affected me deeply and the responsibility of being party to his secret was onerous.

I didn't have to tell him, but I did. I said that our conversation was not for anyone else's ears. As we made our way back to barracks, he was like a man who had shared the weight of his problem; he was more relaxed and had become philosophical:

'I know it's my problem, Will, but thanks for listening, mate.'

And I realized that that was what it was all about. We never mentioned the subject again but I knew that he was grateful for our conversation that day.

Life's a funny old mixture. The weekend following I became of age in the scheme of life's eternal game. She was a member of the Yacht Club and I had discreetly watched in envy as she flirted with the wealthier men who had invited her aboard their boats. Her dark good looks and shapely body were a treat with which to thrill a young man's secret thoughts and lusts. My lack of confidence and inexperience had led me to conclude that she was far beyond my reach. Furthermore, she was 27 years into life's complex pattern of human behaviour and interaction, and I was an emotionally retarded novice at the age of 22 years and 9 months. By the standards of today, I would be classified as a passed-over pensioner beyond help.

I had found my courage and persisted at the Yacht Club dance the previous weekend. Her older partner had clearly been irritated when I stole three dances and she flashed her eyes in pleasure as she watched him sulk. Later she sought me out and gave me a card with her address written in a bold hand upon the back.

'What are you doing next weekend?' she challenged with a smile which made my stomach churn and do three somersaults. It was agreed that I would call for her at her flat the following Friday evening and we would have dinner at the Queen's Hotel.

I had spent the week in torment, fantasising about all sorts of deliciously wicked thoughts, but most of all wondering how the hell I could bring them to reality. My experience was limited to fumbling in the dark while trying to release a bra. One particular field gunner had brought the vicissitudes of life into perspective. I had to laugh at the ironies with which life confronts us in so many different forms. Here was I worrying how to cope with a dream which might come true.

When I arrived, she let me in with an amused smile on her face; it was more a 'I-won't-bite-you' welcome as I hovered tentatively on the doorstep.

'I've got gin and tonic . . . oh, and some wine for later,' she said as she poured the gin generously into the glasses. Then she looked up.

'Let's not go out. I've got some food in . . . there's plenty to eat. I expect you're starving after running about all day.'

Barely an intelligible word had passed my lips. She was totally in charge . . . and I loved it.

The evening was cool and she lit the fire, having settled me into a large armchair with a replenished drink, the taste of which was bitter-sweet, with its large slice of lemon.

'I'll not be long. You relax while I have a bath,' she said softly and disappeared through the door.

I don't know how long I had been asleep, but I awoke in heaven. She was kneeling naked at my feet, her sparkling brown eyes holding me in her gaze while she tortured me into a moment just short of ecstasy.

By morning she had ridden me through the looking-glass of manhood; I would never be the same again. I liked her but I didn't love her in any romantic sense; she was fun, avidly sensuous, hungry and generous. And I have always remembered her gratefully and with warmth.

Before we knew it, Earl's Court was almost upon us. The A team was destined to be chosen for the event but individual members could still be replaced from the B team if they proved to be better than their opposite numbers. Docherty, my left wheel partner, had risen from the B team and I was very much under challenge from the other right wheel number. We had trained with wheels which weighed 140lbs and the wheels we would use at Earl's Court weighed 120lbs. Only after a week from the start of initial training had we been made to wear a shoulder pad. During this early period the wheel had bitten into our shoulders and created an open wound. Notwithstanding the introduction of shoulder pads, our wounds didn't recover until it was all over at Earl's Court. To this day I still bear the honourable scars of the wheel.

The Royal Tournament at Earl's Court in London presents a splendid opportunity for the three Services to revel in pageantry and showmanship: the Massed Band of the Royal Marines, the Royal Horse Artillery galloping with their guns, the Royal Corps of Signals doing impossible tricks on their motor bikes, the acrobatic physical training instructors, and the Royal Air Force Regiment with their precision marching and arms drill – all these played their part. The colour, the glamour, the military music and the large audiences pumped adrenalin and excitement into our veins. This type of show was more popular in those days;

the great British public were our supporters and they turned out in their droves to attend. Recruiting always shot up dramatically during the three weeks of the Royal Tournament.

There were two shows a day, and we competed against a different Division on each occasion. The two teams that were not running would help to rig the arena for the field gun display during the short interval – a matter of minutes – after the previous display. It was customary for those field gunners who were employed in rigging in the evening to pop across the road to the local pub for a couple of pints before the show started.

The choice of the pub was traditional too. It was notorious in those days for being frequented by a large customer base of London 'gays'. They often enjoyed buying pints of beer for all the nice sailors, and their favourites were the field gunners. Usually we would go to the pub in our uniform, so as to be ready to rig the arena on return.

I had gone shopping one evening and was in plain clothes, but had decided to have a quick pint before changing back into uniform. Our team was drinking and joshing with the Fleet Air Arm crew in the corner, so I went up to the bar for a pint.

I recognized the Fleet Air Arm Chief Trainer standing at the bar.

'Good evening, Chief,' I said in a friendly manner as the barman appeared and asked for my order.

'What'll you have Chief? This one's on me,' I called across.

He was a huge man with a boxer's face, which broke into a knowing grin as he winked obscenely.

'I never say no to a lovely lad like you,' and promptly downed the remains of his beer.

There were 72 field gunners in the four teams, and he clearly didn't recognize me. So I decided to correct this oversight so that he would know me in future.

'Excuse me a moment, Chiefy,' I lisped, and minced over to my mates in the corner. I quickly gave them the score; they laughed and agreed to play along. Meanwhile the Chief, who was still at the bar, thought that I had been chatting them up. On my return, he leered with a grin.

'No luck with the lads?' and gave me another one of his winks.

'Never mind them, I won't say no to another,' he said, passing me his empty glass.

For a further ten minutes I acted the part, while the lads roared their heads off every time the Chief waved in their direction and gave them a thumbs up. He was convinced they were laughing at me. Then I made my farewell.

'I hope you'll be here Thursday, Chiefy, it's my favourite night.' I left the pub to the combined laughter of the Chief and the lads, but they were both laughing for quite different reasons.

Thirty minutes later I was waiting to go on with the other forty riggers at the arena entrance. The Fleet Air Arm Chief Trainer was in charge of the entrance. That night I was carrying the 28ft. spar and positioned myself at the back of the group. Then the announcement was made:

'The Royal Navy presents the Field Gun Crews.' The band struck up with a fast moving sea shanty and the Chief screamed,

'Get moving, you're on.'

I'll never forget his face as I pranced level with him, carrying the 28ft. spar.

'Don't forget Thursday, Chiefy, you gorgeous man.' His face screwed up in horrified disbelief.

'You bastard!' he yelled, as I danced by merrily into the arena.

Thereafter, whenever I met the Chief in the pub, he would always reward me.

'Come here, you little bastard, what'll you have.'

It was traditional that on the last night of the Royal

Tournament we would lace some of the events of the evening with a touch of humour. One couldn't do that with events where life might be endangered, such as the Royal Horse Artillery and the field gun crew, but others were fair game. Four of us chose to have a go at the RAF Regiment.

To conclude their display of precision marching with rifles, and having done all sorts of arms drill on the move, they would fire a 'feu de joie', with three blanks from their rifles as a finale before they marched off.

So we bought three plucked chickens and a bag of feathers from a local butcher and made our way up to the internal roof of the arena. There were hatches which opened and revealed the arena about a hundred feet below, and we selected one that was right in the middle.

Came the moment just prior to the triple volley below, and we loosed the bag of feathers, followed later by the chickens in quick succession. Fourteen thousand people roared their approval below us as the airmen marched off among the feathers, leaving three naked chickens lying dead in the centre of the arena.

We didn't win the field gun competition that year. Devonport were much faster than we were. But Docherty and I had the satisfaction of having been recorded as the fastest ever 'first wheels' across the chasm. It was to be another two years before Docherty and I would meet again in Chatham Barracks, under somewhat different circumstances.

The Baggage Store

The return to Chatham Barracks from Earl's Court was depressing. During my time with the field gun crew I had been rated to Leading Seaman and had returned to barracks in the hope of getting a draft to a destroyer. The Drafting Office told me that they had nothing for me for the moment and that I would remain on the barrack list as a supernumerary.

The Barrack Control Office promptly sent me down the road to take charge of the baggage store. What a comedown that was! When I found it, I beheld a bloody great shed full of bags and hammocks – hundreds and hundreds of them. Most of the kit belonged to sailors who were on foreign service leave, sick in hospital, deserters or simply lost and unclaimed. The bags and hammocks were stowed in rows, almost reaching to the ceiling.

The previous Leading Hand in charge had had a crash draft that morning and so my turn-over was given to me by a two-badge stoker. It turned out that he was a right barrack stanchion and had been in the job for two years without getting a draft. He told me that he had a mate in the Drafting Office who kept putting his card down to the bottom of the list.

He proved, however, to be an encyclopaedia of information with regard to the smooth running of the baggage store. There wasn't a wrinkle that he didn't know about concerning baggage store procedures, and he immediately became my right-hand man. I had eight sailors of varying rate and background, which meant that we could work in four Watches of two for weekends, and two Watches during leave periods.

There was a large but cosy office, which was fitted out with a coal stove, a sink and running water, half a dozen battered armchairs, an old radio and two bunk beds. My transport comprised two small Lister trucks for shifting the kit bags and hammocks, and a couple of pusser red bikes.

Within an hour my attitude had completely changed. I had been given my own little empire and wouldn't be interfered with so long as the organization was run efficiently. 'Knocker' White, my two-badge sidekick, told me that those in authority hardly ever visited the baggage store and that while we kept our heads low, we could live quietly in clover. Knocker said that the better of the two Listers was my private transport around the barracks and that he would be obliged if he could use it too. The other Lister was for the lads, to take them up the road for meals and the like . . . when, of course, it wasn't in use for humping bags.

It seemed that Knocker had a close chum who worked in the victualling stores, and that milk, sugar, tea, coffee, jam and bread, baked beans – you name it – were no problem. In fact, any stores for our comfort were easy to come by, since he also had other contacts as well.

To make life even easier, our shed was immediately opposite the NAAFI canteen, and he assured me that he was on friendly terms with the Assistant Manager. Having heard this, I could hardly believe my luck. I would have no duties, either at weekends or during the evenings, and I could sleep in the office at night rather than with fifty others in the barrack mess.

Life was a doddle. On most days no one did more than three or four hours' work. The rest of the time they sat in the office drinking tea, scoffing beans and toast, and reading books or playing cards. We lived in comparative luxury and I made it clear to my team that we would be the smartest and quietest baggage crew that the barracks had ever known. Everyone had to keep their 'nose' clean and observe all the rules of dress and saluting whenever in transit or in the public eye. I made sure that they were smartly dressed every morning, and Knocker did a deal with the barrack laundry to get their washing done for them.

One day not long after I had taken over, Knocker lowered the morning paper he was reading and scratched his head.

'You know, Hooky, I've been thinkin' . . . every bleedin' day there's a long queue of lads outside the NAAFI at 'stand easy'.

What if we hived off some of the trade?'

He went on to explain that the fifteen minutes allowed for 'stand easy' wasn't long enough for everyone to get served with tea and buns. Since we were right opposite, why didn't we provide the back of the queue with a service? We could brew up several fannys full of tea and flog jam rolls or whatever.

We bought the bread and rolls from our NAAFI contact at trade, and began in a small tentative way. By the following week we had fifty regular customers, all of whom said that our brew was much better than the NAAFI's and that we put much more filling in the rolls. Our prices undercut the NAAFI, since we had no overheads, and our trade mushroomed. The regulars knew the form and would enter our shed and be served round the back of the baggage store, and it became an exclusive 'stand-easy' club. When we added up the profits, we found that we could afford further comforts for the mess. We bought an electric kettle and various other bits and pieces which made life more pleasant.

It came to a very abrupt end when the canteen manager came to visit me in my office. He told me that his trade had gone down during 'stand easy' and that he now knew why. Would I like to draw stumps or should he go to the Master at Arms? It was a 'no contest', and we immediately closed down.

Very soon after his visit, my life took a dramatic turn which was to affect me for the next 30 years.

Chapter 11

The Measured Mile

I was walking along the upper barrack road, which overlooks the parade ground, when I heard a familiar voice: 'Willis!'. Approaching me from across the road came Lieutenant Kim, my Field Gun Officer.

'I've been looking for you. Come with me.'

He took me with him without saying a word, and as I marched by his side I tried to guess what on earth he was up to. We arrived at a ground floor office and he knocked, opened the door and ushered me in.

'This is the chap I've been telling you about. Shall I leave him with you?'

He turned to leave and opened the door.

'Best of luck, Willis.' Then he was gone. It was not until twenty-five years later that we met again.

Lieutenant Commander Hadfield was the Personnel Officer for CW candidates and Special Duties Officers. He sat me down and asked me what I intended to do with my career. I told him that I thought that it was too late to do anything other than leave the Navy. My maths was not good enough to pass the HET and it didn't seem likely that I would be sent back to school. Hadfield looked hard at me.

'Well, you're going to school as from tomorrow.'

From that moment everything moved incredibly fast. They

found an immediate relief for me in the baggage store; another Leading Hand had taken over by dinner time. I was made a CW candidate and I joined their special mess that afternoon; the following morning I was enrolled in the Barracks School to join up with others who were already more than halfway through their HET crash course.

Although I worked all hours, the remaining month wasn't enough and I narrowly failed both maths and mechanics. I wasn't alone, however, since five of them failed one subject or more out of the four taken. We carried on with our full-time schooling in preparation for the next examination period, which would be held in three months. This time I felt that I should be able to achieve a pass, and I duly got down to studying as hard as I was able.

Most evenings we would continue working in the mess, and apart from three periods a week in the gym, we didn't do much else. The first time we went to the gym, I couldn't believe my eyes when I found that me old mucker Conroy had been detailed off to be the CW candidates P.T.I. Obviously someone had a sense of humour. Since I had last seen him in the Reserve Fleet, he had qualified as a P.T.I. Furthermore, he had passed for Petty Officer and was waiting to be rated. The transformation and speed with which he had achieved this was incredible.

He proved to be a highly efficient instructor and set out to get the CWs fit. That was no problem for me since I was fitter than I had ever been owing to my time in the field gun crew. This pleased Conroy and he often used me as his assistant in wall bar and boxwork. They had set up an obstacle course within the large gym, and timed all the classes over the course. Conroy was 'chuffed' when I managed to establish a record time, which had only been bettered by one of the P.T.I.s, namely, of course, himself. He still carried his high pitched giggle with him and I warned the other CWs never to laugh if they wanted to live.

We were encouraged to attend a classical music evening once a week, as part of the overall programme to smooth off the rough edges, but most of us didn't need much encouragement. It was held in the Wrens' Quarters at East Camp and presented an ideal opportunity to fraternise during the coffee break. One of the Instructor Officers played 78" records on a record player, and had great difficulty in regaining quiet after each change of record. I remember meeting a particularly exotic Wren called Olga Peniakov, who smoked her Balkan Sobrani cigarettes from the end of an 18" telescopic cigarette holder. Her father was Popski, of Popski's Private Army fame, and she must have been a chip off the old block with regard to her eccentric and avant-garde way of life.

When at the dentist's one day, I met one of Olga's friends, a dental Wren called Kate. She was a delightful redhead and possessed a wonderful sense of humour. We got on well together and I invited her to experience the delights of the weekly NAAFI dance. The main advantage was that I could change into plain clothes at the NAAFI, and stay the night in one of their small rooms for five shillings. The Wrens were billeted just down the road in separate quarters at East Camp. This was on the far side of the barracks and was defended against intruders, rather in the fashion of a prisoner of war camp.

The weeks swept by one after the other, devoted to study and yet more study. And then the examinations were upon us once more. This time I knew that I had to make good because the next Upper Yardman Selection Board was due to take place in about five weeks' time. After the exam was over, I felt confident about all the subjects except good old maths, but I thought I stood a chance. Nonetheless, we carried on studying because

255

those who managed to pass and were selected, would move on to Portsmouth and become preliminary Upper Yardmen, and then continue with further academic studies before the final Fleet Board.

Only recently the Personnel Officer, Lieutenant-Commander Hadfield, had been relieved by another Lieutenant-Commander called Murdock. None of us had taken to him, and we were sad that Hadfield had left us to take charge of the Special Duties candidates as a full-time job. Murdock was now our boss and in a short space of time he had already shown himself to be bad tempered and erratic in his dealings with us, and I had already incurred his displeasure for apparent flippancy. He possessed a very lean sense of humour.

A week later the HET results came through and all but two of our number had passed the four subjects. I had managed to pass maths and mechanics by three marks and was further elated by doing brilliantly in English, geography and history. All our thoughts were now turned to the Selection Board and keeping out of trouble for the next two weeks.

Meanwhile, Kate told me that Murdock had visited the dentist on several occasions and had taken a keen interest in her. She had teased me and said that she thought he was such a nice man. Naturally she was flattered that she had a Lieutenant-Commander as an admirer, but she also thought that he was a bit too smooth to be true. This information made me feel a little uneasy, since the last thing that I needed was to cross Murdock.

About a week later, and after the dance at the NAAFI was over, Kate and I set off down the hill for East Camp to get her back in time for 11 p.m., when her night leave ended.

The Navy took every measure to guard the virtue of its Wrens from all would-be seducers, and the most obvious danger came from Jolly Jack. Preventative measures included the stationing of a Naval patrol wagon outside the East Camp gates from 10.30 p.m. until just after 11 p.m., when the Wrens returned to camp, mostly escorted by their boy friends. In addition, the local residents had complained to the Naval Barracks that they objected to the couples who engaged in heavy 'necking' in the shadows of the entrance while saying goodnight. The Regulating Staff had therefore had floodlighting installed outside the gates, which illuminated the steel fencing and barbed wire and revealed its Stalag defences.

As we approached, we could see the large Patrol Wagon parked opposite the gate. The Leading Patrolmen were dressed in their long black watch coats, white webbing belts – from which hung batons – and Naval Patrol arm bands. The vehicle's windows were caged and a spotlight was mounted on the roof; it seemed that the only thing missing was a machine gun.

I took her to the floodlit entrance, said I would give her a ring in a couple of days, and pecked her goodnight on the cheek. In an instant a Leading Patrolman was at our side.

'Give me yer paybook,' he snapped officiously at Kate.

She looked at him wide-eyed.

'What for, what have I done?'

'It's against regulations. You're not allowed to 'ave carnal contact 'ere,' he said with a leer, holding out his hand for her to produce her paybook for identification.

'Hang on a moment, Leading Patrolman,' I said reasonably, knowing what little Hitlers they could be.

'Those rules are to prevent heavy necking, not a peck on the cheek.'

Until I spoke, he had barely looked at me and that was probably due to the fact that I was wearing plain clothes. But when I spoke and he heard my accent, his tone of voice altered and he said politely,

'I suggest you speak to the Master at Arms. He's over there in the wagon.'

I waved to Kate as she made her escape into the camp and the patrolman and I both walked over the road towards the lethal looking Patrol Vehicle. The Master at Arms was sitting in the passenger seat with his head and shoulder leaning out of the window, and one great gorilla arm hung vertically down the door as he watched our approach with an ape-like grin on his face.

'Master, this officer wishes to 'ave a word wiv' yer,' said the Leading Patrolman respectfully, and before I had had a chance to open my mouth.

I froze. My mind stopped and I couldn't speak as the Master at Arms studied me suspiciously through his red rimmed, gorilla eyes. I just didn't believe it was happening. So I ignored the patrolman's remark and dived in head first.

'Master at Arms,' I said very politely, 'I'm sure you'll agree that a peck on the cheek doesn't constitute necking,' and then gave him what must have appeared as a sickly smile.

'Well, Sir . . . you knows better'n me . . . rules is rules,' he said as he opened the door and got out. He was tall and his arms seemed to extend down the sides of his body for ever. I was praying feverishly that they wouldn't keep using that stupid bloody word, 'sir'.

'May I sees yer ID card, Sir?' said the Master, as the proximity of his dark frame blotted out the wagon from view.

It was pathetic. I fumbled around in my pockets trying to think how to get out of the situation. I didn't dare tell him that I was a Leading Seaman – not after the Master had used the dreaded word 'Sir'. He would 'kill' me if I owned up now, so I would just have to bluff it out.

'Livin' in the Barrack Wardroom, are we, Sir?' he said in a clipped voice, when it had become clear that my ID was not forthcoming.

'Now what would our name be, Sir?' he said, beginning to enjoy himself, and I noticed that his 'sirs' were sounding sarcastic.

'Brown,' I croaked, with considerable originality.

'Right, Sir . . . Lieutenant Brown, I presume?' He stated rather than asked.

I was now reduced to a nodding idiot, whose only wish was to get away as fast and as far as possible.

The Master at Arms, however, allowed me to proceed on my way. This was only because he wasn't one hundred percent sure that I wasn't really an officer. His parting remark said it all:

'I'm sure we'll bump into each other again. Quite soon, *Lieutenant Brown, Sir.*'

As I set off up the hill, I knew that he would detail two of his gestapo patrolmen to follow me. The area was well known to me, and it didn't take me long to lose them as I disappeared into the parkland near the NAAFI. I must have sat for about twenty minutes in the bushes before proceeding with my well-thought-out plan.

I returned to the NAAFI, changed into uniform, and left my plain clothes in the locker. While doing this, I deliberated whether to stay the night or return to my barrack mess, and finally decided to return 'on board' since we had an early start in the morning. That was to be my undoing.

As I approached the imposing main gates into Chatham Barracks, I was feeling confident that my uniform and pusser's Burberry raincoat would do the trick. They would have been looking for someone in plain clothes, and anyway, they would probably have given up looking by now. But then, I didn't know my man, did I?

Without warning, patrolmen in black watch coats and white webbing belts around their middles appeared from the shadows. They had been hiding in bushes, behind doorways and in dark corners; six of them surrounded me in seconds.

'I'm arrestin' you for impersonatin' Lieutenant Brown, Royal Navy, outside East Camp at 2300,' said one Giles-like cartoon Patrolman, without a trace of humour.

'What me, mate? yer must be bleedin jokin' . . . I's bin 'avin a pint,' I said, and then lost control and laughed.

They escorted me into the main gate to the Regulating Office and shut the door. I was by the window while they stood in a long line silently watching me. Not a word was said, and after a while I asked one of them what they were waiting for.

'The Master at Arms is scouring bleedin' Chatham in the wagon lookin' fer you,' he said peevishly. 'He wants to deal with yer personal like.'

We all heard the wagon screech to a halt. He burst in through the door like King Kong, arms almost touching the ground as he homed in towards me. His face was black and wrinkled as though he were in pain, as he stood triumphantly over me.

'You think I'm a bleedin idiot, don't yer?' he spat out, through his clenched teeth.

I reckoned I had nothing to lose by being polite.

'Master at Arms, you know that I'm not obliged to answer any questions until my Divisional Officer is present,' I said in my best lower deck lawyer's voice.

He managed to restrain himself from knocking me down, and was further angered because I refused to give him Kate's name. After telling me that he would see to it that I would never become a 'bleedin' orfficer', I was taken before the Officer of the Day to be charged. Things weren't looking too good and I could already visualise Murdock's face in the morning.

The charge came under the catch-all heading: 'Leading Seaman Willis, with prejudice to good order and naval discipline, did impersonate Lieutenant Brown, outside East Camp gate at approximately 2300 hours.' The Officer of the Day pursed his lips to stifle the grin and rearranged his face to look grim.

Both the Master at Arms and the Patrolman gave evidence to the effect that I had announced myself to both of them as Lieutenant Brown and ordered them to release the Wren. It was a total distortion of the truth.

'Is this true, Willis,' said Warrant Officer Taylor, who had recently been the second Field Gun Officer for our crew.

I told him what had happened and that I was guilty of not owning up when the mistake was first made, and again I refused to give Kate's name. It was clearly a case which had to be referred to the Commander, but the Master at Arms also wanted me to be put under close arrest. Much to his fury, this was denied and I was sent on my way to turn in for the night.

The next morning I was sent for by Murdock. He had been briefed and he was furious. Furthermore, he knew that I had been with Kate and that she too was on a charge. The Master at Arms had gone to the Wren Officer and demanded a line-up of all those with red hair, and who had also been ashore the night before. Kate was the only one.

'This is the end of your career, Willis,' he said, eyes bulging and looking at me with venom,

'I shall see to it that you're sent back to sea.'

The following day the Commander heard the damning evidence given by the Leading Patrolman, and which in the meantime had been further embellished. I was given Commodore's Report. Murdock gave me no support whatsoever, and told the Commander that he was dissatisfied with my behaviour and was sure that I was not fit to go before the

Selection Board. I left the table all gloom and doom. Then I had an inspiration. I went off to see Lieutenant-Commander Hadfield and told him word for word the whole truth. He told me that I was a stupid idiot and deserved a good boot up the backside, but that he would see what he could do to mitigate the outcome.

Meanwhile, I found out that Kate had been condemned to four days' window cleaning and stoppage of leave, and she hadn't done a thing wrong. The story had done the rounds in the barracks like an Australian bush fire, and I got lots of salutes from people who knew me. Even my Maths Instructor greeted me with a salute.

'Good morning Lieutenant Brown, how's your maths today?'

But I was worried stiff that the Commodore would have my CW papers torn up and that I would not go before the Board.

Murdock took me to the Commodore's office, berating me all the way and telling me that I hadn't got a chance of remaining a candidate. Apparently I was not to be lined up for Commodore's defaulters, but was to be seen separately . . . and probably shot.

Commodore Collard was sitting at his desk; Murdock and Hadfield stood on either side of him as I was marched in and stood rigidly to attention.

Collard didn't mess about with the details, he simply opened fire with the most terrible verbal broadside. It must have lasted a full minute before he was done, and by that time I stood about one foot high and felt very foolish. Neither Murdock nor Hadfield were invited to say a word and remained silent throughout; Murdock, however, looked his furious self.

'You've been an ass,' said the Commodore, 'but I am pleased to note one thing out of this stupid affair.' At this point his face softened as he continued,

'You did at least demonstrate that the age of chivalry isn't quite dead yet.' He dismissed me, and as I marched to the door he added,

'By the way, best of luck with the Board, Willis.'

I had been saved by the bell – Commodore Collard's bell. But I knew one thing instinctively: Hadfield had encouraged him to ring it.

The following week I passed the Board by a whisker. The Chairman was a well known gunnery officer, Captain Roberts, referred to as 'two-gun Roberts'. He had heard of my recent stupidity, but possibly let me through when he read in my report that I had been in the Field Gun Crew. Anyone who was sensible enough to play with guns couldn't be all bad. I remember him saying that he was in two minds about sending me back to sea for a couple of years, because then I might make a better officer. Unfortunately there were too many like-minded officers at the time who couldn't see that the sooner those selected were taken into the fold, the better they would be trained and moulded for their new role. Maybe he was just scaring the hell out of me – who knows?

Anyway, I packed my bag and hammock and joined Victoria Barracks. I was now one of the preliminary Upper Yardmen who would be honed ready for the Fleet Board in three months' time. Could I keep my nose clean till then?

Oily Qs

The successful CW candidates from all the Ports of Division were now merged into one group in preparation for the next vital test. We had, in effect, become eligible for further consideration. We were now to be dusted off in preparation for the Fleet Board and if we passed that, we would be sent to

H.M.S. *Temeraire* for one year as fully fledged Upper Yardmen. During that year at *Temeraire*, we would be subject to three further critical examinations, when we might fail and be returned to the Fleet. As we slowly climbed the ladder– as did the Upper Yardmen of yesteryear in sail – none of us could afford to slip on any of its rungs.

There were about twelve of us – half had already fallen by the wayside – and it was expected that about four of us would fail the Fleet Board. We immediately noticed, however, that both officers and senior ratings responsible for our training treated us quite differently from hitherto. There was a subtle change in attitude. Much more was now expected of us and we also felt that we were being given serious consideration for membership of the exclusive club. In short, they now demanded that we demonstrate officer-like qualities (OLQs) at all times.

OLQs now became both the bane and the humour of our daily lives. They were mostly subjective qualities, which did and could, in the eyes of the beholder, change from individual to individual; these qualities were affected by both time and fashion. Naturally a senior officer's perceptions would differ considerably, in terms of priority, from that of a junior officer. But it wasn't as simple as that. A particular junior officer might have been influenced by a right old stickler, while another might have served under a so-called 'enlightened modernist'. Those of us who passed the Fleet Board were destined to walk through a minefield of uncertainty and prejudice until such time as we had learned where the mines were buried. But we entered enthusiastically into the spirit of the new game, which was known throughout the Navy as the pursuit of 'Oily Qs'.

The more obvious considerations included: plain clothes dress – otherwise now known as 'dog robbers' – what to wear and what not to wear, table manners, and the way in which one held one's knife and fork, drinking formalities – 'Do have the other half,' even if the chap was on gin and tonics – and never saying 'Good morning' to a senior officer unless he had already inclined to the opinion that the weather was fine. The list was endless, and as one became more familiar with the subtleties, degrees and nuances, one learned to elicit smiles of approbation from one's superiors.

Our most enthusiastic mentor in 'Oily Qs' was an eccentric Instructor Officer, Lieutenant Thomas. No matter how many times he shaved away the black stubble each day, the shadowy outline remained on his great chin and cheeks. He was a caricature of 'Desperate Dan,' albeit a meticulously dressed and well-spoken Desperate Dan. He frequently donned a monocle and often practised catching it between cheek and eyebrow. His subject was history and he was a superb teacher. He brought the past alive with a multitude of colourful historical titbits. The scandals, the spice and the misdeeds of the past were served up in the vernacular and laced with dry English humour. His command of English, combined with an enthusiastic, bubbling delivery, brought the characters to life in our presence as he spoke. He was also deliciously irreverent and a natural born actor, who knew that he was teaching us the rules of a complex and necessary game.

On Saturday mornings it was his delight to take us to the Queen's Hotel for a 'half'. We would wear our 'dog robbers' and the obligatory hat. In those days, a hat or cap was essential for officers when walking 'ashore,' since it would be doffed in response to subordinates, salutes, or raised in deference to superiors. Without a hat one just had to gape and look foolish. The style of hat or cap, however, was important. A flat shooting cap – especially when supported with a suitable gun dog and walking stick – was senior officers' territory, but was approved to be worn by juniors without the additional props. A pork pie, though, was positively spivvy and only worn by sharp practitioners and Special Duties Officers who hadn't yet got the buzz. The trilby was very acceptable, preferably in dark brown, and hideously misshapen by wind and rain. Harris tweed sports jackets, suits and the like, were de rigeur, and if it was cold or raining, one could wear an ill-fitting navy blue, pusser issue Burberry – officers' beltless version only. Snazzy blue blazers with gold buttons and badges were definitely out, but a Gieves reefer with black anchor buttons was most certainly in – if you could afford it.

Hence one usually had to achieve the appearance of a country gentleman who was probably on his way to inspect the estate or maybe shoot pheasants. The overall impression had to lend an air of casual but rich shabbiness, later to be brilliantly illustrated by MacMillan as Prime Minister, and also a brilliant poseur. The unrepresentative surroundings of ships' dockyards and the sea crashing over the nearby breakwaters merely accentuated the juxtaposition, and indicated that one was probably off one's usual beaten path.

In those days the Queen's Hotel was one of the acceptable officers' haunts. This was all the more so if one frequented the 'snug' bar. It was invariably devoid of women, and on a Saturday lunchtime smelled of stale beer and looked rather like the black hole of Calcutta. Everything was dark; the navy blue curtains hung heavily and reeked of cigarette and pipe smoke, the tables and chairs were oak, and pseudo-beams crowded the deckhead above, while the light from the small leaded windows was meagre and full of shadows. Row upon row of silver-plated half-pint tankards caught what light there was, and hung twinkling above the heavy oak bar. The optics catered only for brandy and gin.

For those with deep pockets, gin and tonic – or maybe

Plymouth with a tincture of angostura – or 'horse's neck' (brandy and ginger ale with ice and lemon) was the usual choice. This applied to most naval officers aboard ship. But on shore and without duty free, a half of bitter in a silver tankard – never a pint – was the acceptable alternative to spirits. And it was important to know how to hold the tankard, both when drinking and between sips. If one was right-handed, it should normally be held close to the upper right chest in readiness for the next sip.

It was considered to be incredibly bad form to ask a chap whether he would like *another* drink. It implied that the man was either a drunkard, couldn't be got rid of, or was permanently on the bum. But to ask him whether he might like 'the other half' was quite different. In that situation he was almost doing you a favour, even if he was on large gins at double the price and clearly pissed as a fart. We learned all these niceties from Desperate Dan, who humorously explained both the merits and the absurdities of each OLQ.

Sometimes he would take us to the Keppel's Head, just outside the main dockyard gate, and once frequented by the likes of Rodney and Nelson prior to joining their Fleet at Spithead. Before Rodney's West Indies jaunt and the Battle of the Saintes, Rodney couldn't have used it much because he was constantly pursued by creditors who waited for him to appear on the Hard at Portsmouth. Apparently he was forced to be picked up by boat from a deserted beach near Gosport in order to elude them. Anyway, he picked up so much prize money in the West Indies that he could probably have afforded to open an account with Gieves, the naval tailors, on his return.

Each morning we attended colours on the parade ground armed with a cutlass. This was early preparation for sword drill, and we would march past the rostrum flashing our cutlasses in salute. This was done to the music of the Royal Marine Band on an ancient 78" record, and was broadcast over the tannoy system. The distorted music blared raucously across the parade ground, and every morning it sounded as though some Panamanian military coup was taking place. We would then spend the rest of the day either at instruction, school or sport, and I found plenty of time to go sailing in the naval whalers and dinghies.

We lived in a semi-world of make believe, putting on what we supposed were the airs and graces of naval officers, and demonstrating our new-found OLQs whenever in the company of our tutors. Yet at the same time we were still sailors dressed in ratings uniforms

The day of the Fleet Board arrived and we were taken to HMS *Sultan,* where the board met. I seem to remember that about eight officers and a president constituted the board, and the latter was an Admiral. The procedure hadn't changed much from that employed for many years, and that which was used during the Second World War. We all changed into PT gear and lined ourselves up in the gym to have numbers pinned to our chests and back. Then the fun and games started. They confronted us with an imaginary chasm (ever since the Boer War the Navy had loved chasms), and provided us with large oil drums, half a dozen planks, lots of rope and several large climbing ropes which were secured from the ceiling and hung down in the middle of the chasm.

One of the board officers then posed a task to be performed, which involved getting something or some people, or both, across to the other side. He then invited us to discuss amongst ourselves how this should be done. Everyone wanted to be seen as a natural born leader, and consequently the discussions quickly developed into an Irish parliament. Nevertheless, everyone was also aware that they couldn't be seen to be hysterical loud mouths and so we all tried to be frightfully reasonable at the same time. At this stage, the officer appointed a particular person to take charge and get on with the task. So one by one we were given the opportunity to be the leader.

All through my naval career I had cursed the fact that my name began with W. The Ws' were followed only by the Ys in the alphabetical order of things – not too many Englishmen's names began with an X or a Z – and everything was done in alphabetical order. There were no Ys present at the board and therefore I was the last on the list. One of the early candidates had been a Chatham man, who knew that I was both very fit and athletic; so he chose me to launch myself into space on the end of the climbing rope to the other side of the chasm. Two persons had already fallen in during previous tasks, and he was well pleased when I made it to the other side. Thereafter, I was chosen to leap into space or climb the rope by every leader who took charge. By the time it came to my turn to take charge, I was not only exhausted but I didn't know who else would make it across the chasm. My first and second choices promptly fell to their 'deaths' and I was beginning to fear that I would run out of men. The third one got over and we finally came to the end of the morning's events.

The afternoon was devoted to an interview with the naval psychologist and followed by the main board interview. Once again I was last, but this time I felt that circumstances were now all in my favour. As each white-faced candidate emerged from the psychologist, we would make him re-live his experience. But after about half a dozen such wash-ups, I had become utterly confused since no comprehensible pattern emerged, and I was fast becoming a manic depressive. We had a Royal Marine candidate, who was apparently fascinated by ghosts and things spiritual. When asked by the psychologist what his favourite hobby was, he had tried to interest the psychologist in the occult. The Marine failed to achieve a new conversion or indeed to pass the board.

When my turn came, I steered clear of all controversial subjects, including my father, and strove to appear to be impossibly bland and normal. Once he nearly caught me out; he asked whether I had any strong feelings about anything, and I just saved myself in time by saying, 'Yes, the Navy,' and left it at that.

The main interview was a bit of a trial, since I detected that the board was now weary of asking the same questions and there was a danger that in desperation they would pluck weirdo questions out of the air. The Engineer Commander kept going on about boiler tubes, and the Instructor dwelt heavily on my maths; but I was probably saved by the President, who was a keen sailing man, and I listened attentively while he spent ages telling me of his experiences.

They discussed us in private for a further hour and a half while we nervously chatted and speculated in hope. Then, one by one, they started to call us in for the result. It was easy to tell as they emerged from the room who had been successful and who had not. Four failed and eight of us passed.

We were sent off home on leave for ten days and were ordered to join HMS *Temeraire* at South Queensferry in Scotland. The 'Upper Yardman' course would take a year to complete, and if we were successful, we would be promoted to Acting Sub-Lieutenant.

The Measured Mile

In 1954, South Queensferry was a small Scottish village on the south bank of the Forth. It was dominated by the Forth Bridge, which towered over its eastern edge and then swept its way majestically north across the Firth to North Queensferry. The Navy still had a small harbour next to South Queensferry, which had been used by small destroyers in the First World War but was now used occasionally by minesweepers and other small craft.

The Upper Yardman establishment comprised a large Victorian house on the hill overlooking the Firth of Forth. It accommodated the Captain, a number of officers and about twenty Upper Yardmen. Some of the officers lived locally or in drab naval married quarters.

Each term a new batch of seamen and other 'specialisations' – engineers, aircrew and supply – joined *Temeraire*, and the senior terms departed as Sub-Lieutenants. The specialist candidates would leave after two terms and continue training at their respective specialist training establishments, while the seamen remained for three terms at *Temeraire*. There were four of us in our group of seamen, and throughout we underwent our instruction together.

The staff, including the Captain, consisted of four Seaman Officers, five Instructor Officers and a small ship's company of cooks and stewards. *Temeraire* was allocated two picket boats and a fifty-square-metre yacht for seamanship training, and it had its own sports field. We were virtually self-contained, and isolated from all outside influences. The village was about a mile away and Edinburgh was ten miles. There was no leave during the week, and our only day out was on a Saturday or Sunday. The bus service was almost non-existent and initially going out meant getting a lift with one of the staff officers who owned a car. The lowest priority on our agenda, however, was shore leave;

we were there to undergo intensive schooling and instruction, which was designed to bring us up to the standard of our future Dartmouth equivalents. If we qualified, we would join the general list and become full career officers in the Royal Navy.

Our biggest and most immediate culture shock was that we now lived as officers in the wardroom. We had our meals with the Captain and the staff officers, and we all sat down together for dinner each evening. Nonetheless, we still wore our ratings' uniforms, except that we now had white flashes on our shoulders and a white band on our caps. This signified that we were Upper Yardmen and as such, officer candidates.

During the first two terms our time was dominated by schooling. Most found that the curriculum for applied mechanics and maths was difficult. I found it to be sheer hell. My understanding of the basics was pathetic and I tried to learn by rote, but inevitably stumbled whenever the problem was couched in a different form. I wasn't the only one to suffer, but we were so pressurised that there was no time to consider anyone else's problems but our own.

Lieutenant Commander Selwyn was responsible for maths and mechanics and gave us prep. to do each evening. It took me till midnight to get through it, and increasingly I began to dislike him. He gave me no respite and I dreaded each day as he would come to list the evenings prep. I would even call out in despair as he named the seemingly endless stream of problems we would have to solve that night. The man was heartless and utterly indifferent; he would smile when he heard me groan as I wrote each prep. notation in my book, and probably add another for good measure.

The evening's work was done in the privacy of our own small cabin. As the hours passed and I realised that there was so much more to do, tears of frustration would roll down my cheeks and stain the page as I fought to untangle my mind. By now I hated the bastard intensely, and I was damned if Selwyn was going to make me look the fool I felt. The hate became my daily motivation, and when I handed in my completed prep., I would crow silently to myself: That's got the bastard. He never thought I would do it. And then it would start all over again as he called out the next evening's prep.

The days merged one into another, and we became immersed in the demanding grind of the classroom. This was cleverly spiced with occasional sport or a few hours on the river, to wash our minds clean for the next onslaught.

Prior to lunch and dinner, we would gather in the ante-room for a pre-meal half pint of bitter and a chat. Our Captain was a man called Marriot, who often brought his Labrador dog to sit at his feet while we chatted before lunch. This casual chat had its own canons, which were observed and played by us all. Although we were wary, we soon became relaxed in the company of all the staff officers, and even Joe Milne, the First Lieutenant, didn't bite unless you asked for it. But it was different with the Captain. When he entered the ante-room it was the unspoken signal to form a circular screen around his position. He and his dog would be in station zero, the centre, and each of us would have some erudite question already stored in our brain.

The first eager man who wanted to shine would step one pace into the ring, clear his throat, fire his profundity into the air like a star shell, and then wait for it to bloom in the Captain's mind.

'Sir, I wonder whether you think the political situation will improve in Egypt?' He would then mentally reload with a supplementary question, and resume his station on the screen.

The Captain, having located the source of the question, would gauge the person while pondering the answer.

'Interesting . . . yes . . . well it can't get much worse. All depends on Eden, I suppose.'

As the Captain paused for breath, the next opportunist would move smoothly into position and fire his own profundity at the target.

'Sir, they say that it takes a year to paint the Forth Bridge . . . and then they start all over again.' The questioner was clearly a new boy, since the Forth Bridge was an old chestnut and didn't win any points; this sort of crass observation would merely flicker momentarily, then fade quickly as the Captain wrestled to find yet another original reply to this tired subject.

It would, nonetheless, be the cue for all to gaze hypocritically in wonder towards the bridge through the ante room window, and find to our amazement that the bloody great lump of Meccano was still there.

'Ah . . . yes . . .' the Captain would say with resignation, 'Hmm . . . You know that the old battle fleet had to strike their topmasts . . . before going underneath . . . and another thing, if the navigator arrived under the bridge bang on time, the Captain would buy him a drink.'

Then some prat who was low on brownie points, would blurt out,

'Gosh, sir, you must have enjoyed striking the topmast . . . and I expect you won a drink from your Captain, sir?'

The Captain's face would tighten and he would remind the prat icily that in the first place he was a gunnery officer and not a navigator, and in the second that he hadn't served in the First World War. Whereupon, the Captain would impatiently close the audience, the questioners would turn pink and escape to the heads, and the rest of us would follow the Captain to lunch, grateful that we had kept our mouths shut.

Trying to score points so obviously was a dangerous game.

The staff had seen it and heard it all before. One had to do one's homework before venturing into the minefield and it was wise to read up on the subject beforehand. A quick flip through *The Times* could be rewarding, while there were some who swore by the *Readers' Digest* since they were sure that Marriot wouldn't dream of reading that sort of magazine. All the staff officers were on the alert for those who kept quiet and held their council. One had to join in and voice one's opinions, otherwise one would score low marks for social graces, lack of confidence and general knowledge. This was also tested daily in written form. We kept a journal and had to write at least one page a day, which was handed in weekly and read by our House Officer. Subjects could embrace naval affairs or general knowledge, and in order to fill the seven-day quota, there was plenty of plagiarising. Old magazines and articles from the *Readers' Digest* were much in demand, but I found it was more trouble than it was worth. It took so much time to transpose the article and readapt it into one's own style, that one might as well have written an original. Furthermore, the staff weren't often fooled, so it wasn't worth the candle.

By the end of the first term I had made some considerable progress, but we still had much to learn before reaching the required standard. I failed our 'in-house' examinations in maths and mechanics by ten marks or so, and knew that the following term would be one hell of a challenge. At the end of the next term we had formal and final academic exams which had to be passed.

After Christmas leave at home we settled down to the long slog through the spring term. A new intake had arrived and included Charles Wylie from my Mediterranean days, plus Bobby Newall, Len Cavan, Pip Barker and Tony Davidson. They were a lively and welcome addition to our numbers and there was a further bright light to look forward to that term. We would all go to London for an educational week to see the traditional sights, and for the accompanying staff to observe our conduct as young 'gentlemen' in a civilian environment. It was a short 'couth' course in plain clothes.

We had enormous fun in going to Edinburgh and ordering our dark pin-stripe suits from Austin Reeds, as well as a rolled umbrella and the obligatory bowler hat, which we would be expected to wear in London. Len Cavan was a well-built Canadian affectionately known as Davy Crocket. He had bought a bowler which was too small and he looked like a younger version of Hardy from Laurel and Hardy. Furthermore, Canadians had more adventurous tastes in clothing and he had bought a Mediterranean blue suit to go with it. The First Lieutenant, Joe Milne, winced and raised one eyebrow but accepted that some colonials had unusual tastes. There were several Australians and a Kiwi as well, all of whom used to come to Britain for their training in those days.

The staff timed our trip to London to perfection. We departed just when our minds were about to blow the full set of fuses. What a splendid sight we made on Waverly Station; dressed to the nines, swaggering along, bowler hatted and swinging umbrellas. How we laughed when we thought of our former shipmates and what they would say if they could see us now, poncing like peacocks in our finery. I knew what Nobby would say, as he cheekily pinched my cheek with a grin: 'Hell man, no offence. One never knows unless one tries.'

We trudged round all the museums, we visited the Albert Hall and we saw the ravens and jewels at the Tower. Then we took in a show, probably *The Mousetrap*, flogged all the way out to Kew gardens, and swaggered some more in the Inner Temple.

But the best trip of all was a visit to No. 1 Court in the Old Bailey.

We arrived when a man was on trial for producing and possessing pornographic material, in those days a serious offence. The case was well under way and the defendant was under cross examination. I had never witnessed the full majesty of the law in progress. There was the red-robed judge, raised high in his chair like God and harbouring his power, while below him sat the clerk of the court. And in the front stalls were the wigged counsel, some lolling while others fussed with their papers. But as if this wasn't enough to send a tingle of fear through the innocent, the grandeur of the impersonal setting formed an imposing backdrop, and the air was redolent with power. This was the law taking its inexorable course towards justice. I was glad to be a spectator.

The defendant was a small, sharp-featured cockney, with a 'Spiv's' pencil moustache. In fact he looked just like my old 'Buffer', but without a moustache. He was dressed in a brown suit with heavily padded shoulders and he wore a loud tie. The dock seemed to dwarf him and he gave the appearance of an inquisitive sparrow, as he frequently bobbed his head at the prosecuting counsel.

'Now tell me in your own words, what happened on that fine sunny day by the river,' said the prosecuting barrister in a relaxed and friendly manner.

The sparrow bobbed his head and then hunched alternate shoulders, as though warming up and just about to take off.

'Well, it were a luverly sunny day, so my gel and me went fishin'. My mate 'ad caught a right real wopper a couple a weeks before, like,' added the sparrow gratuitously, as he exercised his wings again.

'I see, and what happened then?' said counsel coaxingly.

'It were very 'ot, and she loves 'er sun . . . so she took a few fings orf to give 'erself an all-over tan, like,' said the sparrow, clawing the dock nervously and moving his weight from one foot to the next.

'And anyway, the fish weren't bitin' . . . so I finks to meself: 'Why not take a few snaps fer the family album, like? So I does.' concluded the sparrow lamely, darting his head toward the judge as though looking for confirmation.

Counsel for the prosecution uncurled slowly to his full height, clasped the lapels of his black robe firmly in either hand, and with head held high, went in for the kill.

'I see. *So you took a hundred filthy photographs because the fish weren't biting?*' thundered the prosecution with righteous indignation.

From that moment onward the day was lost for the sparrow. No matter what he said by way of explanation or in mitigation, the prosecution thundered back: '*You took a hundred filthy photogaphs because the fish weren't biting?*'

If my memory serves me aright, he was sentenced to seven years. I was really sorry for him, especially as it would be only a few years later that the law would change dramatically and the crime would have warranted a fine only.

In no time at all London was but a distant memory as we got back into the daily slog. Selwyn continued to be the single-minded focus of my hate as the time drew near for the final academic examinations. He ploughed deep furrows in my brain and cast the seeds of knowledge into my fallow mind. So far as maths was concerned, I was just plain thick.

Meanwhile Captain Marriot had been relieved. Our new Captain was called Carrington, a sharp and dedicated career officer who was said to be in the fast lane. He held firm views about the qualities required of Upper Yardmen and he made an immediate impact on our conduct. Gone were the sanguine, 'father figure' ways of Marriot, who could give a blast of anger with the best of them but was relaxed and tolerant at most times. In its place came close, cold, analytical inspection. We learned to weigh our words carefully in his presence, and loose cannon ball remarks became collectors' items. Spontaneity became a luxury that we could ill afford, since censure was immediate and we sensed instinctively that each disapproving glance was logged indelibly in his mind.

Carrington was single and a single-minded man. All conversation was geared to things naval, and every mealtime we shared was laced with naval conduct and politics – sadly not with salt, wind and spray. He was deep and heavy and his conversation didn't elicit response. Carrington was, nonetheless, devoted to his cause and spent all his hours pursuing his aim. This was to identify those not worthy of promotion, and to smooth the paths of those that were his chosen. Most Saturdays he would invite six different Upper Yardmen to dinner. Naturally it was a royal command and we knew that our every word and move would be observed and weighed.

One such evening I found myself sitting next to a fellow Upper Yardman called Peter Hill. He was a poseur par excellence and was gifted with a pseudo-cultured and penetrating voice. His every action and remark were presented with an actor's skill for the benefit of the Captain. We were halfway down the table from Carrington, but his false and monotonous conversation droned on solely for the Captain's ears. It consisted of his borrowed views – all Carrington's – about naval beliefs and what one should aim to achieve. Finally I could stand his cant no more.

'For God's sake, stop talking shop. It's me you're talking to.'

Carrington heard me and stopped dead in mid-sentence.

'I should have you know, Willis, that I always talk shop, as you put it, and I'm pleased to hear that Hill has the good sense to follow my lead. You would do well to take note.'

As is the situation in all institutional organisations, the staff were bound to have their favourites and the Captain was no exception. The House Officers, Lieutenants Cobb and Hunt, were pretty well straight down the middle, but with one or two exceptions. In fact, looking back, I don't think that we could have had a more reasonable and fair-minded bunch of officers, and during the time that I was at *Temeraire* we were led by good men. Indeed, Lieutenant Nicholas Hunt was to become the Commander-in-Chief Fleet, less than thirty years on. John Cobb retired early as a Commander, and I believe that Joe Milne, the First Lieutenant, became a four-ring Captain. My only blind spot lay with Selwyn, and so far as I was concerned, common sense and reason didn't enter into my hate.

I passed all my examinations except applied mechanics, and I failed that by several marks. A number of us had failed various examinations, and the form was that we all had to go before an impartial 'Fail Board'. This was convened across the water in Rosyth Dockyard, and it was with a sense of foreboding and sick stomachs that we waited our turn to be interviewed.

Two of the four of us were failed. This meant that those who had failed would be returned to the Fleet and carry on as ratings as though nothing had happened. It was incredibly cruel. They should have given them the option of leaving the service. I was most upset by one lad's failure in particular. We had been close chums for a number of years and I could see that the decision had hurt Purvis deeply. Those who failed were made to disappear quickly, as though they hadn't really existed; within an hour they were packed and on their way to Edinburgh Station without any farewells. They just vanished. But more of Purvis later, since they couldn't keep a good man down for too long.

The term ended and I had been reprieved. I experienced an immense sense of satisfaction at having got through, but I didn't celebrate. The mixed feelings had left me emotionally drained; the strain of the past two terms hit home suddenly as the tensions poured like a septic abscess from my mind. I had never thought that it was possible for me to reach the standard of maths required. The only thing that had kept me going was that bastard Selwyn. And only now did I realise that he had known all the time. Had he been kind and considerate, I would have failed, and this understanding came home to me in an instant, like a blinding revelation. Selwyn had dragged me kicking and screaming, by the scruff of the neck through the nightmare and into the light.

He was a wise old bugger. He was grinning wickedly and his eyes were sparkling as he saw me coming across the ante-room, my right hand already outstretched in thanks. I was incoherent with emotion and kept mumbling, 'Thank you, sir. Thank you, sir.,' as he continued to grin and wring my hand.

'You see,' he said quietly, 'You weren't thick after all,' and added, 'I think we could both do with a drink, don't you?'

I laughed as I brushed away the tears from my eyes, and went and bought him a bloody great 'horse's neck' with two shots of brandy. I will never forget Selwyn; he was the watershed of my life.

We started the final term as the senior Upper Yardmen. This term we would concentrate upon seamanship and navigation. The navigation was in two parts: pilotage – coastal navigation – and celestial navigation. I had fears about the latter, because the theory would involve mathematics, but I felt confident about the pilotage because I had already passed my HET while serving in *Loch Scavaig*. As for seamanship, I thrived on the subject and had had plenty of practical experience upon which to build.

We had an additional incentive during our final term, which was to join a destroyer or frigate for three weeks' sea time. Each of us would go to a different ship and we would be assessed by the ship's Captain on completion. Meanwhile, we set about learning the theory of astronomical navigation.

To my amazement I found that I both enjoyed it and had few problems. Selwyn was our Instructor Officer, and it was so satisfying not to be the 'no-hoper' any more, and to look forward to the evening's prep rather than dreading it.

We had much more time to ourselves and nearly every weekend we would go to Edinburgh, quite often to the University dance on a Saturday night. We even had time for the occasional girl friend, and our social life was no longer a thing of the past.

I was sent to HMS *Tumult*, a destroyer, and I joined her at Portland in Dorset. It was strange to be back on board a ship again, dressed as a leading seaman but living in the wardroom. The officers immediately made me comfortable and at home; they treated me like a midshipman, and naturally I got all the grotty little jobs that no one else wanted to do. When at sea, I spent most of my time on the bridge as Second Officer of the Watch and for the first time enjoyed the thrill of taking the 'con' under the eagle eye of the First Lieutenant or Navigator. It was a happy wardroom and they were full of fun.

One day in harbour, a 'chummy' ship, berthed on the jetty opposite us, had invited our wardroom to an RPC for drinks at 1800. I was left alone to hold the fort while the other officers were gone. About an hour later, while I was sitting reading a paper in one of the wardroom chairs, I heard a voice say,

'Hello, where's everyone gone then?'

I looked up and saw a Sub-Lieutenant eyeing me quizzically

from the wardroom door. I jumped to my feet and invited him in, explaining where the others were and saying they wouldn't be long. Then I asked him what he would like to drink. He was somewhat hesitant but decided he would take me up on the offer and sat down. I poured him a drink and then decided that it would be polite to join him, so poured one for myself too. I passed him his drink and sat down saying 'Cheers' as I took a sip of my gin and tonic. For a moment I thought he was going to choke on his drink, and I wondered whether I had put in too much gin as he stared at me in disbelief. Thankfully, the Quartermaster gave two pips over the tannoy on his bosun's call – to warn me the officers were returning. As I rushed off, muttering an apology, he was still gripping his glass tightly in some sort of shock. I met them over the brow and warned the First Lieutenant that there was a visitor waiting in the wardroom.

When I returned to the wardroom two minutes later, they turned towards me and laughed, but I noticed that the Sub-Lieutenant was red-faced and sheepish. Apparently he had immediately reported my behaviour to the First Lieutenant:

'Sir, your steward actually had the nerve to join me for a drink when I got here,' had said the Sub-Lieutenant indignantly.

Another amusing incident occurred in a similar vein a week later. I had been told to meet a party of visiting sea cadets and to show them round the ship, and I went to meet their bus and escort them to the ship. As I waited on the corner just outside the dockyard gate, I noticed one of my favourite fraternity come out of the patrol headquarters from across the road. He was a pug-faced Leading Patrolman, already looking for someone to harass. Portland, at 1000 on a Sunday morning, was usually deserted, and I was the only person in sight.

He spotted me immediately and stopped. I stared back at him and smiled, knowing that to smile at a Leading Patrolman was like throwing a petrol bomb.

'You, come 'ere,' said the Patrolman with military charm.

I turned away, shaded my eyes with one hand – à la Pinafore – and looked up the road with exaggerated concentration.

'Did yer 'ear me?' he snarled from across the road.

I turned slowly towards him and smiled again.

'Surely, Leading Patrolman, you're not speaking to me?' I asked in surprise.

'Report to me right now – this instant,' he blustered, while pointing his finger at the road in front of him.

'Take me to the Duty Regulating Petty Officer at once!' I commanded, in an exaggeratedly officer-like tone of voice, and marched across the road towards the patrol headquarters.

'No, I ordered you to come 'ere,' he whined, still pointing at the piece of road at his feet.

He followed me protesting into the presence of the RPO, who was sitting behind his desk clutching a bacon sandwich in one hand and a mug of tea in the other.

'RPO, in future please brief your Leading Patrolman properly before letting him run riot on a Sunday morning,' I said formally, noting his bacon sandwich and mug of tea. He rose from his seat in bewilderment and looked questioningly at his Patrolman. But I was determined to retain the initiative.

'You, of course, RPO, will be aware that I am an Upper Yardman, and as such have officer status,' I said pompously, not knowing whether it was true, but noting with satisfaction that he spilled some of his tea as he nodded his head in uncertain agreement.

'Therefore, RPO, I would be obliged if you will tell him to desist in future from bawling, "Oy, you, come 'ere" from across the road.' I added this primly with all the affected wardroom manner I could muster.

The RPO found his voice.

'He's new, Sir,' he said appealingly, as he gently placed his breakfast on the desk.

''Asn't been 'ere long. He wont be doin' it again,' he said meaningfully, glaring at the silent Patrolman, whose face was in shock.

I savoured my harmless revenge and later drank a derisory toast to the *Ganges* Master at Arms and the persecutor of Lieutenant Brown R.N.

I had enjoyed every minute of my time in *Tumult* and couldn't wait to get back to sea. The Captain and the First Lieutenant had given me a good report for my time spent in the ship, and this would carry weight in my final assessment. But meanwhile we sat our seamanship and navigation examinations and fast approached the day when the final decision would be made. I was particularly jubilant to have gained top marks in astro-navigation, and Selwyn had done me proud once again.

We, the senior term, were now being measured for our uniforms by the Gieves representatives. The staff were very pro-Gieves and other tailors didn't stand much of a chance, even though they were less expensive. There had been, however, a significant number of occasions when failure had followed even after the uniform suits had been made, and the sailor was returned to the Fleet. Nothing could be taken for granted.

It was at about this time that I received a sudden shock. One of my allotted miscellaneous duties was to be in charge of the Loan Clothing Store. This included items such as oil skins, sea boots and socks, gym shoes and other oddments. The First Lieutenant had carried out a crash muster and found that I hadn't been able to account for half a dozen or so missing items. He gave me a severe blast and told me that it was both his and the Captain's opinion that I was lacking in organisational ability.

I took every word to heart. There were three and a half weeks to go before we would be told if we had passed. I became a fanatical organiser overnight. Within twenty-four hours I had conducted a search and located two left sea boots, one right gaiter, one sou'wester and three gym shoes. With the greatest ostentation, I mustered all the Upper Yardmen twice weekly for loan clothing musters – it happened to be well within earshot of the First Lieutenant's office – and they signed for every individual item. The Upper Yardmen thought that I had gone mad. Anything which needed to be taken charge of, I volunteered for immediately. My methods of accounting were immaculate and I returned to my 'secondary occupation' days, when I was seldom to be seen without a clipboard.

Meanwhile, the senior term were told to give some thought to organising a night exercise. We and the staff would have the task of detecting and catching the attackers and would make use of the boats and all available transport to best advantage. Our next meeting would be in three days' time for further discussions and planning.

I arrived at the meeting armed with the entire written operational order, including: nominal lists of duties and tasks, ordnance survey maps, charts, moonrise and moonset, height of high and low water. I had planned it to be a surprise. My plan swept the board and no one had any detailed material with which to argue against my proposal. The First Lieutenant smiled knowingly and commented that his boot up the arse had done wonders. One of my group was livid that I had taken all the glory, while the others knew damned well that I needed the organisational brownie points and laughed at the whole charade.

Mother and Father had long prepared to come to the Passing-out Parade, and arrived as South Queensferry four days before the event. They booked in at the local inn, the Seal's Craig, overlooking the Firth of Forth, and there they settled down to await the outcome. It was all very unnerving, having them just down the road, and before we had officially been told the results. Mother was permanently nervous and kept telling me to speak nicely to the Captain, and Father was bored out of his mind by the end of the first day. So, never at a loss to find something with which to keep himself busy, Father asked the landlord if he had any odd jobs that needed doing.

'I ken that I can find a wee challenge,' said the landlord, and promptly set him to work building shelves in the cellar. This kept Father occupied and happy for three days, and the landlord was pretty pleased too. When it was finished, Father painted a plaque which read: 'Erected during the painful labour of Acting Sub-Lieutenant H.A.N. Willis RN.'

The Captain sent for us one by one. My name was Willis, so I was the last to enter once again. The other three, 'Sandy' Sanderson, Tony Norris and 'Pony' More, were celebrating and shaking hands. My heart was pounding as I opened the door and saw Captain Carrington seated behind his desk. He didn't offer a reassuring smile or welcome.

'Sit,' he said. Then having perfunctorily flipped through documents laid upon his desk, he looked up at me.

'Well, do you think that you deserve to pass, Willis?' he asked.

'I did my very best, Sir.' I answered quietly as he fixed me with a critical stare.

'Against my better judgement, you *have* passed. But I don't think that I would wish to have you in my ship.'

Nothing further passed his lips. He nodded in dismissal. No qualification, no explanation – nothing. And I left his presence hurt to the quick, the joy of passing having been instantly snuffed like a candle.

They wondered why I hurried passed them to my room, emerging only five minutes later when I was composed. They were sure I had failed – but then I smiled and they cheered with relief.

Later, at the Seal's Craig, Mother burst into tears and laughed with relief while Father whooped and danced around us both like a grinning Indian warrior; and then I noticed. He was brandishing his naval sword which hitherto had hung proudly on display at home for many years. As he passed his prized possession into my hands I saw his name engraved upon the scabbard catch; just below it I saw another name inscribed: H.A.N. Willis. I hugged him hard and cried.

The letter arrived during my leave: 'My Lords Commissioners of the Admiralty direct Acting Sub Lieutenant H.A.N. Willis to repair aboard HMS *Whirlwind* at Chatham on . . .'

And after all those years it seemed that I had still hearkened to the bosun's call . . . and what was more, Dad's sword now bore *my* name.